Up River

DARREN WOODHEAD

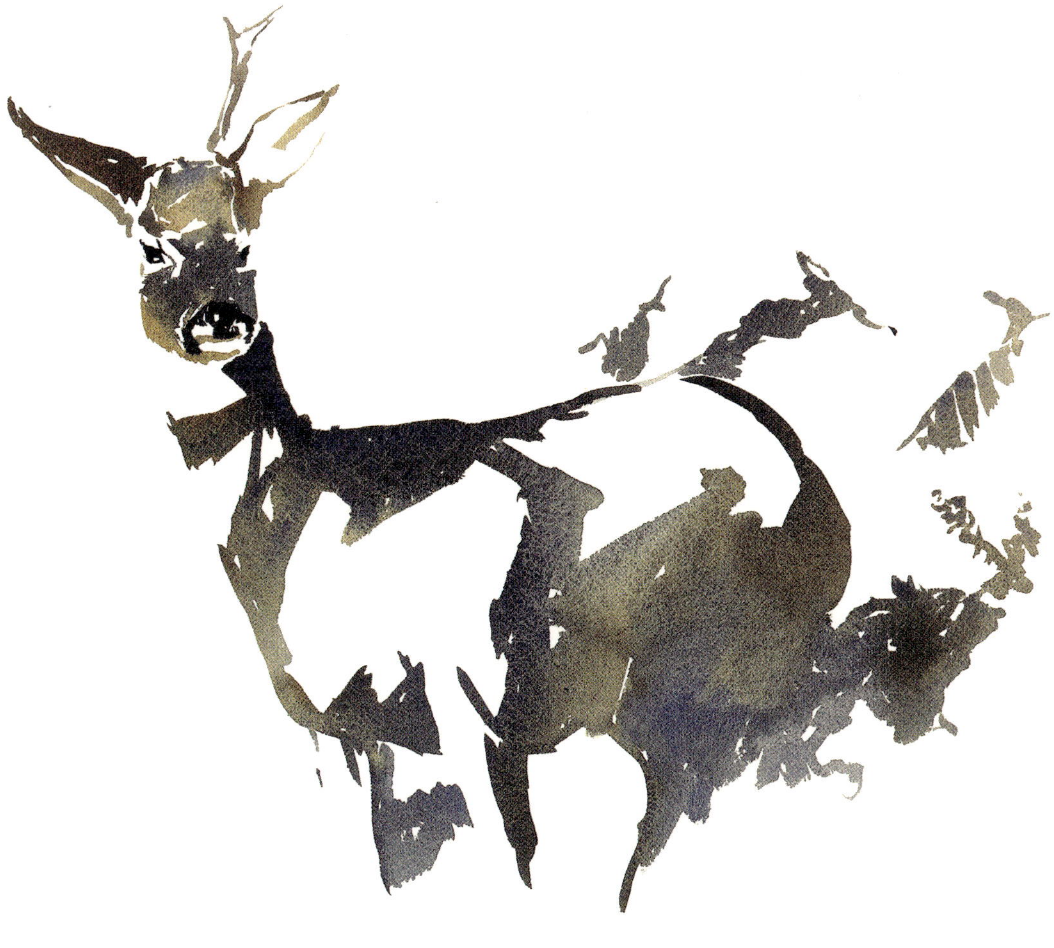

'. . . One needs real knowledge of the birds and beasts one paints and of the shifting scene around them – a naturalist, like the elephant's child, must have insatiable curiosity: "How long", says the viewer, "did it take you to paint, that picture?" The actual painting? – an hour maybe – plus fifty-odd years' experience.'

ERIC ENNION
The Living Birds of Eric Ennion

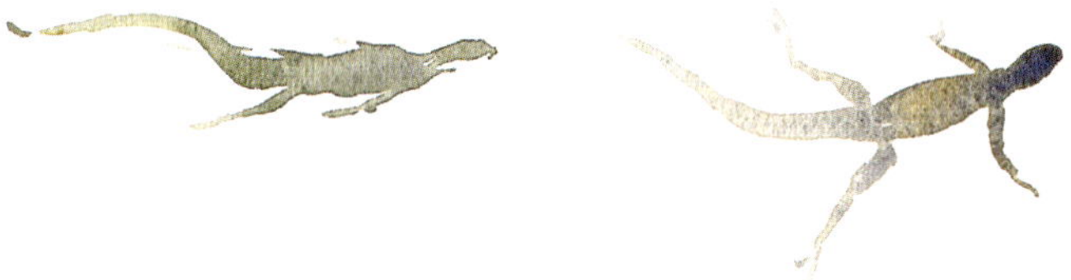

Up River

The Song of the Esk

DARREN WOODHEAD

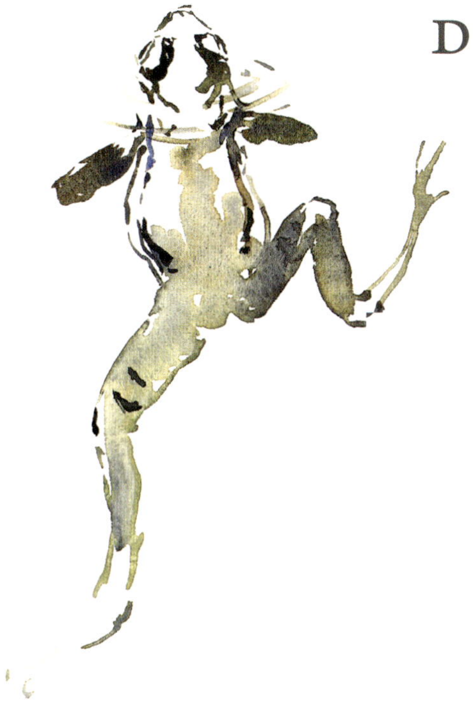

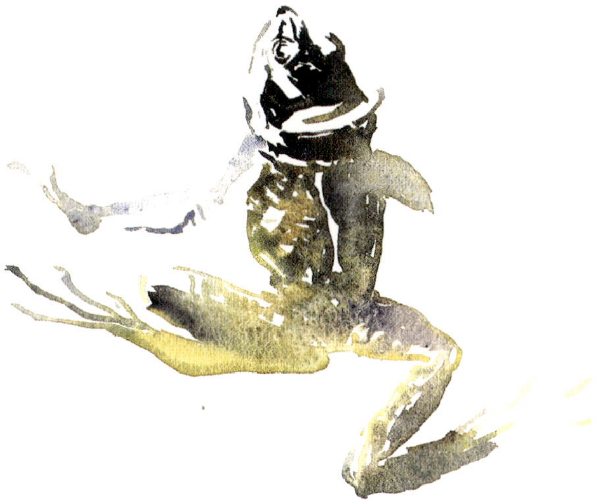

BIRLINN | 2009

For Pasci, Corin, Keelan, Mum and Dad, and to the memory of Nan and Sue, and for The Orcome Trust *and all who live in and around Carlops*

First published in 2009 by
Birlinn Limited
West Newington House
10 Newington Road
Edinburgh
EH9 1QS

www.birlinn.co.uk

ISBN: 978 1 84158 834 6

The Publisher and Artist gratefully acknowledge the support of The Orcome Trust and Keir Sword of Royal Mile Whiskies towards the publication of this book

British Library Cataloguing-in-Publication Data
A catalogue record for this book is available from the British Library

Book design by James Hutcheson
Typeset in Arno Pro and Trade Gothic

Printed and bound in Slovenia

Half-title page:
Roe Buck above the Glen,
4th November 2008, Amazondean
(watercolour, 380mm x 560mm)

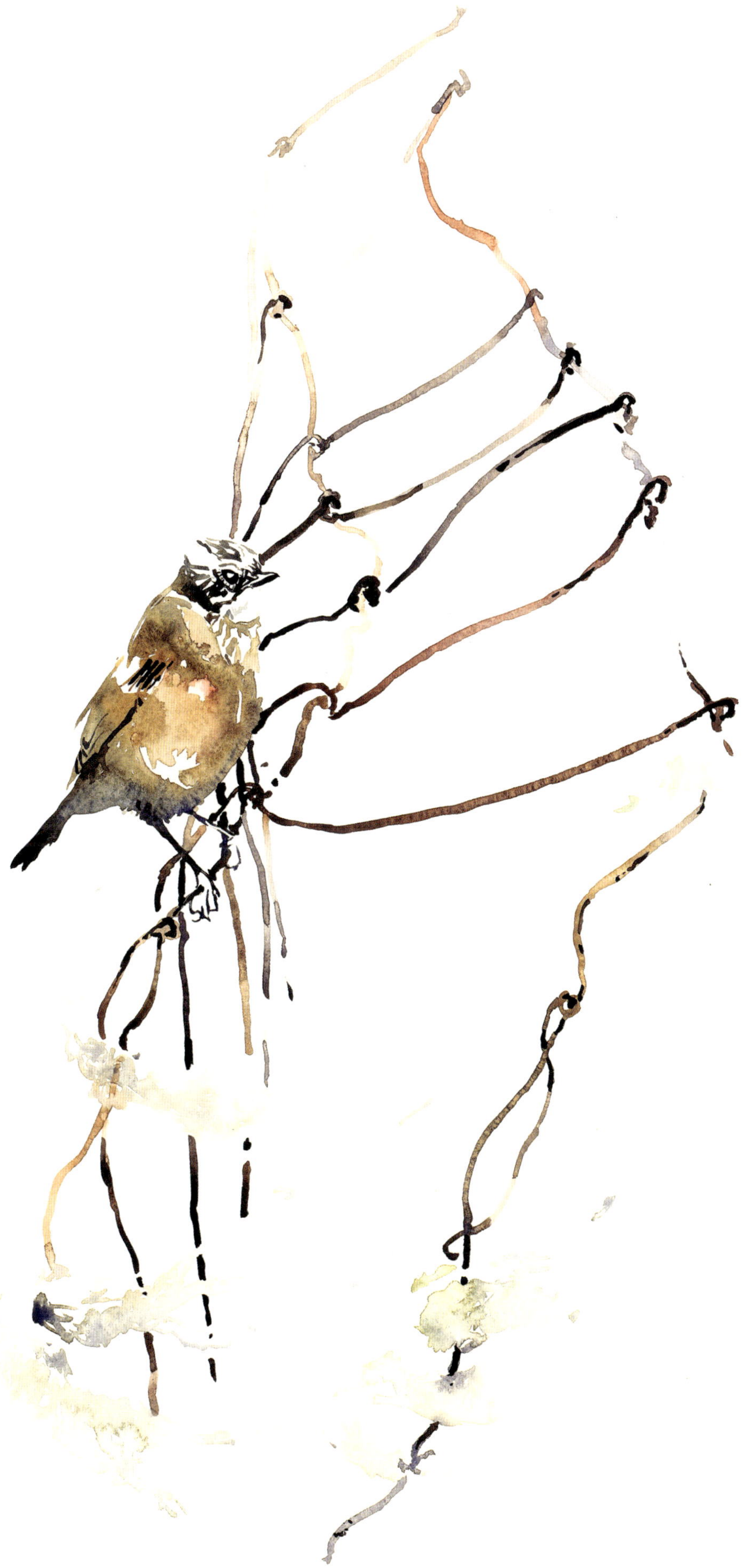

Contents

Juvenile Stonechat on Pentland fence, 30th June 2008
(watercolour, 560mm x 380mm)

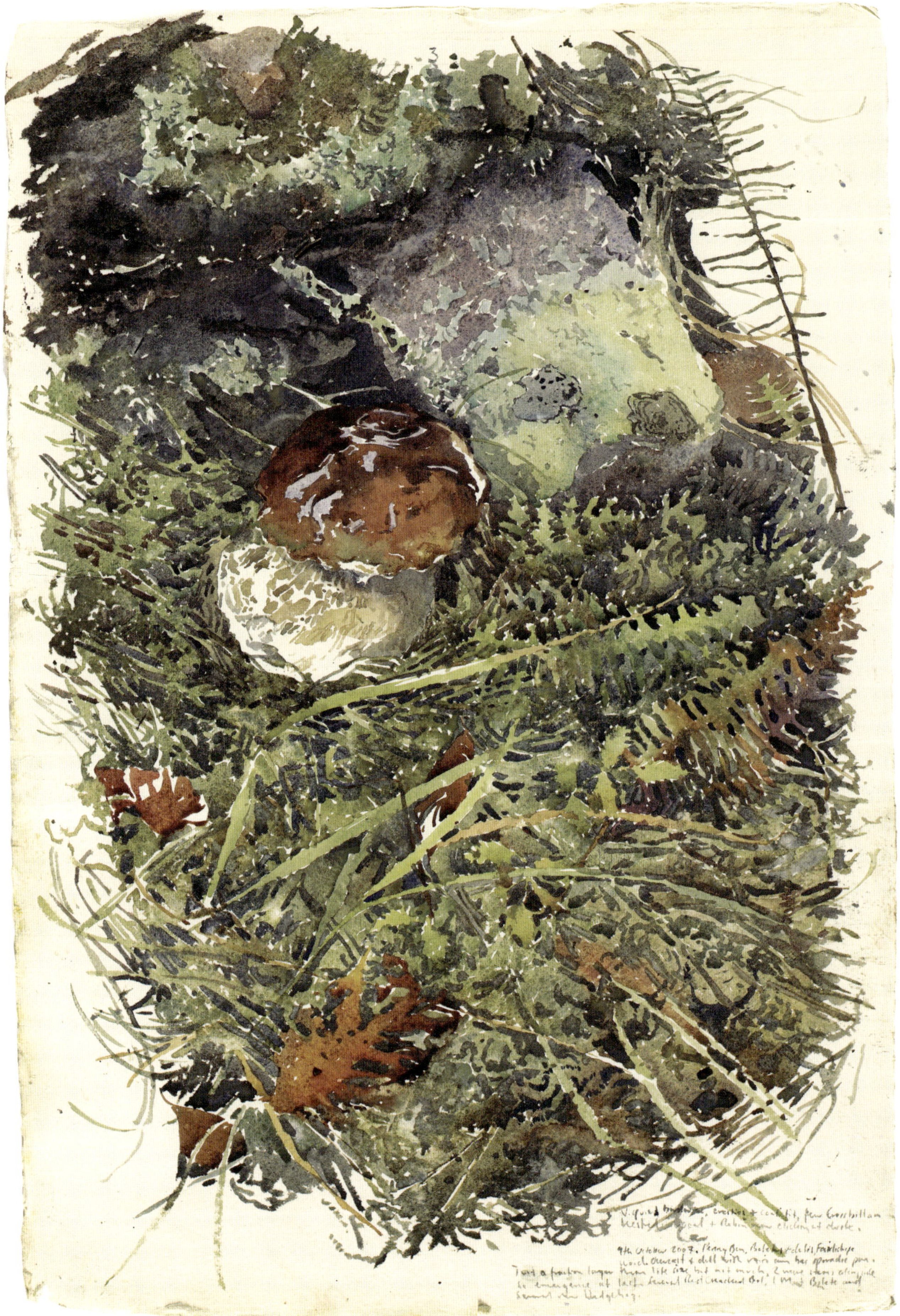
9th October 2007.

Foreword

Cep nestled in moss against lichened rock
(watercolour, 560mm x 380mm)

9th October 2008, Penny Bun, *Boletus edulis*, Fairiehope Wood. Overcast and dull with rain becoming sporadic p.m. Just a fraction larger than life size but not much, two more stems alongside so emergence at last. Several Red-cracked Bolete, one Matt Bolete and several new Woodland Hedgehog also. Very quiet bird-wise, Goldcrests and Coal Tits, Few Crossbills a.m., Kestrel in wood and Robin now clicking at dusk.

When Victoria Crowe suggested that we consider offering an artist residency for a year and described the work of Darren Woodhead, we embraced the concept enthusiastically. Never having offered such a residency before, we had no preconceived ideas of what might evolve. But Darren threw himself into the project with characteristic zeal and was often been seen out in the countryside in all weathers, recording a unique scene with his usual skill and originality.

Darren's enthusiasm is infectious, and at his demonstrations in Carlops village hall he took his audience along with him; and like the Pied Piper, children happily followed him into the hills. We are so delighted to have helped contribute to the creation of this wonderfully original book in which he has captured so much of the wildness and tranquillity of a very special place just a short distance from the bustling city of Edinburgh.

John Kennedy
Chairman of the Orcome Trust
May 2009

The area covered by Darren Woodhead in this book is part of Scotland that is very close to my heart. It was here, nearly forty years ago, that my husband and I came to live and work as artists and teachers. At Kitleyknowe we met the retired shepherd, Jenny Armstrong, whose life became an important subject within my own artistic career. The paintings and drawings I made over some twenty years became a visual record of the landscape and a rural way of life. In this area our own children grew up and became part of the community, with a love of the countryside in all its varied seasons.

It is therefore a great source of pleasure for me that the Orcome Trust, many years later, created this unique collaboration with Darren. What he has produced with the community workshops, the exhibitions and a permanent archive of artwork for the area has given insight and pleasure to many local people. With this book, however, he is reaching many more and giving the wealth of our local 'natural world' a permanent recognition. Thank you, Darren!

Victoria Crowe
May 2009

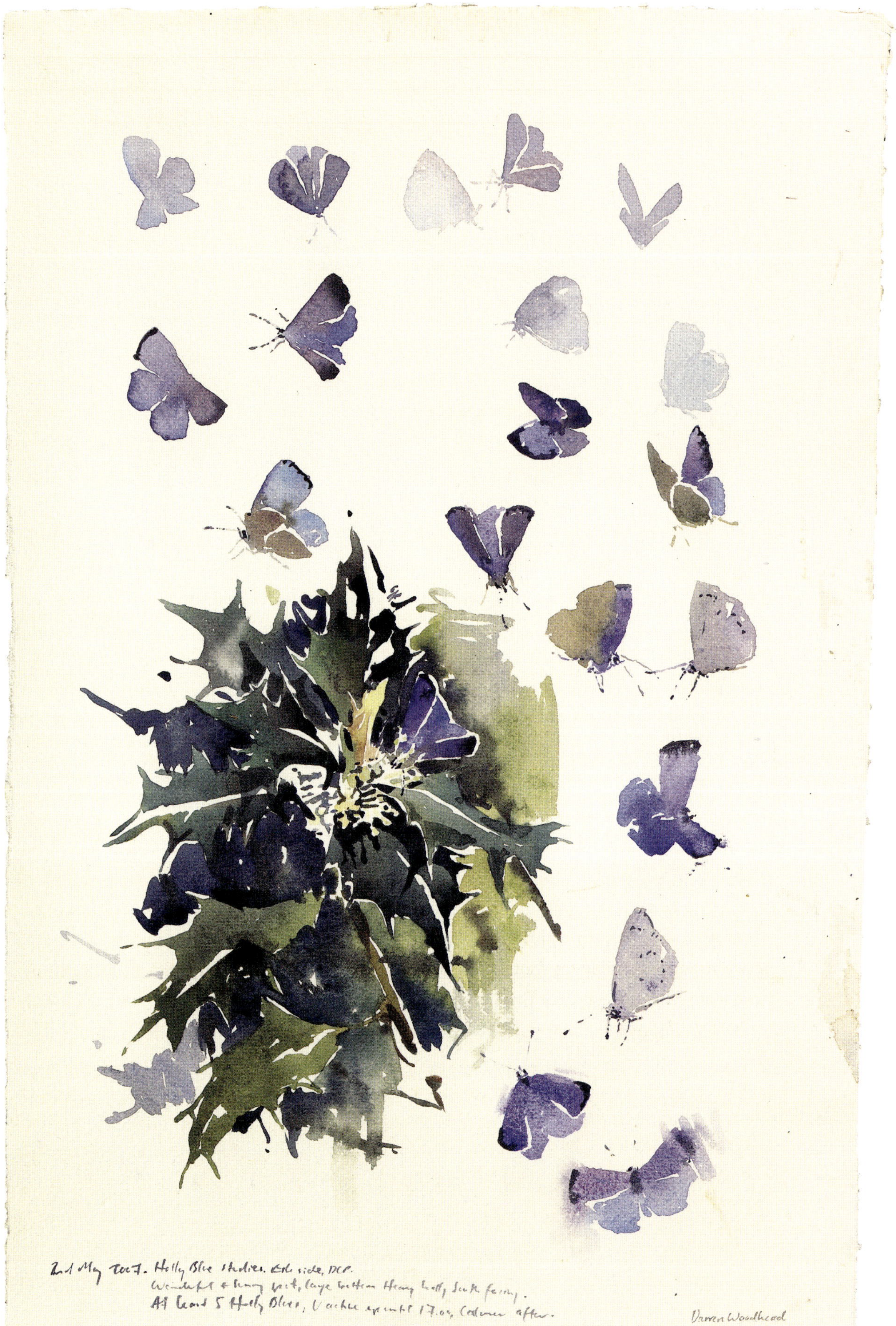
Holly Blue studies.
At least 5 Holly Blues, V active up until 17.00, calmer after.
Darren Woodhead

Introduction

Holly Blue butterflies
(watercolour, 440mm x 285mm)

2nd May 2007. Holly Blue studies beside River Esk. Wonderful, sunny spot, butterflies among a large base heavy Holly south facing. At least five Holly Blues, one active up until 17:00, calmer after.

My first Holly Blue butterflies in Scotland – a beautiful species more common in the south but now spreading northwards. I found them purely by good fortune. I saw them during a week of fabulous weather that early May, but when I visited the same area during May 2008, I had no such luck. The weather was much more unpredictable that year, and maybe I just chose the wrong days to look for them. It would be wonderful if these butterflies became a regular sight here.

For Darren Woodhead, a sheet of white paper is a pool of light in which paints dance. All works of art glow in the mind. This is where Darren hunts, catching fleeting thoughts and feelings. His pictures are not nature studies – nothing so mechanical, dry or prosaic. They are not sights fixed on a board, pinned down, measured: they are feelings caught on the wing, fireworks in the mind of excitement, love and inspiration.

How can mere paint make paper flame? That's the magic that Darren describes so clearly in his writing. With typical humility he makes it all sound so simple. But few artists alive today have such skills at their fingertips, and not many have had in the past. There were the Chinese masters of the watercolour art that flowered so exquisitely during the Song Dynasty nearly a millennium ago. But Chinese artists never carted their rolls of paper, their paints, brushes and water bottles out into the countryside. These stayed neatly arranged on table-tops, attendant on the artist's passionate remembrance. For Darren, watercolours are his hunting gear. He has no studio. Nothing is touched up afterwards. Everything, the slightest stroke, is done outside, in the elements. This is what makes his achievement so exceptional and his paintings so full of life and light.

What Darren does apparently so 'artlessly' is to play with our perceptions. Look at his Lapwing flock: it is a wonder in itself to be able to paint a moving mass of birds, each one individually active and totally convincing in its behaviour, posture and sense of busy purpose. Anyone who has tried to draw just one knows the problem – birds just don't stay still, even for an instant. To draw a dozen moving all at once is little short of miraculous. Artists who try to paint birds today tend to work from photos. Darren never ever does that. At best, snaps freeze the subject; at worst they kill it. Like rouged corpses, paintings worked up from photographs never totally succeed in concealing their base of rigidity and coldness. Darren's creatures, his whole creations, pulse with life, but then their foundation is not grey and static but movement and light. A river of white runs through his paintings and it is the paper itself. This white can be a drift of snow, a lifting mist, the smart, swelling breast of a Plover or the piercing glint in a Buzzard's eye, but always you discover to your surprise that these brilliant whites, each so different in feel from a distance, are, when you look closely, nothing more than patches of the same plain, untouched paper.

Darren builds up his lights by carving out the darks around them, with washes and stokes, some broad or tiny, some sharp-edged, others fading away to nothing, creating closeness and distance, solids and spaces. So skilful is he now, after fifteen years of persistent painting day after day, that he can work without any preliminary drawing (though when he does draw, his line is vibrant). He uses a very limited range of colours: rose madder genuine, aureolin yellow and cobalt blue as his primaries, from which he mixes most of his hues, together with a few additional pigments: ultramarine, alizarin crimson, burnt umber, raw sienna, cobalt turquoise, cobalt magenta and occasionally Payne's grey. From these he can create the green shine on a Lapwing's wing, the proud glow of a Bullfinch's chest, a sky heavy with snow – all unnameable colour mixtures of rare subtlety. He never uses black, for darkness is created by the obliteration of light. Nor does he ever resort to white pigment, for no thick paste, however bright, could add anything to the luminosity of the paper itself.

Darren sets out on his search at dawn, stopping when his sees something that makes his eyes light up, and is soon surrounded by palette, water bottle and bundle of brushes, often on his knees sunk into bracken, grass or earth – the closer into nature the better – with a large sheet of paper spread before him. Then the dance begins, the celebration of that specific, unique moment in time, to be praised, held and enjoyed to the full while it lasts. And, this being Scotland, more often than not the experience changes while it lasts, often dramatically: winds pick up and rage, rain drizzles then lashes, snowfall follows sunshine, all within hours. Darren has an umbrella rigging, but he likes it best when the weather contributes to the action. Rain dapples his washes, pools form that he works into edges, gusts of wind streak the paint away from his brush and often, since he loves working in winter, stains freeze before drying to leave delicate crystalline traces across the surface. As he settles into the scene it comes more to life; he begins to respond to the different rhythms within it – the imperceptible growth of Lichens, the spreading reach of branches, the busy searching of a pair of Goldcrests, the slow stare of an Owl. Often in his quiet absorption he shifts his gaze a little with a premonition that something else is happening – a Hare fending off a half-hearted attack by a Buzzard, a Fox tossing a Rat, a Deer nibbling the upper leaves of a Hazel. This is the real subject matter of his art, the life of nature going on, continuously confluent with our own but for the most part ignored by us, as close to us and as distant from us as the dismal stream of traffic that pounds along the trunk road above the glen where Darren works undisturbed.

The upper gorges of the Esk have changed him; the environment is more intimate than the open beaches where he first made his reputation at the river's mouth, and his skill goes on developing. His art is becoming at once more expansive and richer, freer yet at the same time also more intricate. His vision has widened to embrace not just the creatures that have fascinated him from childhood, but their whole environment. Within a softly suspended, drizzle-drenched mist, in the middle of an impossible tangle of twigs and branches, Lichens, leaves and berries, a fuzz of shades from light greens to browns to deepest crimsons that no one but Darren would ever dream of painting, a Blackbird sits, pale-beaked now after the hectic spring, quietly waiting till the weather gets better, its eye shining with a glint that is, of course, within all this dampness, only a patch of dry paper. This is a meditation on the nature of awareness within an environment, the bird's as well as our own.

Those who have been brainwashed by the marketing of today's art world might be surprised to see Darren's work described as contemporary art at all, let alone cutting-edge. Of course, no one can deny that his art is contemporary, because he's producing it now. But he also has a legitimate claim to be considered at the very forefront. On one level, his work pushes its medium to the limits of possibility. On another, it explores a terrain that is vital to our future, not just the nature of consciousness, but our consciousness of nature. There are few things more urgent for us to ponder than our relationship to the natural world. Darren's art is part of an artistic history that has been sidelined by the self-promoting pundits of modern art. All painters who concern themselves with nature are arrogantly dismissed as 'wildlife artists', despite the long history of such subject matter, from the Lascaux caves to ancient Egypt, from Leonardo to Stubbs. In the early years of the last century, artists began to turn from painting dead specimens to showing animals alive in the wild; the Swede Bruno Liljefors was a pivotal figure, and more recently British painters like John Busby and David Measures have taken their sketchbooks and watercolours into the woods and fields. Darren Woodhead has been inspired by all of them, and his work should properly be seen as a flower on this great

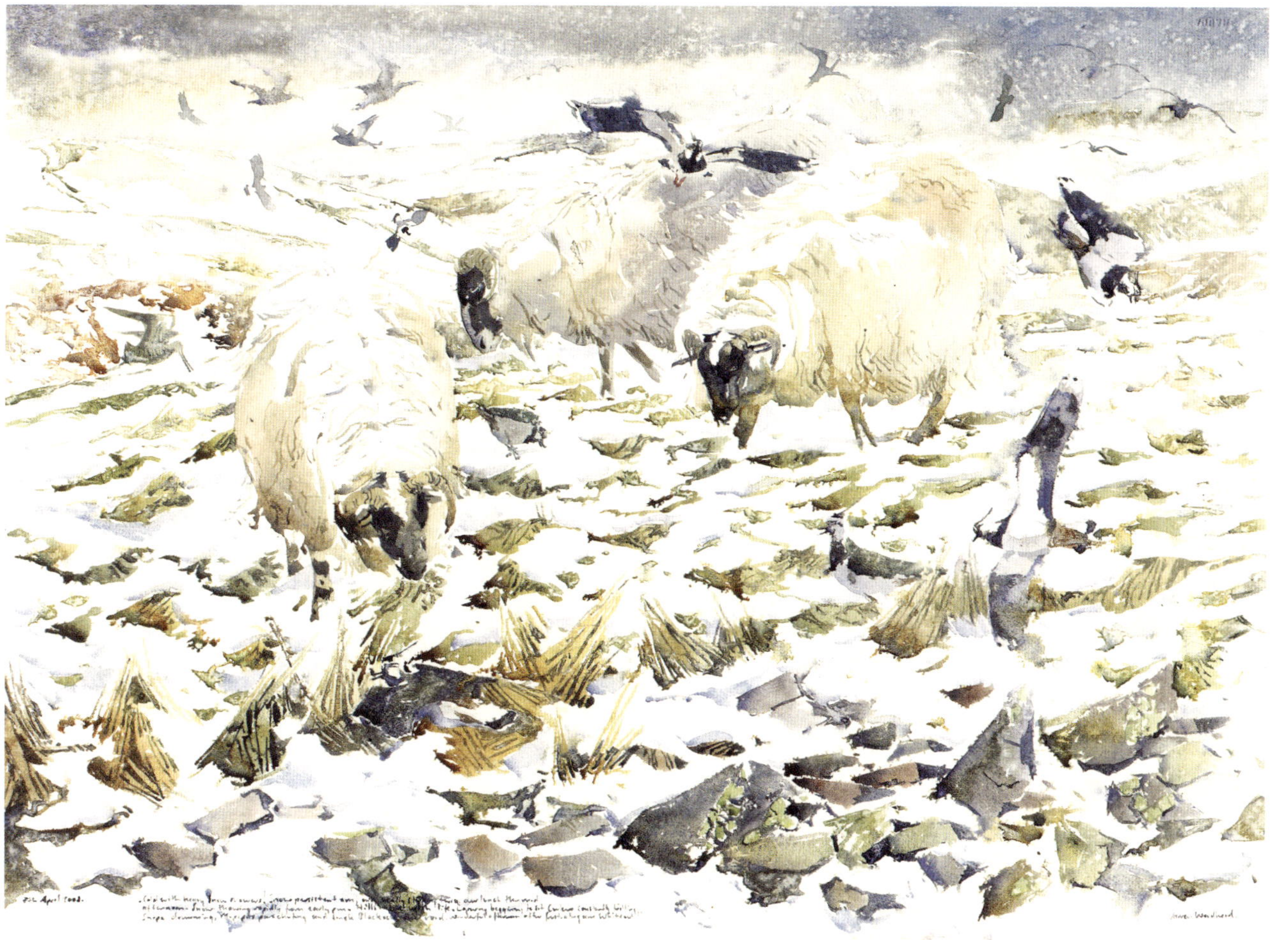

Spring Among the Hills,
7th April 2008
(watercolour, 560mm x 760mm)

Cold with heavy snow showers. Snow persistent a.m., only really stopping twice over lunch then mid afternoon. Snow thawing rapidly from early p.m. Hills alive with life, Lapwing beginning to sit, Curlew constantly trilling, Snipe drumming and Meadow Pipits parachuting. Wonderful afternoon after frustrating morning whiteout.

branch of art. The high priests of conceptual art and installations might dismiss it as nature studies, but in fact it ranks among the best art being created by anyone today. Art has to be created. It can't be something just found or thought – trite one-liners, adolescent philosophies. Art is the form of feeling. And the better it is formed, the more feeling it can contain. That's why Darren Woodhead's work shines like a beacon: it illuminates that parallel universe, close at hand, that we ignore at our peril. The natural world from which we came and which we are all part of, whatever we might like to claim.

Julian Spalding
Former Director, Glasgow Museums and Art Galleries
April 2009

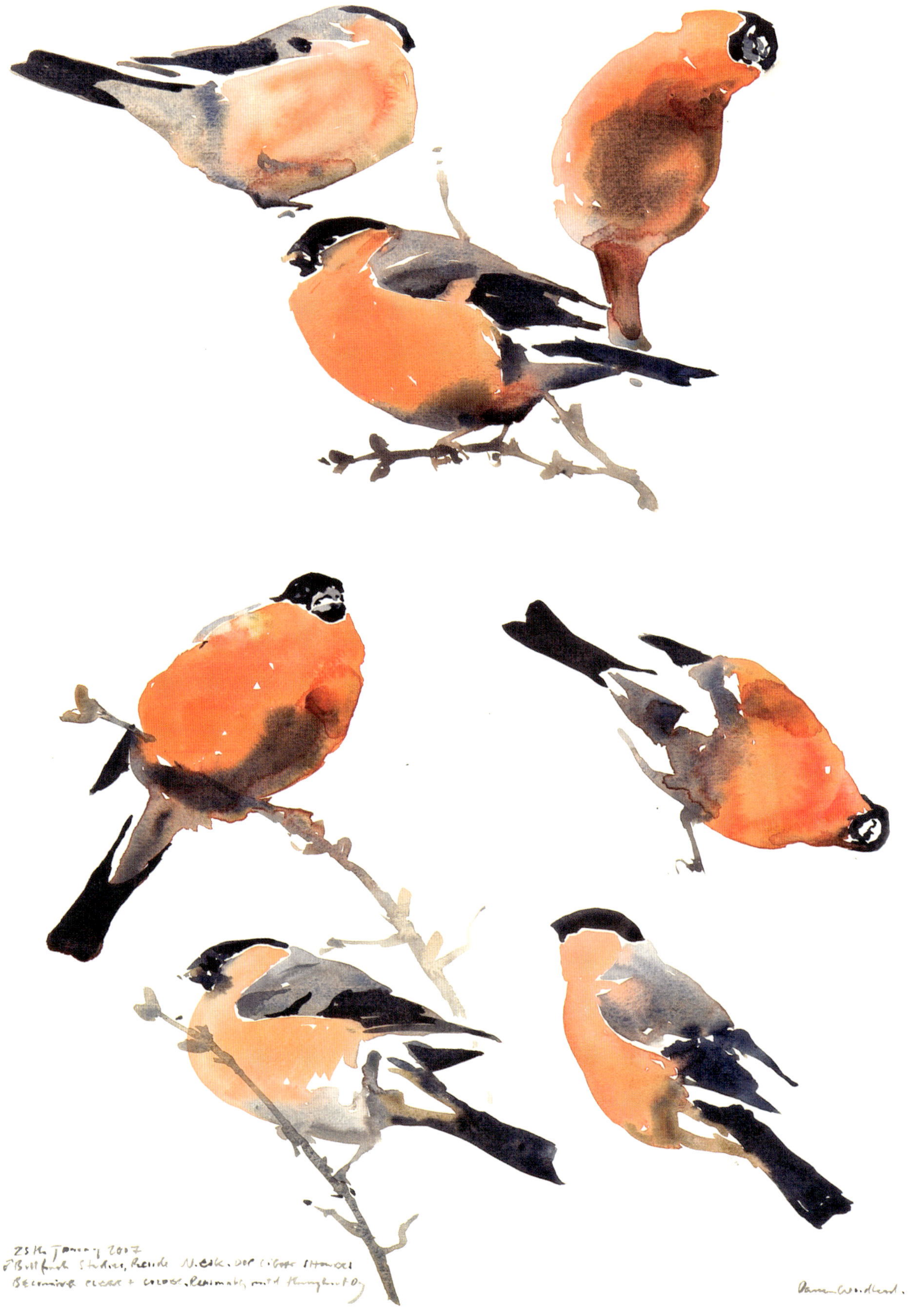
25th January 2007

The Song of the Esk

Male Bullfinch studies
(watercolour, 594mm x 420mm)

25th January 2007, Male Bullfinch studies beside North Esk. Light showers becoming clear and colder. Reasonably mild throughout day.

Tuesday, 16th January 2007. Instinct trusting a good forecast, I head up to the Borestanes once again to work from the source of the Esk. Heavy frost and wonderfully clear. Cloudless conditions lasting till dusk, when the low winter sun was dulled by a grey, chilly haze. Intentions of searching for Mountain Hares but, as always, best plans go to waste. No sooner had I crossed the white, crisp banks of the North Esk Reservoir than my eyes focused on six Roe Deer feeding on the hill above. With rattle of tin palette, I begin to paint, then, amazingly, a hunting Short-eared Owl drifts past over the deer. I am torn. I have waited so long to see Roes out in the open, but here is my first Owl by the reservoir in the most ideal of light. I begin working without worrying, the page brimming with a mixture of Owl and Deer shapes, at one point both interacting, a young Roe inquisitively sniffing at a vole-fattened Owl. Frustration at how quickly ice forms on my metallic mixing surface, transforming my delicate brush into a cement-like laden bulb. Paint becomes hard to move around the page yet the most beautiful icy rosette forms on my depiction of sedges.

This was one of many intense memories and highlights of a unique residency that I have just completed. I was very fortunate to be granted a very special project to work on, centred within a stunning part of the Scottish Borders around the village of Carlops, around sixteen miles south of Edinburgh. This aim of this book is to show the results of this opportunity, and I hope that the essence of the area I was so kindly invited to portray will shine through in the following pages.

The content of *Up River* differs from my previous book, *From Dawn Till Dusk* (Langford Press, 2005), which depicts the coastal strip of East Lothian near my home at Musselburgh. So many new elements and challenges had to be overcome in order to capture the character of this inland area – the colours, the light, not to mention the weather. The area's unique and intense natural beauty is enhanced by an enormous variety of animal and plant life, and I hope that the book shows just some of the richness and diversity that the Carlops area boasts.

Throughout the book, many of the paintings are annotated with notes about events that happened around me whilst I was working. These notes are as important a part of the finished work as the images themselves, and recall those unexpected occurrences that influence the way a painting develops. Never setting out with a specific subject in mind allows me to depict the events of the day as they happen – so often it is the surprise element that gets the pulse racing and allows hand and eye to work in unison.

The book is arranged in chronological order, so it is in a sense a journey over the three years of my residency, but at the same time it is also a journey into the way my work developed during this period. Each year was different, characterised by its own particular events, and subjects changed according to the fluctuation of seasonal and yearly variations. For example, the summer of 2006 was memorable for Butterflies, yet 2007 and 2008 were much less so. A cold and wet July and August both years meant that I had to focus my attention elsewhere. The difference between the years is a major factor in the feel of the book: for the whole period it was the same eye that was observing, though it was being led to different subjects.

The time I spent in the area was life-changing for many reasons. One of my most memorable painting days was followed hours later by the birth of my first son, Corin, and since then, I have been blessed with my second son, Keelan. Many new friendships were formed and different inspirations have developed. Though birdlife, insects and mammals are still flourishing interests, my work has moved on. Mycology for example now plays an important part in my life. The excitement of the day's hunt is almost as thrilling as the return of Geese skeins overhead.

The Residency

In January 2006, whilst in conversation with the painter Victoria Crowe, a trustee of the Orcome Trust, I was asked if I would be interested in an Artist in Residence position working around Carlops, an area I had driven through before but never explored. The position would be unique. I would be a visiting artist working on location but also forging close links with the local community. The residency would be funded through the Orcome Trust, which is based at Newhall and supports a wide range of local projects, though this was the first time it had sponsored an Artist in Residence.

Meetings with the Orcome Trustees set out clear aims for the project. I was to work throughout the seasons, capturing the landscapes as well as the flora and fauna of the area and recording my observations through painting, drawings and notes. I was to be introduced to the community to discuss the scope of the project, and would also present a lecture at Carlops Village Hall with slides and examples of my work. During the summer I would hold several weekend workshops open to people from the area. I would also hold an exhibition of works towards the end of the year and, finally, present a report on the project together with a gift of works for the Trust's archive. An essential element of the residency was that my work would create an extensive and invaluable archive for the area.

The project was of huge personal interest, as I would be tracing the Esk, my adopted home river, which enters the sea near Musselburgh, up one of its two tributaries and back to its source in the Pentland Hills. The estuary of the Esk has inspired my work for several years, and I had been planning for some time to wander along its banks as it meanders into the hills. But for one reason or another, I had yet to venture that way. Now, thanks to such an exciting project, I would finally be able to trace the river back to its source, following its path through the hills, heaths and woodland.

That journey began on one crisp, cold February Saturday morning in 2006, when a reconnaissance trip via the Saturday market at Carlops village hall paved the way for the project ahead. After meeting several members of the local community and demolishing a nourishing hand-made pie and coffee, we followed the snaking track beside the steepening valley which encloses the North Esk on its journey from the Pentlands. The expanse of barren, windswept hills, sliced by narrow gullies and neatly wooded valleys, gave way to an oasis beyond – the North Esk reservoir. Beyond the ridge and out of sight lay the Borestanes, where the trickle of water, silenced by shrouds of heather and moss, begins its journey downhill. As a Buzzard pair soared overhead, my attention was drawn to the small pale dots of sheep that littered the hilltops, as well as the views out over the vast raised bog and moor that sits behind Amazondean and Kitleyknowe. Stands of Beech and Scots Pine dissected bleached ochre-green fields and washes of rose-madder subdued the heath beyond. The distinctive horizon of the Moorfoot Hills in the distance beneath the icy blue sky gave a thrilling sense of distance and space in the crisp winter light.

Geographically, the area I was to record in paintings and words is in the midst of the Pentlands, which stretch south-westwards from the outskirts of Edinburgh down into the Borders. The drive down the A702 from Edinburgh leads you along the eastern edge of the hills through a somewhat bleak landscape. But this topography is deceptive, and one is unaware from the main road of the valleys and deans that intersect, or the reservoirs and streams that feed the land. The highest crest of the hills is Scald Law, at 579 metres, and alongside Carnethy Hill, Southern Black Hill and the Kips, it stands as guardian in a line of hills that mark the north-eastern border of my residency area. The area takes in the estates and localities of Eastside, Spittal and Paties Hill, as well as Bavelaw, Fairliehope and Carlop Hill. Carlops, the village central to the area, sits at an altitude of 300 metres, which although not significantly high, means that it experiences weather conditions very different from those that I am used to on the coast, as I found out first-hand on some very notable occasions.

The locality contains much historical and cultural significance, such as the carvings on Harbourcraig rock made by Covenanters prior to the Battle of Rullion Green in 1666. It is also the setting for both Allan Ramsay's play *The Gentle Shepherd* and Victoria Crowe's magical paintings inspired by Jenny Armstrong, which are published in *A Shepherd's Life*.

Amidst this strong historical significance, my most important task was to describe the countryside in my own particular way, and although that day the expanse of landscape in front was new to me, it recalled memorable childhood days spent in the Yorkshire Dales or adventures among undulating Welsh hills. Inevitably, it takes time to absorb a new location and get a feeling for it, but a detailed tour of the whole area with Patricia Kennedy of the Orcome Trust, which included meeting several of the local landowners, helped me to familiarise myself with the area.

During the first year one of the most exciting yet challenging experiences for myself as an artist was familiarising myself with the sheer variation of environments and habitats. Coming off the exposed rolling hills, where views either side appeared limitless on clear days, I could head almost directly into the aptly named Amazondean, where in the height of summer the matted tangles of green are like a jungle. Rust-coloured Scots Pines clinging to steep valleys give way to elegant lines of Beech, bowed by the relentless onslaught of the wind. The land then opens out to fields of livestock where concealed gullies are hidden from all but the most inquisitive. This hugely varied landscape is home to a wealth of plants and animals so easily missed by the crowds that speed all too fast along the main trunk road that dissects the area. Within sight of the road Red Grouse babble from the heather-clad hills criss-crossed with the tracks of Hare and Roe Deer. Distinctive mounds showing prominent signs of Badger habitation lie at the side of seas of Thistle stems, themselves indicative of thriving insect communities. The North Esk chuckles along to the chorus of Dipper song, and in the distance Curlews, the watchmen of the hill, are alert to any sign of danger. Swathes of Rooks and Jackdaws make their way to communal roosts, and in the distance their much larger relatives, the Ravens, can be heard croaking high above. The scene is completed as the high-pitched calls of Pink-footed Geese momentarily obscure the bleeting of Black-faced Sheep.

During my first few visits I was immediately lured by the isolation of a Raven family alone in its precipitous territory in a corner where the wind never ceases. The interaction with other birds was so gripping that I forgot about my cold, stiffening fingers. Immersed by the coming and goings of late winter and the beginning of spring, I was unaware of the explosion of life that the coming season would bring. Caught out in a late fall of snow, I endured an eventful struggle back to the shelter of lower ground. Here, the painting of the frail stone bridge at Kitleybrigg became my stepping stone into the landscape: I began to feel at home and free to paint.

The altitude of the land seems to exaggerate the speed at which seasons change. As the year progresses, the colours and pace of life intensify dramatically. The lonesome croaking of early breeding Ravens gives way to the electric display of the Lapwing. A clearing in the swathes of greens in the dean becomes alive with activity in the first weeks of May, and from late spring follows the manic hustle and bustle of summer. With bursts of colour and an explosion of scents and smells, I found the sheer scale and speed of change often difficult to keep up with. Caught in the crossfire of so much activity, it was even stressful at times. Whilst working on a Thrush family I became aware of a family of Tawny Owls, as well as a host of new arrivals such as Warblers,

Sheep tracks and scree slope
(watercolour, 560mm x 380mm)

Monday 6th March 2006. View looking north from Silverburn Quarry towards Carnethy Hill. Wonderful morning. Still remnants of Friday's snow. Clear and frosty start though sun thawing snow quickly.

Redstarts and Spotted Flycatchers. Within the same week, Green Hairstreak Butterflies also emerged, brushing their metallic green wings together whilst perching on Cotton Grass and Blaeberry. No sooner had I began working on one thing when another was in full view, it seemed.

The 24th May 2006, for example, was a bitterly cold morning with a gusting westerly wind bringing hail and rain showers. Sitting below the sycamore that held the Mistle Thrush nest, the leaf-cover above held the first signs of the coming season and the Scots Pines bristled to the calls of newly fledged Chaffinch. The appearance of Green Hairstreak Butterflies nearby and the surprise distant song of a Redstart added to the awakening of the woods that week, and it didn't stop there. On 30th May, after a cool grey start, the trees were alive with birdsong, and any preconceived ideas of a grey day were thrown well out of the window. As the sun burnt the low lying cloud away, I will never forget how, among the intense golden greens of fresh leaves, a proud male Blackcap announced his territorial intentions to deafening effect.

As the year progressed the Thrush family that I had spent so much time watching fledged, and the quietening woods made way for what was to be a classic Fungi season. Beneath the branches that began to bend with a staggering abundance of berries, underfoot the fruiting bodies of Fungi covered the forest floor. As I found myself stepping aside more and more often to avoid these curious shapes among the leaves, I decided I had to learn more about them. A foray out with Mike Jones of Fairliehope began a quest to become familiar with Fungi, to learn and appreciate the splendid variety of shapes, colours and forms. I was suddenly finding and admiring Chanterelles, Penny Buns, varieties of Amanitas and the subtly spectacular Horn of Plenty. Autumn 2006 was a Fungi year par excellence and I enjoyed it to the full.

With the first signs of winter arriving in late October, I began to focus on the ever-present symbols of the hills – the sheep. They typify the sights and sounds of the landscape and are the essence of that area of the Borders. It would seem unnervingly empty without their presence. That first winter gave many opportunities to work in differing lights, from complete white-outs to crisp sunshine, and it took time to truly capture the character of these animals within their changeable and often hostile environments.

The first year was a huge success. The talks, demonstrations and workshops were well attended and the exhibition was a triumph. On the opening night the village hall was packed, and people, warmed by freshly mulled wine, immersed themselves in the images inspired by a landscape and light they knew so well. After an enthusiastic welcome by John Kennedy of the Orcome Trust, I presented a talk in which I introduced the work I had done so far, and which was on public view over the whole weekend. The workshops, too, generated enthusiasm as well as exciting results. One weekend saw a dozen or so of us venture into Amazondean amidst driving November rain; the crinkled results once the paper had dried held so much life and atmosphere that the camera can only dream of. The rosy-cheeked smiles of people richly engaged in conversation and clenching mugs of hot tea and chocolate said it all.

The feedback from all who were there was enthusiastic and encouraging, and was a precursor to some great news that arrived the following spring. Whilst excitedly waiting for the arrival of the first Lambs, I heard that the Trust had been so impressed with that year's work that they wanted me to stay a second year. And so the project progressed, the documentation continued and the archive grew.

Technicalities and Working in the Field

'The artists' job is to see, interpret and distil,' Eric Ennion, *The Living Birds of Eric Ennion*

In order to enhance the experience of looking at the paintings and drawings in the book, I thought it would be useful to document briefly my way of working and the materials I use. As an artist, I have always worked outside, in the field. Every piece of artwork you see here has been completed directly from life whilst I was observing the subject in its natural environment.

I have always been a keen observer, inquisitively

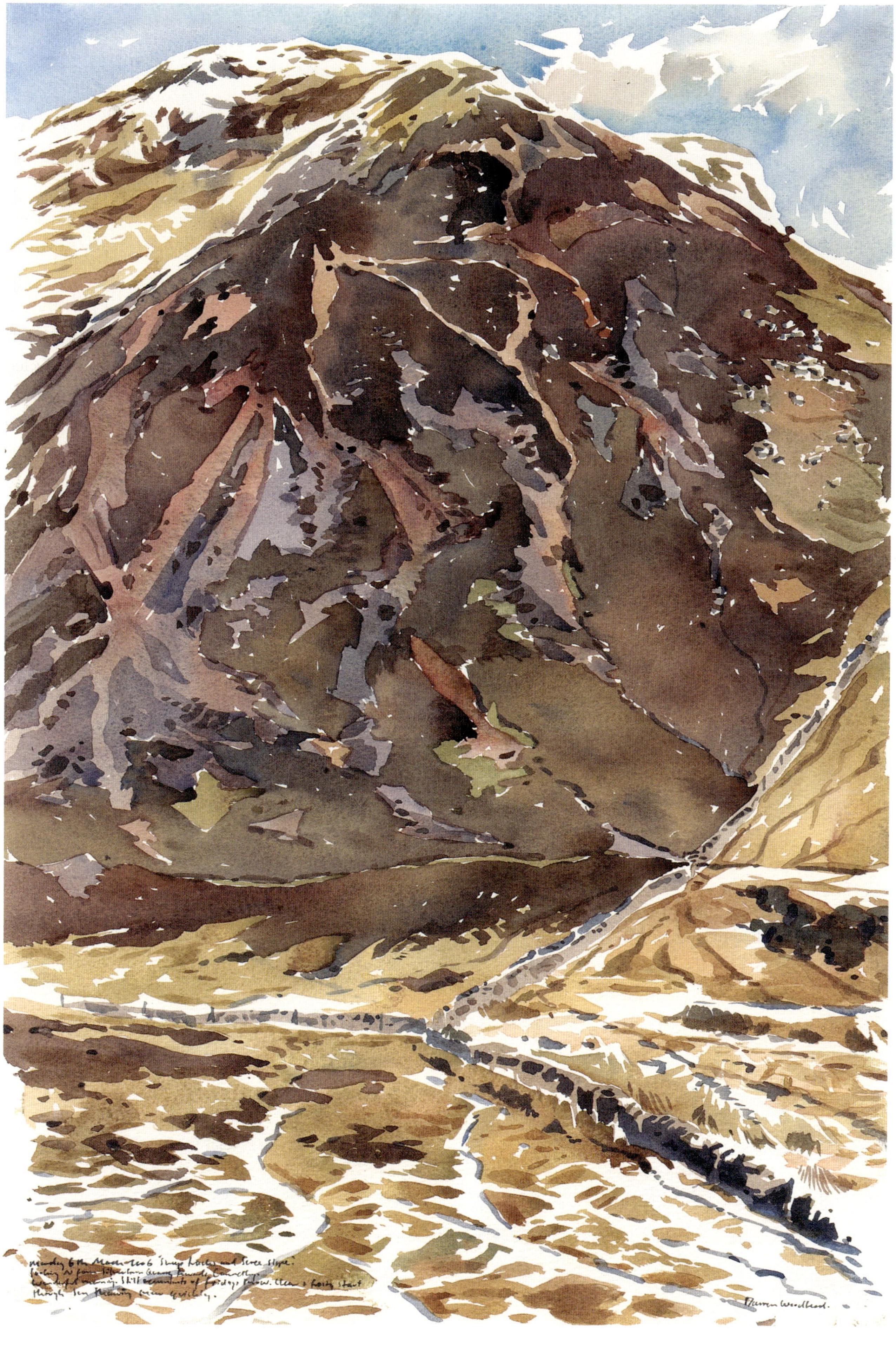
Darren Woodhead.

wanting to know and understand by spending as much time as possible being out and observing the natural world. Countless childhood hours spent kneeling behind the sofa creating images on reams of A4 paper has helped to develop a visual memory that can act like a camera lens as it records those fleeting moments. At that early age, as yet still unfamiliar with the idea of working outside, a school outing would invariably result in me trying to draw what I had seen (with varying results) as soon as I got home.

Eventually I found myself looking at paintings and drawings by artists such as Eric Ennion, Charles Tunnicliffe, John Busby and David Measures. Their work encompasses the energy of the moving object that had been lacking in my early efforts and seemed so natural and easy. Deep in every line and every mark, as well as showing technical confidence, they display clear knowledge of the subject matter and a sense of honesty that I found captivating. Many years passed, during which my early interest became a passion and then an obsession. Understanding the animal, bird or insect was the key to capturing it convincingly in a painting or drawing. This could not be achieved without experience; and so my journey began. As I progressed I encountered many more inspirational figures, among them the great Swedish painter Bruno Liljefors, a master of portraying predator/prey relationships in environments he knew so well. In Liljefors' work the viewer is given a real and profound glimpse of nature, a sense of being there as the action depicted actually happens.

There is an excitement and an exhilaration that comes from watching an event in the natural world as it unfolds. Whether it be a fleeting encounter with a wild animal or the changing quality of light in a woodland glade, I find the intensity and challenge of the moment invigorating. The experience embraces sound, atmosphere, light and mood. There is no time for deliberation; the image has to be recorded speedily and instinctively. But working outside obviously has its pitfalls. Nothing ever stays the same for any length of time, and subjects are always going about their daily lives with an obvious disregard to the figure sketching nearby. Never do birds or animals stand on plinths and pose as we should like them to do. They are concentrating on feeding, migrating, resting – on simply surviving. In fact it would be a bad thing if they did pose for us. That excitement and essence that makes seeing something that we do not normally see so special would be lost. I believe strongly that if we are lucky enough to see animals in their natural habitat, then this is how you should attempt to record them.

Drawing moving objects demands high concentration and, crucially, the ability for the memory to act as a camera shutter. This skill has to be constantly exercised, and it is easy to tell if I have gone a period of time without working, as the results will show in the work. It sounds such an easy process to see and remember, but in that split second between taking the eyes off the subject, mixing the colours and applying it to the paper, the link can be broken and something vital can be lost. When I am out I am generally out for the day, and like to sit in a place where I can dissolve into the background and become just another element of the landscape, enabling life to continue around me. I find it amazing how easily a figure can become 'accepted' into the environment – several times I have been working and looked up to see a bird looking down at me, or, as has happened recently, a Roe buck smelling the air metres from me then barking as it tiptoed on.

I find the best results come when I'm totally absorbed in work; when I'm working almost without thinking. I remember having a conversation some years back with Robert Greenhalf, the wonderful painter and printmaker, about this exact subject. In a certain frame of mind things can happen so easily and the results can be exciting; yet conversely, when one tries too hard the day can be a slog and the end product disappointing.

I carry a folder full of varying sizes of paper and am never too concerned about the amount I use. This helps to encourage that freedom of thought and expression essential to allow ideas to flow and materialize. For me, becoming zoned into the atmosphere is part of the experience. At the same time it's amazing how one can be totally absorbed in the act of painting one thing yet somehow intuitively aware of other events going on around. No doubt I miss much when I'm engrossed in painting, but how often do I seem to look up just at the right moment to see a Peregrine chasing Thrushes or a Roe Deer family passing by? Perhaps there is a certain state of mind that allows one to be totally absorbed with one thing yet open to what else is happening, or perhaps it is just coincidence. Whatever the cause, such serendipitous events have made so many days, and I never pass on the opportunity to include them in my paintings.

Equipment

Working outside means that all my equipment has to be portable. This limits the amount that I can comfortably take with me. My everyday painting materials are carried in as small a rucksack as I can get away with. Any larger, and I would no doubt soon fill it with non-essentials! I make sure that it is packed with the smallest and lightest utilities in order to make as much room as possible for art materials. Also included is a small waterproof, which is used as much to shelter from the wind as from rain, as well as a couple of heavy polythene bags that I can use to protect paintings. I use a small waterproof blow-up mat as a seat, and packed alongside is a lightweight telescope and an equally light tripod, which I use as a support. One of my most inspirational ideas was to purchase some DIY knee-pads that are cushioned as well as waterproof. These have been a godsend as I always tend to kneel when I paint, so thankfully the days of cold, wet knees are now long gone!

With regard to art materials, I always carry paints, brushes, a water container, palette and water bottle. For many years I have used artists' quality paints in large tubes. For me they have a huge advantage over small cakes of paint, as I find I can squeeze out a significant amount of paint, which is essential for the large washes of paint I need. It is a necessity for me to have instant access to strong, bright tones. These colours are arranged in a rough order on my metal folding palette, which is now unfortunately beginning to show its age. Thankfully, however, it still keeps the paint from leaking too much into the bag. For many years I used an enamelled metal plate for mixing, but the mess created by a day's accumulation of wet colour became tiresome. For the last few years the folding palette has been a revelation. If for any reason I do not use all the paints, they will keep and can easily be used on another occasion. For the colours, I regularly carry a couple of browns such as raw sienna and burnt umber, aureolin yellow, rose madder genuine and crimson alizarin for reds, ultramarine and cobalt blues with another couple of bonus colours such as cobalt turquoise or Payne's grey as reserve stock. All these are kept in a small plastic box that used also to hold pencils. By relentlessly using the same colours I try to get to know them and all their possibilities so that I can mix them instinctively as I launch into a painting.

In one pocket of the rucksack I keep a brush case which holds half a dozen medium to large brushes of varying quality, some pure sable, others synthetic, and a couple of favourite oriental-style goat-hair brushes. Most of my work is done with a favoured couple, the large oriental goat-haired brush being irreplaceable. This type of brush holds so much water yet sheds it easily, unlike some other real-haired brushes that just seem to drink paint into their ferrules. A small plastic water container is filled by water from a collapsible water bottle, which I try as much as I can to refill from local sources.

I have a passion for paper, and for watercolour paper especially. There is such beauty and elegance to its touch and feel. The charm and character of a particular paper can be in its grain or texture, as well as its deckled or torn edges. These features are so precious in themselves that, if at all possible, I always show the full page, including its edges, when it is framed or reproduced. There are many different makes of paper, each of which possesses a certain character, and I regularly use a coarse handmade paper for its rawness and strong organic feel. Although it is possible sometimes to choose a certain paper that I think will suit a certain image, in the heat of the moment it is not always possible to lay my hands on my preferred stock, and I often just grab that which is nearest to hand.
All that is then needed is fuel in the way of food, my

binoculars, possibly an umbrella and the day is set.

As I always tell students, watercolour sounds the simplest medium of all to master, requiring just water, paint and paper, yet in my experience it is the most complex of all. Being a transparent medium, you will see every single mark made. There is no chance to hide or erase a wrong line. Every decision you make will have a bearing on the finished image, from the type of colours chosen to the paper and the water in which you dip your brushes. Even then, just when you think you have it sorted, the atmospheric conditions around can have an effect. It is impossible to be in total control of the medium; you can guide it to some extent, but when you use lots of colour and water together, as I tend to do, other forces come into play. You have to both let go of the watercolour in order to let it do some of the work, yet at the same time exercise a delicate, precipitous control. A contradiction in terms, I know, but unless this is fully appreciated, the excitement and possibilities afforded by the technique cannot be explored to the full.

Being at the mercy of the weather can be both a hindrance and a blessing. Working out on the hill, especially, is a lonesome experience, yet magical at the same time. On many occasions sunny days have deteriorated beyond recognition to a thick grey mist at best or white-out blizzard at worst. Such conditions can bring failure as well as success. On one memorable occasion I was painting a Long-eared Owl sitting high up in a snow-covered Pine, only to see the image on the paper disappear not once but twice during the double onset of heavy snow showers. Snow acts like salt and sucks any wet paint up like a sponge. Now, those two Owl paintings exist only in my memory. I have experienced paintings and even drawing boards ripped away by sudden gusts of wind, or paper drenched to a pulp. Scraping inches of snow away from paintings has become a normality, and I have even watched helplessly as a page I was working on flew off down a cliff face, was tossed around as violently as a weak autumn leaf, only to land metres away from its original position relatively unscathed. The ensuing battle with weather and conditions is very much part of the struggle of working direct in brush from life, and always conveys a sense of actually having been there.

The vulnerability of watercolour lends itself to working out of doors. Earlier this year, as I painted in a squall of hail and snow, I laid a wash of deep intense grey sky, overdoing it I thought, only for it to lighten considerably during the last stages of drying. Such is the nature of watercolour. I may guide the colour onto the paper but I watch as colours change and develop, as much as the affecting elements around it allow. It is this that excites me about watercolour – the way that it exudes a life of its own. Add to this the way in which rain can stipple the paint or how ice rosettes can decorate and mark a surface and you have a medium that can bring to a painting much more than just a sense of colour.

I have become a watercolour purist, beginning the painting, tackling the entanglement of vegetation and ending the written notes in brush and colour alone. Of the one hundred and thirty plus paintings that appear in this book, only half a dozen or so have any pre-drawing in pen or pencil, and these exist solely because these implements came immediately to hand at the time. Pure brush has now become my way of working. It has a flow, an elegance and a delightful subtlety of mark. It has a traditional beauty, which allows the artist with a swift flick of the wrist to change a needle-fine line into a block of heavy colour – perfect for switching from detail to shadow. It allows freedom whilst also enabling precision.

Creating a painting direct in brush is riddled with complexities and problems. Of highest priority is the white of the paper. For example, when working on the painting of the Buzzard nest on p. 83, I painted the chicks first, leaving areas of the paper white so I could put in the brighter pine needles later. The darker shadows were used to define and lift the thin needles, lastly leaving the white down of the birds to be suggested by the warm glow of the hills and the silhouetted branches and needles behind. Any wash of colour or water, no matter how slight, will deaden the luminosity of the surface. I never use white or masking fluid, which can make a painting heavy or

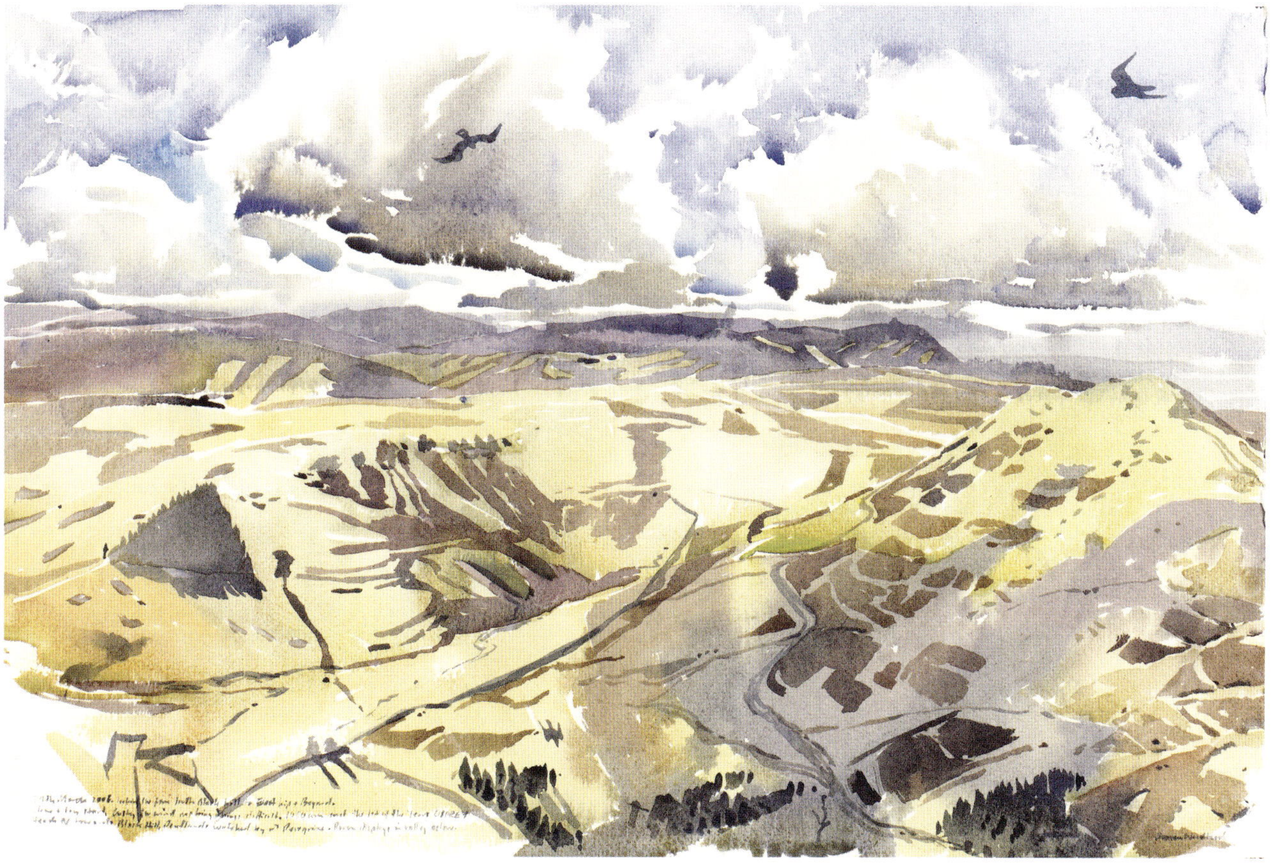

Osprey passing over South Black Hill
(watercolour, 380mm x 560mm)

29th March 2006. Looking south-west from South Black Hill to West Kip and beyond. Clear icy start with a gusting westerly wind making things difficult. 10:50 and first of the year's Osprey heads north towards Black Hill, Pentlands, watched by male Peregrine. Raven displays in valley below.

A first trip to view the area from one of the cairns proved a delight. A bitterly cold day backed by a raw strong west wind, but bright and clear. Among the darkened hills to right of centre is East Cairn Hill. Below is where the Borestane marks the source of the North Esk.

unduly harsh. New white paper can be daunting, but it can also create space and room to breathe. Therefore, whenever I am creating a painting, whatever I decide to leave white I have to work around, projecting ahead to an extent, the area that I am going to leave untouched. By working this way, I can never tell what a painting is going to look like until the very last colour is applied. Because I do not give myself a definitive outline to work to, the edges of my subjects can be moveable. Only when I apply a final colour next to a subject do I decide where its edge lies. I have spent fifteen years or so developing brushwork, pushing the boundaries with a method of working that is both direct and instant and characterised by a mystery as well as an unpredictable excitement that I find no other medium allows.

It has been a rare privilege to be absorbed into a new landscape and locality, to be able to open myself up to an endless supply of subjects and themes. I have strong ties around Carlops now. I am inspired by the landscape, the wildlife, the plants, the light and the atmosphere of the area. I feel now that my work is firmly rooted there and am extremely fortunate that I have been able to work and develop as an artist in this very special place.

Darren Woodhead
Musselburgh
May 2009

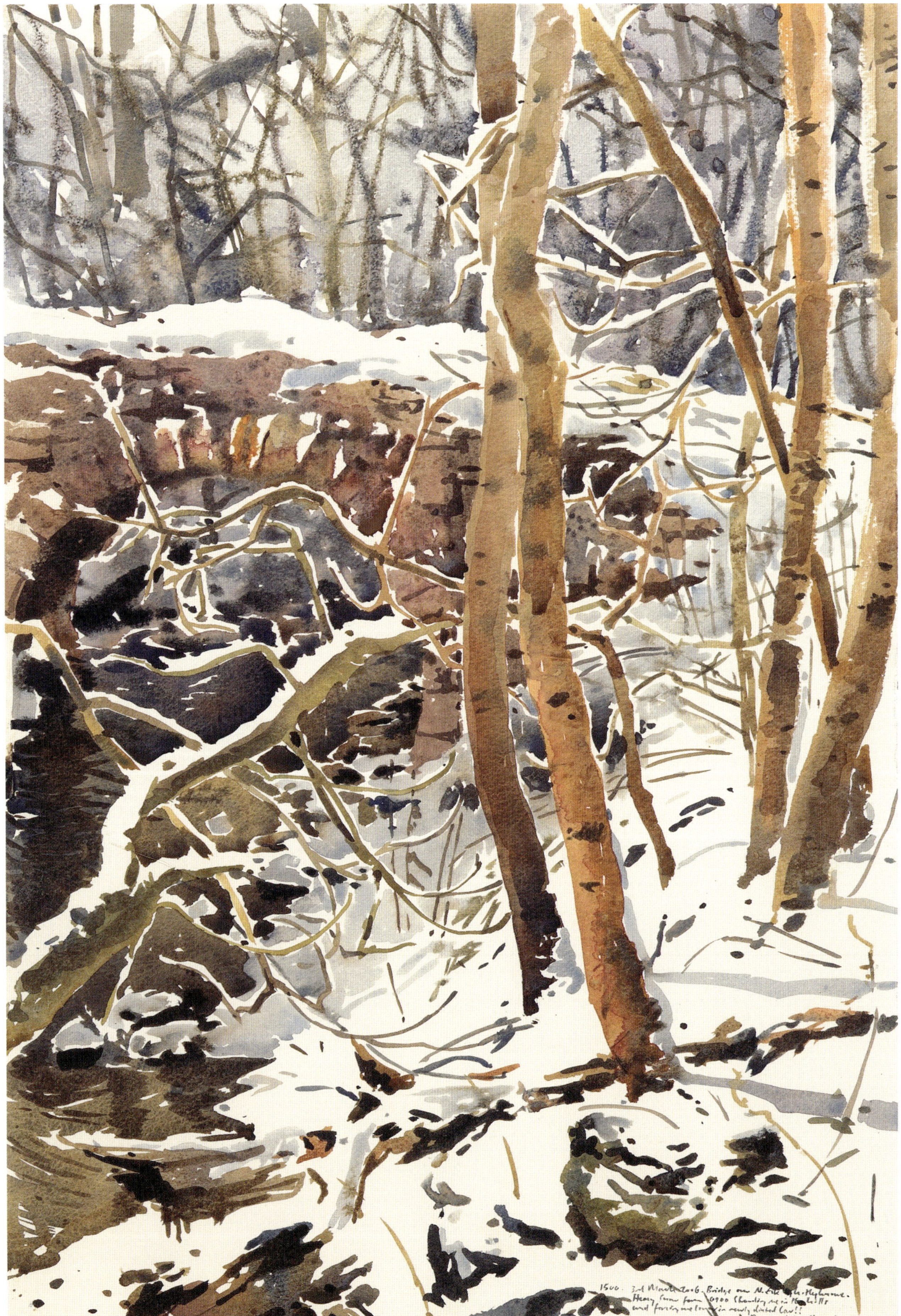
1500.
Darren Woodhead.

2006
Towards the Source

Lull after sudden heavy snowfall over stone bridge and Rowans, Amazondean
(watercolour, 560mm x 380mm)

15:00, 3rd March 2006. Bridge over North Esk by Kitleyknowe. Heavy snow from 09:00 stranding me in hills forcing me lower in newly dented car!

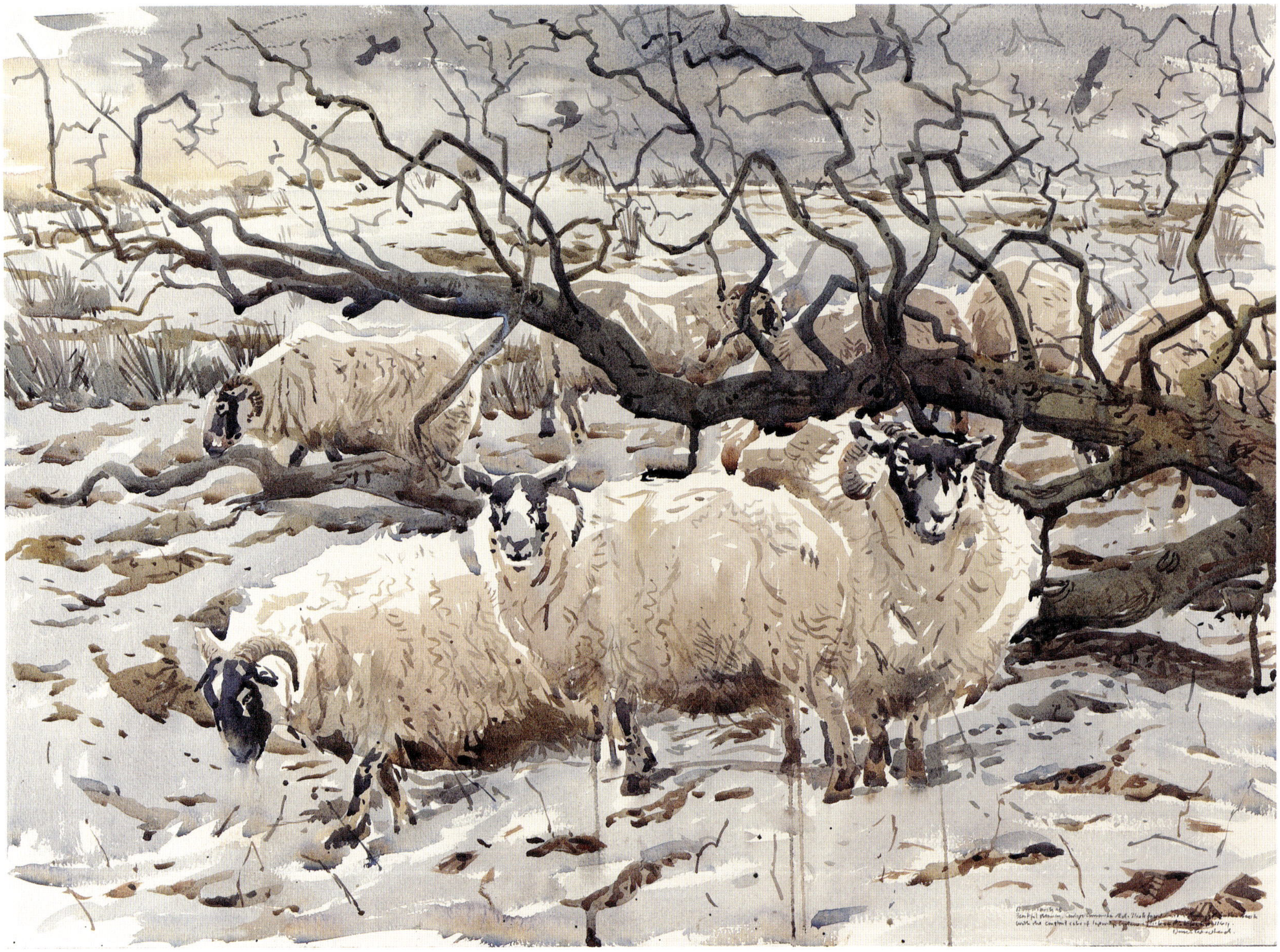

Early morning light towards the moor
(watercolour, 560mm x 760mm)

12th March 2006. Beautiful morning beside the Carlops to Lamancha Road. Black-faced Ewes among fallen Beech, with constant background echo of Lapwing, Curlew, and a flock of Pink-footed Geese passing.

Lapwing and Curlew seen on the moor behind sheltering Ewes whilst a skein of Geese head back north towards the clearing horizon – true signs of spring.

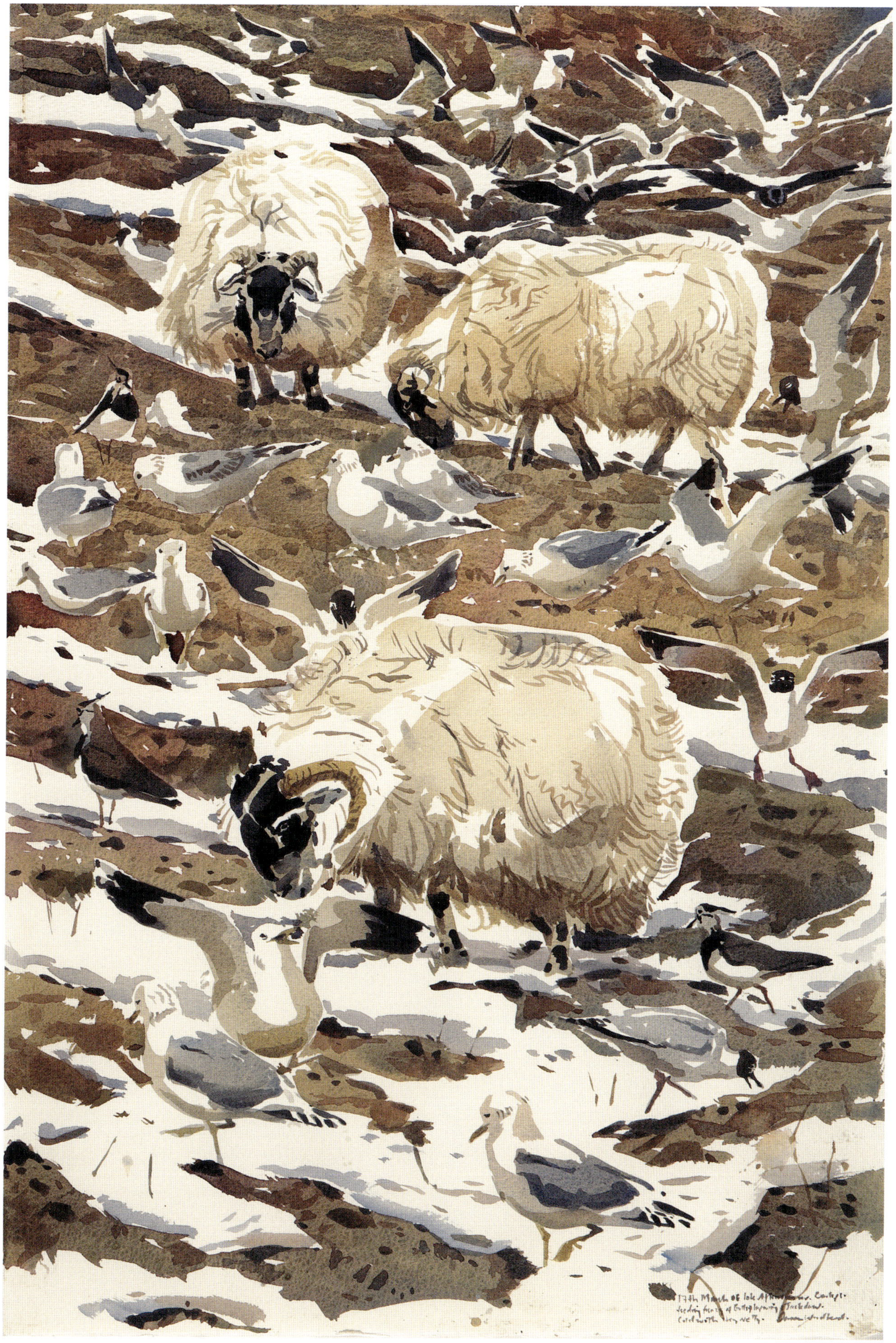

Ewes among thawing snow
(watercolour, 560mm x 380mm)

17th March 2006. Late afternoon near Carlops. Feeding frenzy of Gulls, Lapwing and Jackdaw. Cold with strong north-easterly.

A strong sense of the season ahead. The rapidly melting snow exposed grazing for the ewes, and worms for the voracious birds. Already streams of hooded Black-headed Gulls are visiting their nesting grounds in the hills, and Lapwings are spectacularly defending their territories.

Scratching Badgers in view of
Harbourcraig, Carlops, 31st May 2006
(watercolour, 380mm x 560mm)

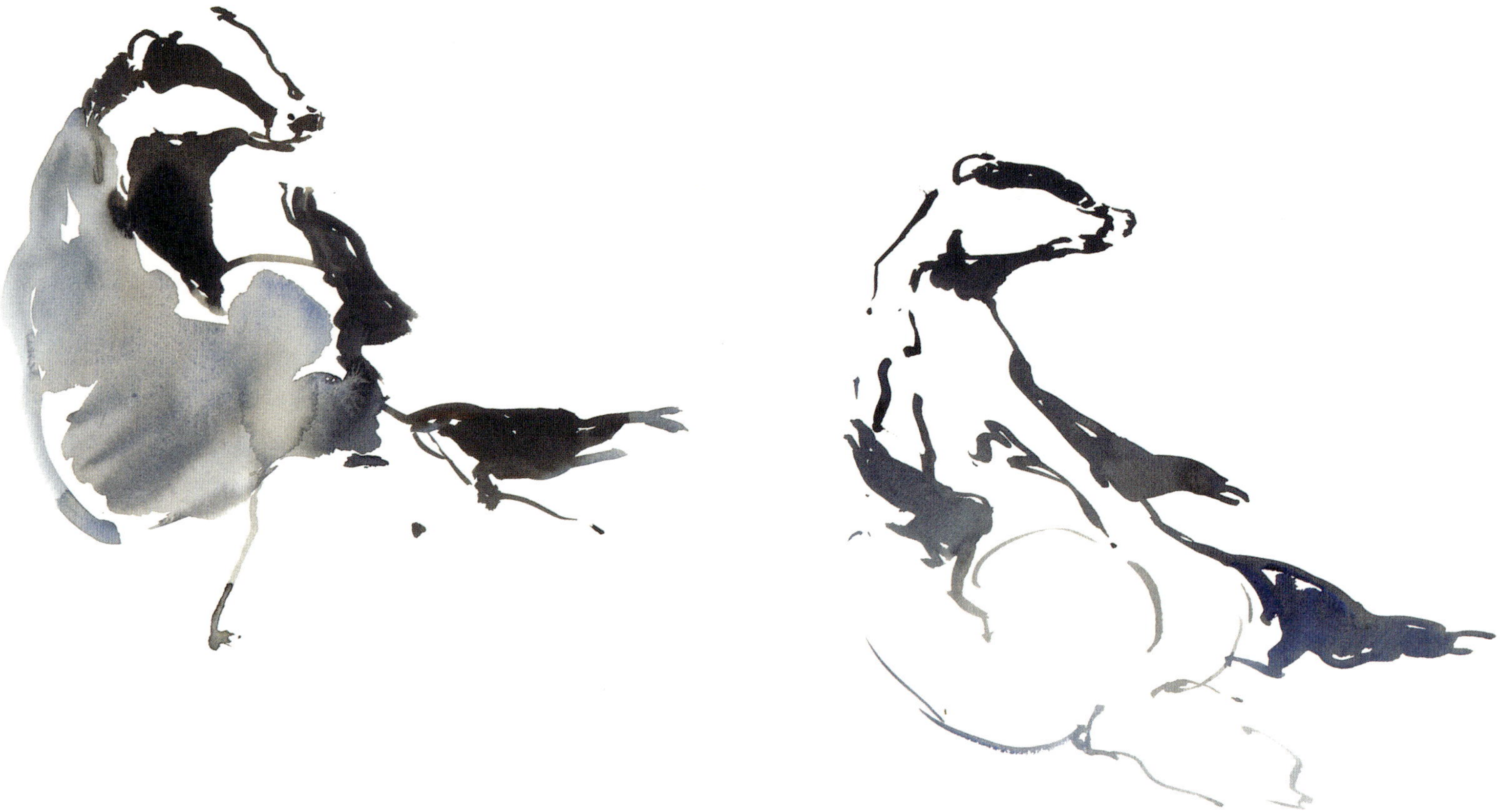

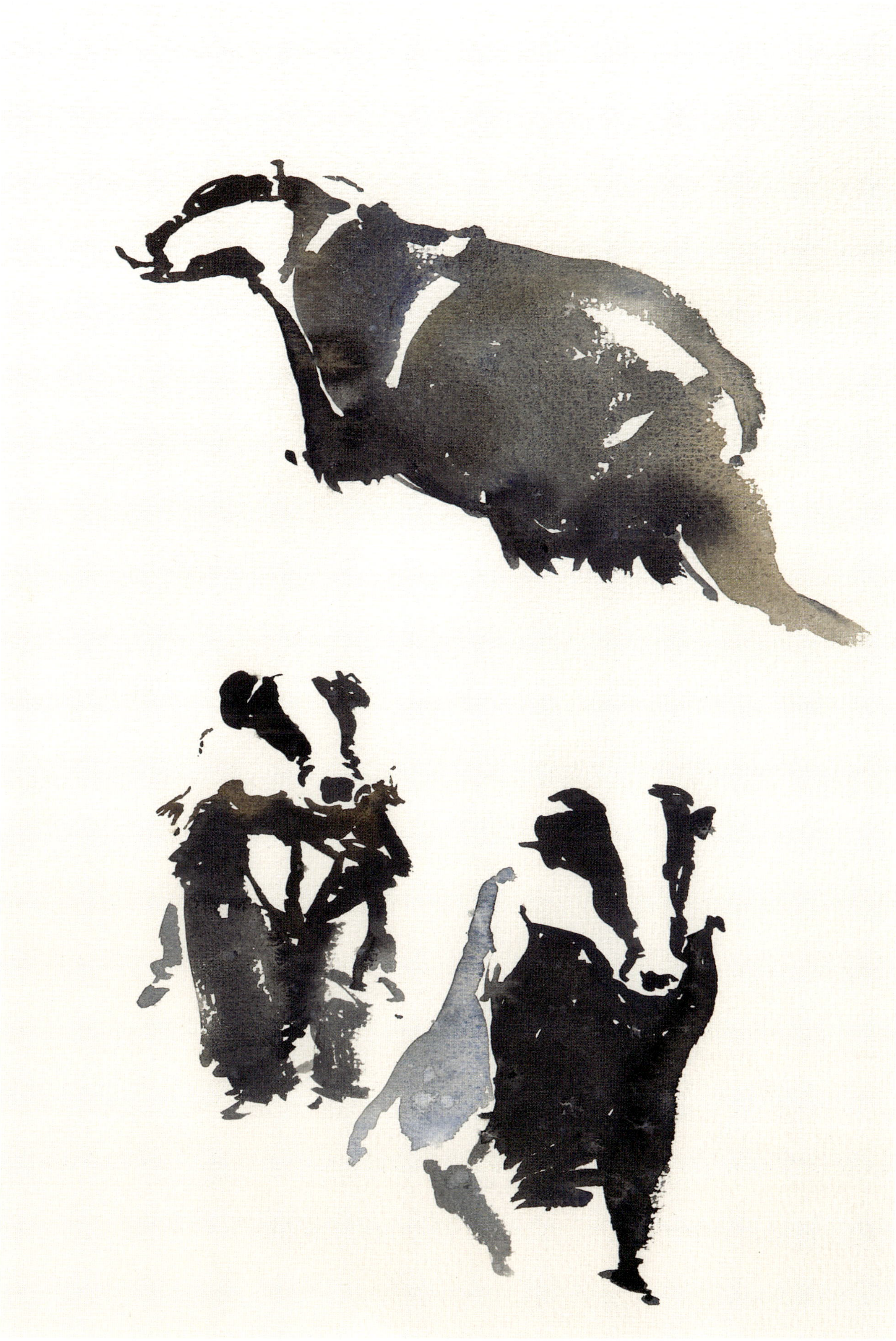

Badger Cubs
(watercolour, 400mm x 300mm)

31st May 2006. Near Carlops, Borders. Overcast after beautiful day. Light spots of rain, 20:50–22:30. Badger active when arrived. Cubs out 21:15 but in sets 21:50. Adult Badger off over hill 22:00.

That May I made several magical visits to a Badger set, positioned against the backdrop of the hills. The long May nights were perfect for watching these generally nocturnal mammals. More often than not, an adult would disappear over the hill close to ten o'clock, but other activity was much less predictable. Seated some distance away and downwind, I was able to watch the comical antics of cubs, chuckling as they emerged from the set. Even the distance between us could not hide the sound of a frantic satisfying scratch, which clearly brought relief after a day spent underground.

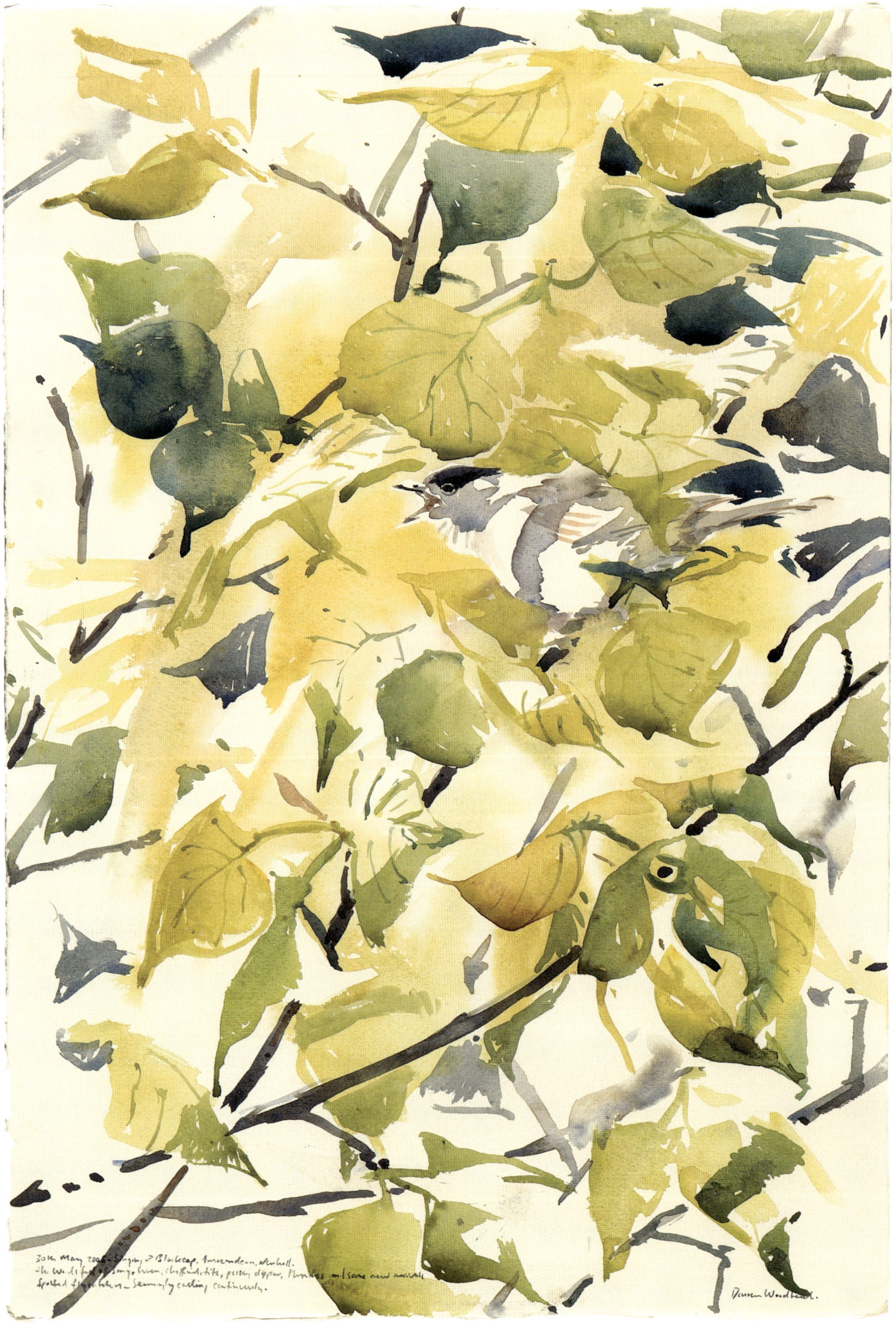

Darren Woodhead.

The Song of the Esk
(watercolour, 560mm x 380mm)

30th May 2006. Singing male Blackcap, Amazondean, Newhall. The woods full of song, Wren, Chaffinch, Tits, passing Dipper, Thrushes and some new arrivals; Spotted Flycatchers seemingly calling continuously.

A stunning day among lemon-green new leaf cover, where the woods of Habbies Howe are alive with spring song. One of a few images painted of a boisterous Blackcap warding off contention for its precious territory in a clearing below Newhall. Of its many neighbours, the arrival of such a healthy population of Spotted Flycatchers was a warming surprise during a worrying time of national decline. They are among the last migrants to arrive, heralding summer to the woods and completing the music of the dean.

One of the first paintings produced in the area on a very memorable induction day indeed! It was a crystal-clear morning, exceptionally cold and icy, the ground frozen solid after several days of low temperatures. I headed up to the Borestane to begin working from the source of the North Esk. Without any warning, a front of cloud engulfed from the north-west, bringing at first the odd flake of snow but within minutes a full blizzard. I tried in vain to paint, but the conditions were impossible. The grouse that I watched disappeared under the horizontal sheet of white blowing in. Snow covered every surface immediately and my palette and paper became a mound of multicoloured crystals. Packing my gear together I headed back, slipping, sliding on the ice beneath the new snow. Sula was in her element, but even she was caught out, endlessly finishing sprawled out like a newly born animal trying to stand. Had it not been an hour's stumble back to the car in very heavy conditions it would certainly have been hilarious. We managed it back to the car with the only misfortune of a torn pair of trousers. Phew!

The car wouldn't make it up the hill; it had no chance, even in reverse. I had no choice but to begin the long trek to John Aitken's farm at Carlopshill, snow continuing to accumulate, to ask for some help. John was in, like any sensible soul, and agreed to help instantly. His truck struggled and could not make any ground up the hill. The spinning vehicle then careered back down the slope in my direction giving a new feature on my front wing! There was no choice but to call for the tractor. William, John's son, towed me clear and if only that had been the end of the story. In order to make my way off the hill a couple of major hurdles lay ahead. In my two-wheel drive, negotiating the incline from Fairliehope was perhaps the most unnerving of all. The tractor went down with the occasional drift, the truck with a definite wobble, and then me. As soon as I turned the corner the car went into a slide, and so did any hope of ever being able to stop or even control it. After what seemed an eternity I had steadily bobsleighed down the slope but then began to approach the hairpin that dropped off steeply into the ravine. With brakes pointless I tried to slow by guiding the wheels into the occasional large drift alongside, but with no let-up in the pace I grasped the door, expecting I would have to jump ship. Miraculously, the car stopped within feet of the edge and I was then able to shrug off the beating that my pride had taken. I had been well and truly christened into the area, and my thanks and praise go to both John and William. The sight of the bridge was my salvation that day. The snow only lay for a period of five hours or so, and the day finished as clear, cold and quietly as it had begun.

Peregrine studies,
30th May 2006
(watercolour, 560mm x 380mm)

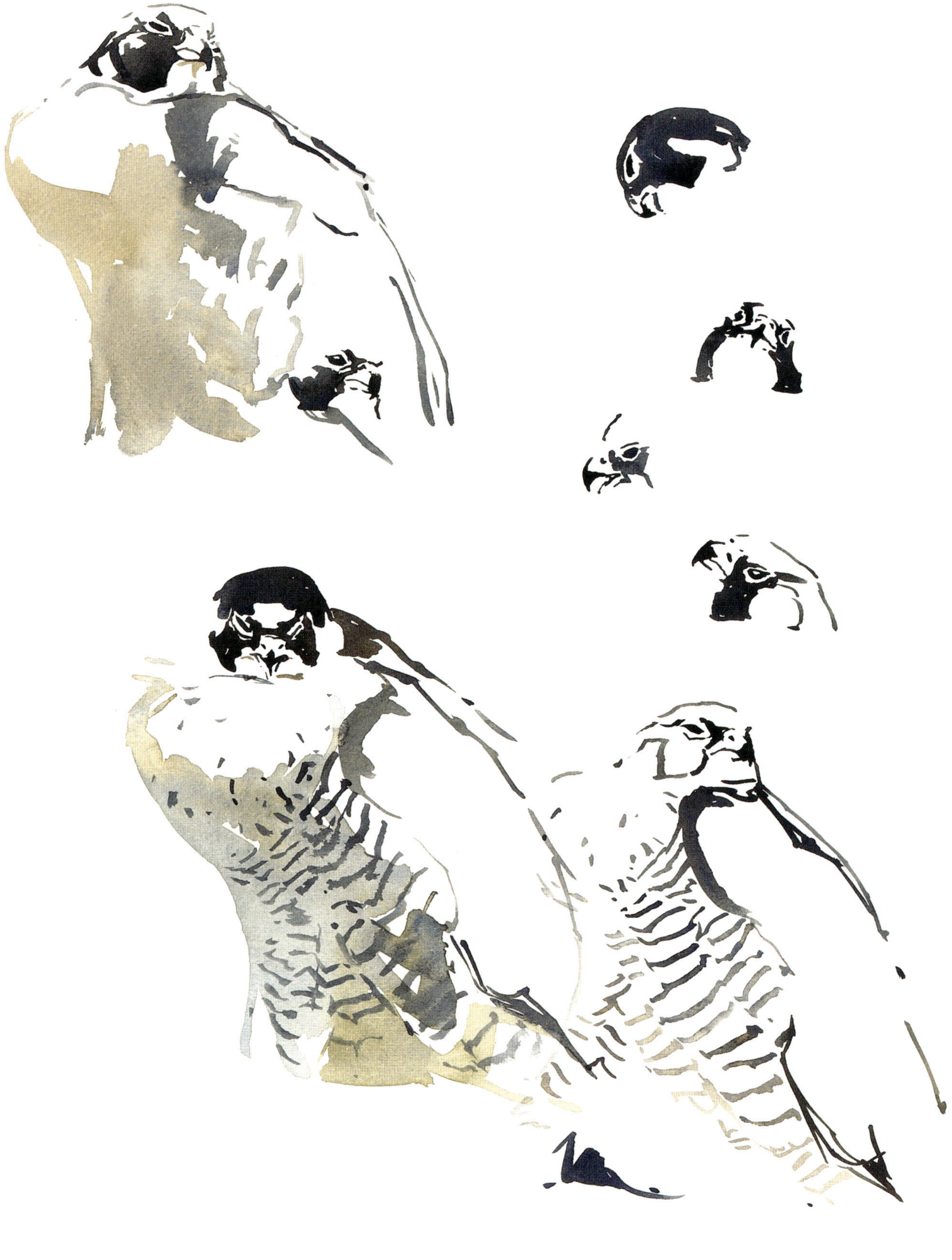

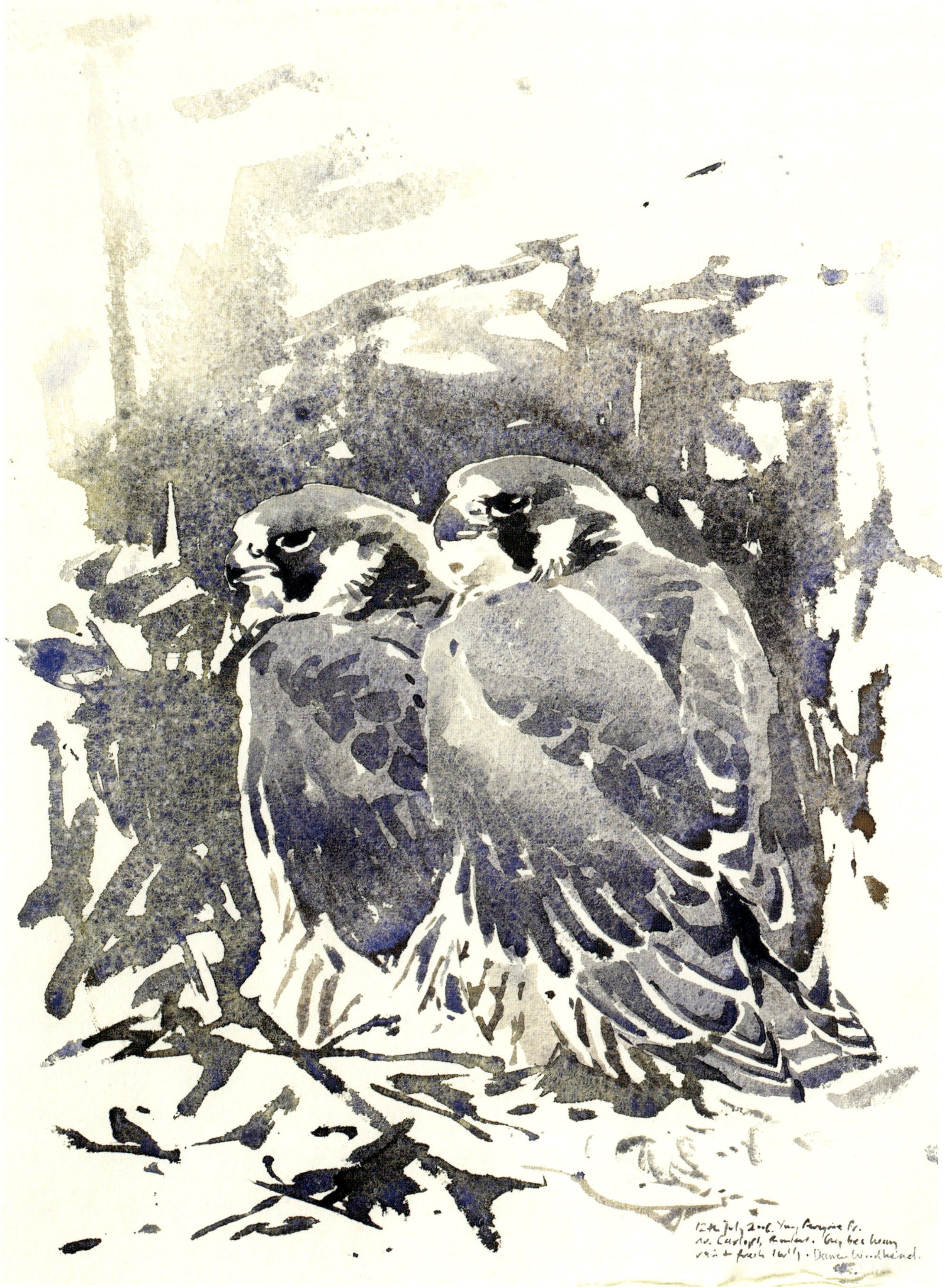

Young Peregrine pair
(watercolour, 360mm x 280mm)

12th July 2006. Young Peregrines near Carlops, Borders. Grey becoming heavy rain and fresh south-westerly.

A bad forecast yet I desperately wanted to spend my birthday out painting. Equipped with umbrella, it was tied to an adjoining fence and guyed down in prospect of the arriving weather. I painted frivolously, the buffeting coming from wind and rain limiting the size of image I could produce. Painting was one thing, getting it back to the shelter of the car another!

It was a year of both tragedy and success for local Peregrines. This family, tragically displaced after their eggs were taken earlier in the spring, moved to another patch where they raised two youngsters, becoming one of the highlights of that summer. Their early setback meant that they were a month later in producing chicks than a neighbouring pair, and the last summer evening I saw them was memorable.

Globe Flower

(watercolour, 380mm x 280mm)

22nd June 2006. Globe Flower Studies, *Trollius europaeus*. North Esk Reservoir. Gusty wind but milder than of late. First Black-headed Gull fledgling and calling alone. First painting as a daddy! Only the single flower in full bloom.

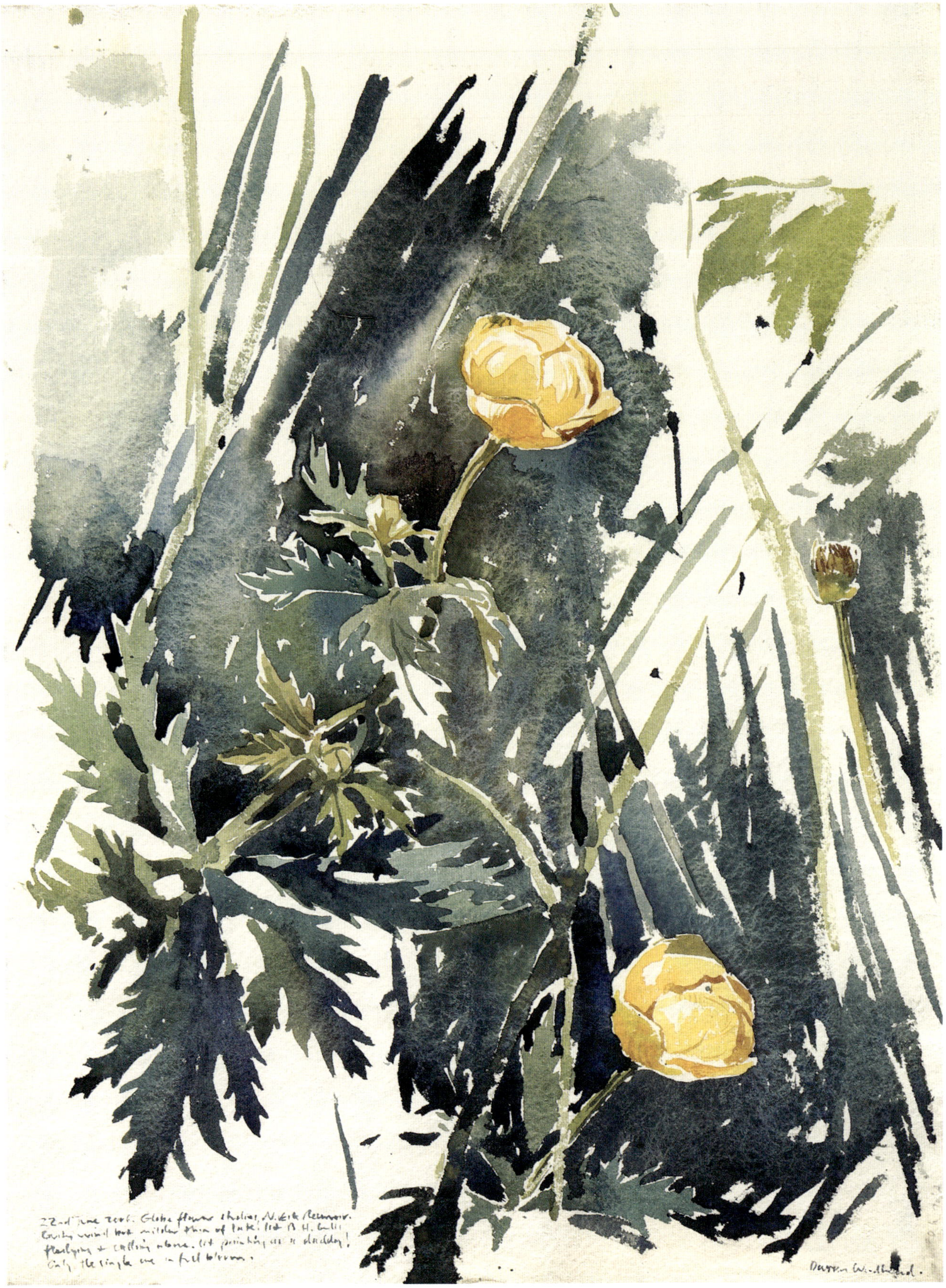

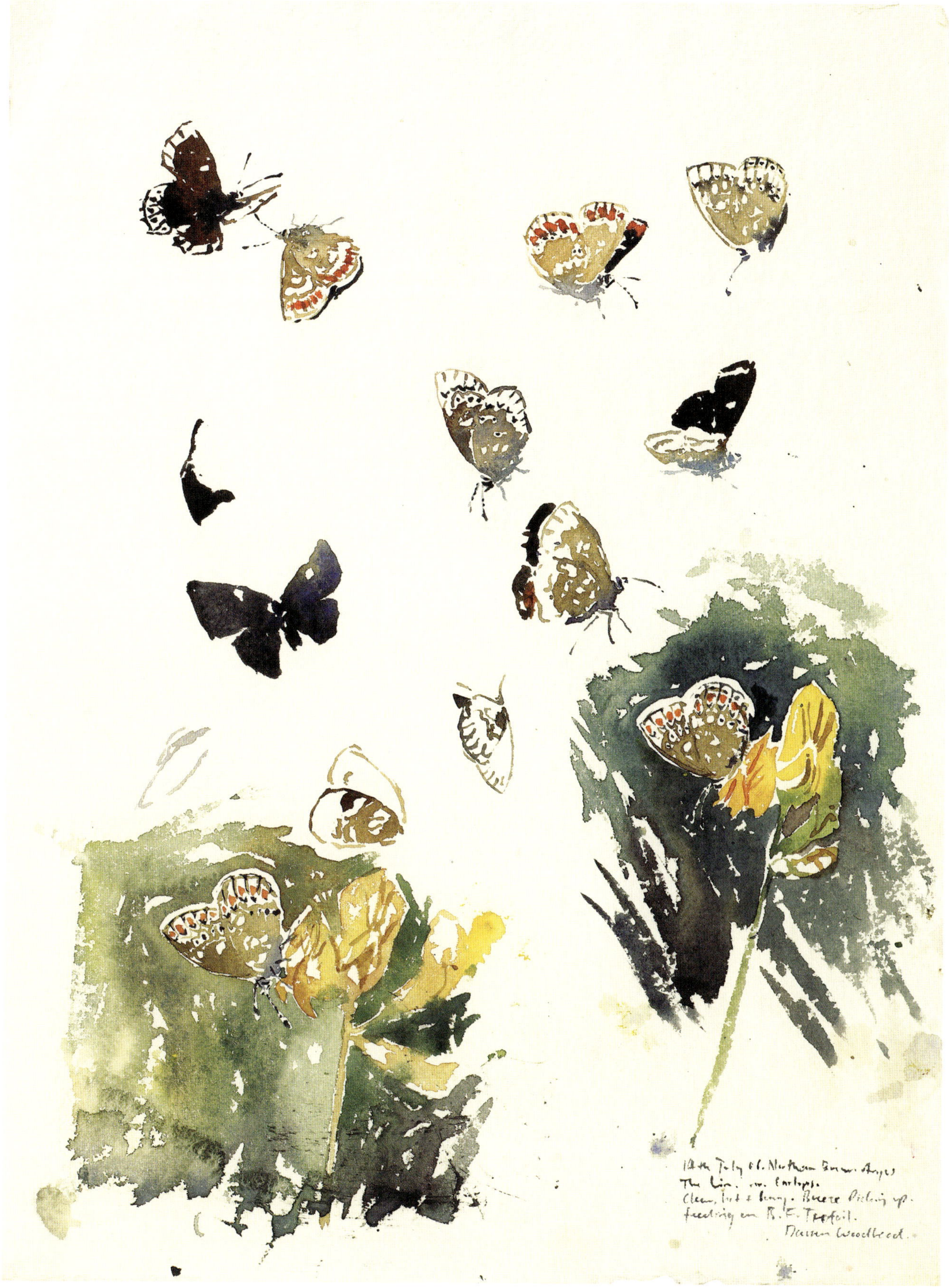

Northern Brown Argus
(watercolour, 380mm x 280mm)

14th July 2006. Northern Brown Argus at The Linn, near Carlops. Clear, hot and sunny. Breeze picking up. Feeding on Birds-foot Trefoil.

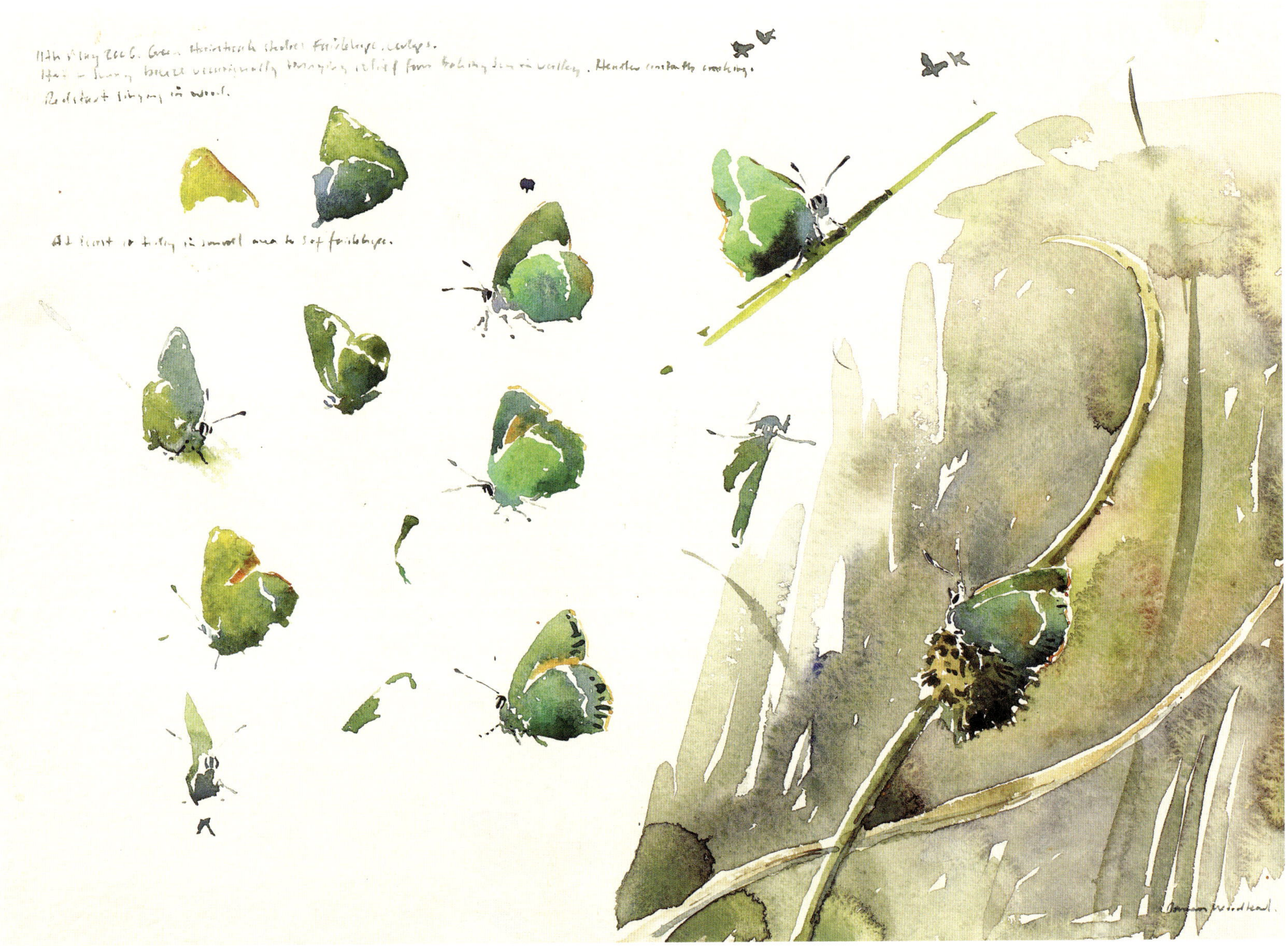

Green Hairstreak butterfly
(watercolour, 280mm x 380mm)

11th May 2006. Green Hairstreak Studies, Fairliehope, Carlops. Hot and sunny with breeze bringing relief from a baking sun in the valley. Heather constantly cracking. Redstart singing in wood. At least ten today in small area to south of Fairliehope.

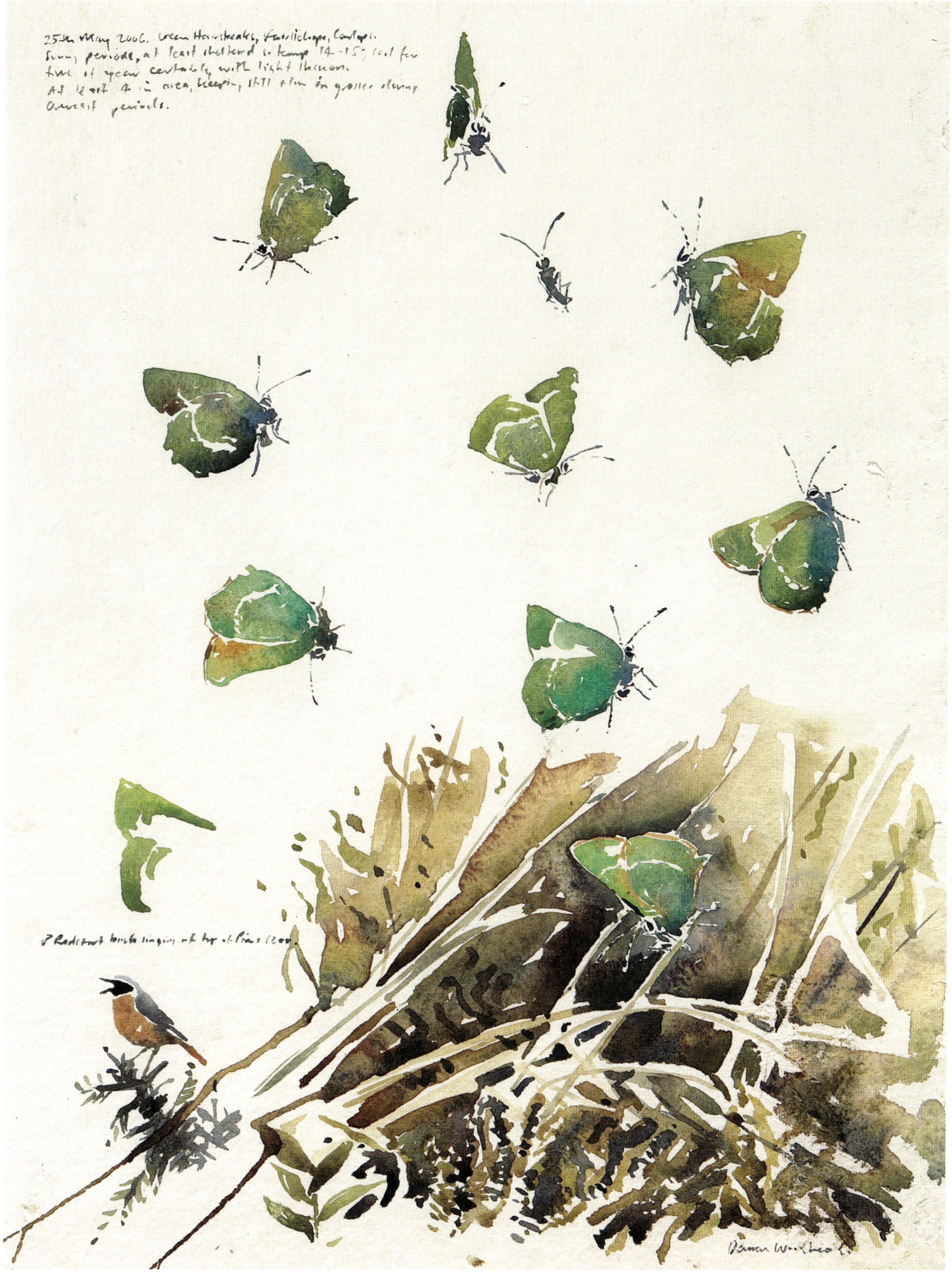

Green Hairstreak butterfly
(watercolour, 380mm x 280mm)

25th May 2006. At least sheltered so temperature fourteen to fifteen degrees, cool for time of year certainly, with light showers. At least four in area, keeping still and low in long grass during overcast periods.
Male Redstart back singing in top of pines 12:00.

Painted Lady, Dark-green Fritillaries and Common blues *(watercolour, 380mm x 280mm)*

27th July 2006. Sunny periods and hot. Wonderfully fresh Painted Lady on Knapweed, feeding alongside path and into verges. Very worn Dark-brown Fritillary.

Male and female Common Blue hovering together for good ten minutes. Female flight slower more dropping, male fluttery and shimmering wings.

Both dropped into grass several times, once, male landed next to female and presented abdomen.

16:20 fresh Dark-green Fritillary landed at my feet, again on Knapweed.

Female showing abdomen to hovering male. 14:30 newly fledged Peregrine flies directly at Curlew on wet marsh. Curlew reacts by trailing wings as if injured or perhaps to increase potential size? Peregrine then continues making several lazy grabs at other waders.

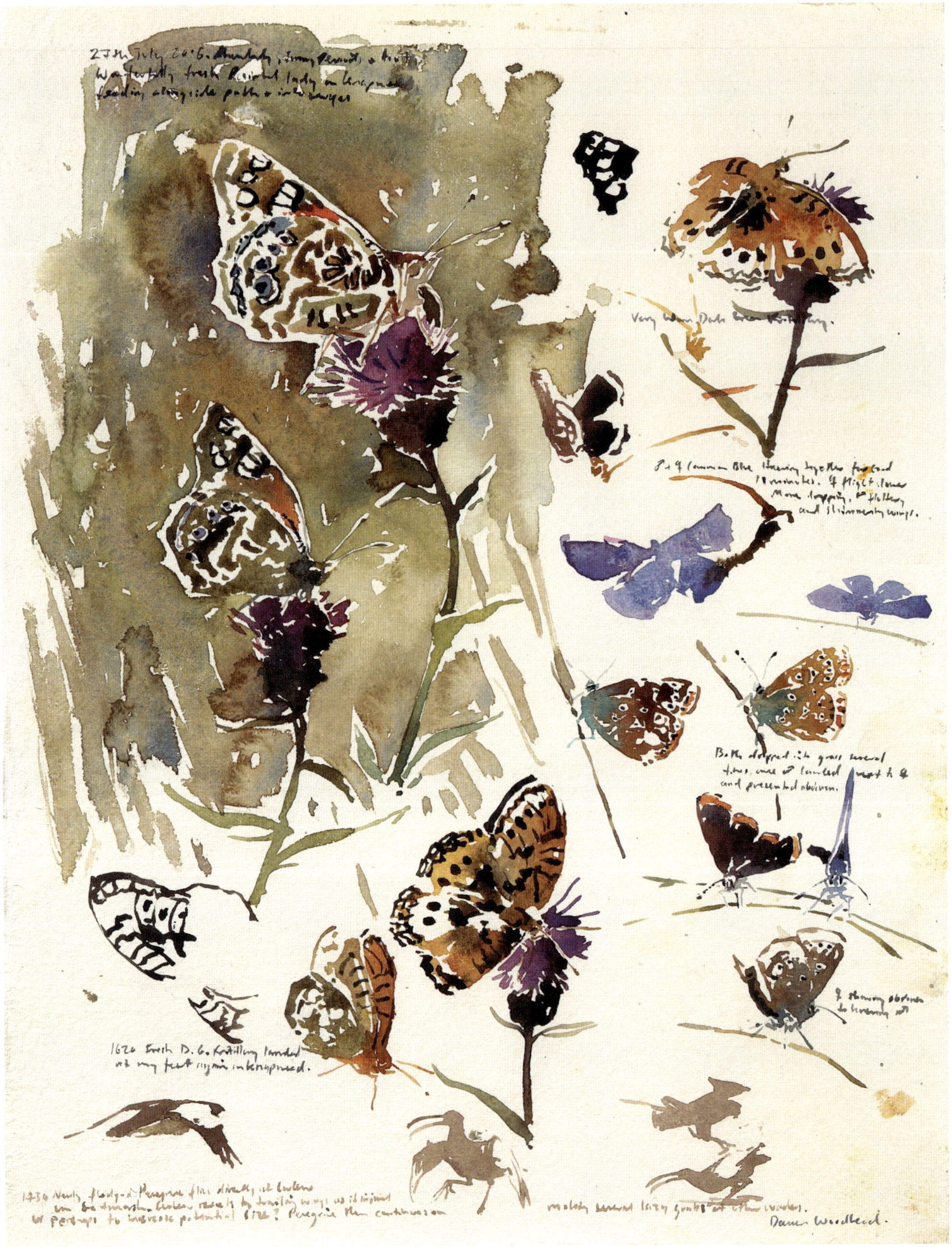

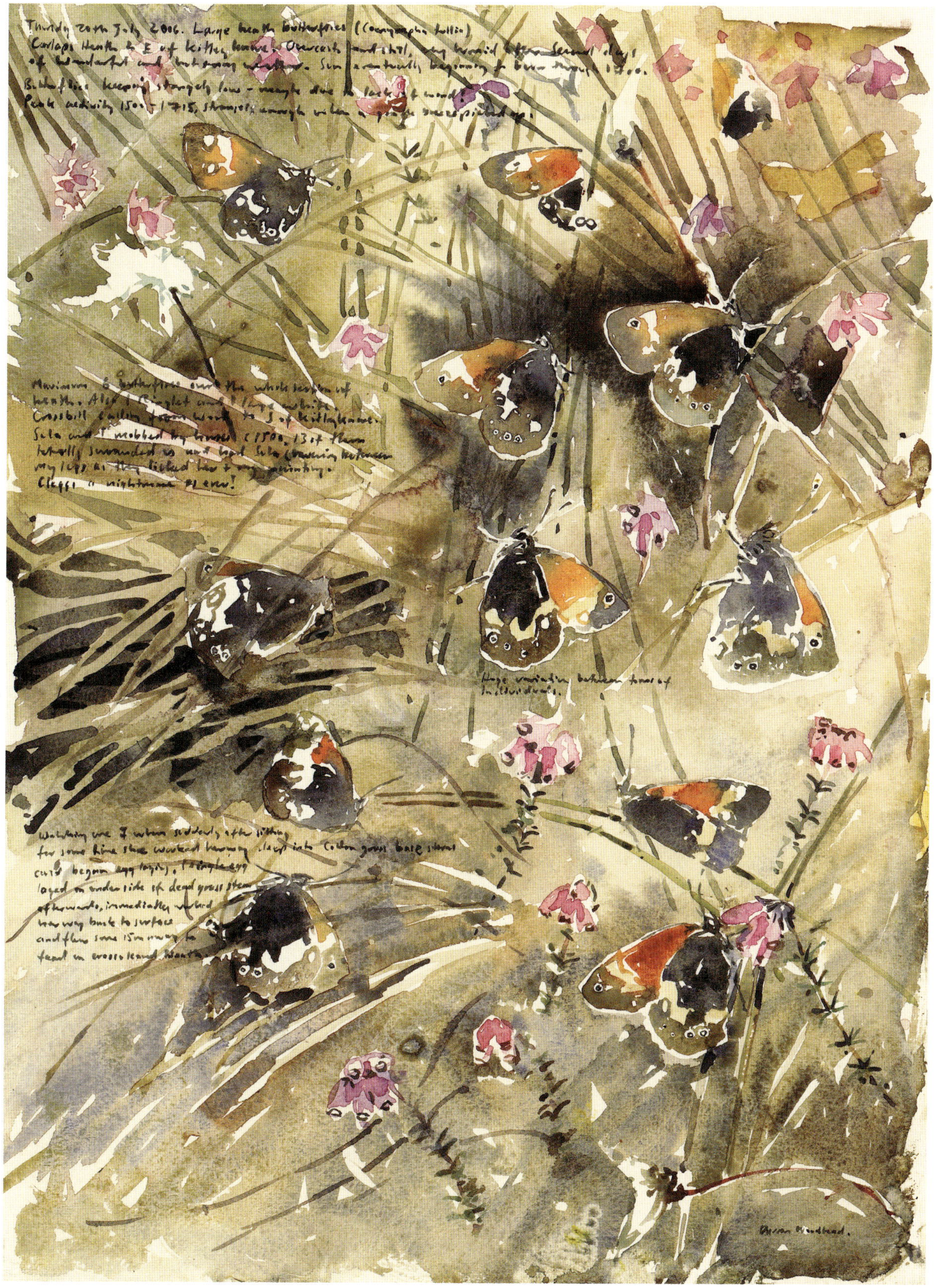

Large Heaths among Cross-leaved Heath and Cotton Grass *(watercolour, 380mm x 280mm)*

Thursday 20th July 2006. Large Heath butterflies (*Coenonympha tullia*) , Carlops Heath to east of Kitleyknowe. Overcast and still. Very humid after several days of wonderful, hot and sunny weather. Sun eventually beginning to burn through 17:00. Butterflies keeping strangely low – maybe due to lack of wind? Peak activity 15:00–17:15, and strangely enough when a gentle breeze picked up.

Maximum six butterflies over the whole section of heath. Also one Ringlet and one Large White. Crossbill calling from wood to South of Kitleyknowe. Sula and I mobbed by (Icelandic) horses around 15:00, thirteen of them totally surrounded us and had Sula cowering between my legs as they licked her and my painting. Cleggs a nightmare as ever!

Huge variation between tones of individuals.

Watching one female when suddenly after sitting for some time she worked her way deep into Cotton Grass base stems and began egg laying. One single egg laid on underside of dead grass stem, afterwards immediately worked her way back to surface and flew some fifteen metres away to feed on Cross-leaved Heath.

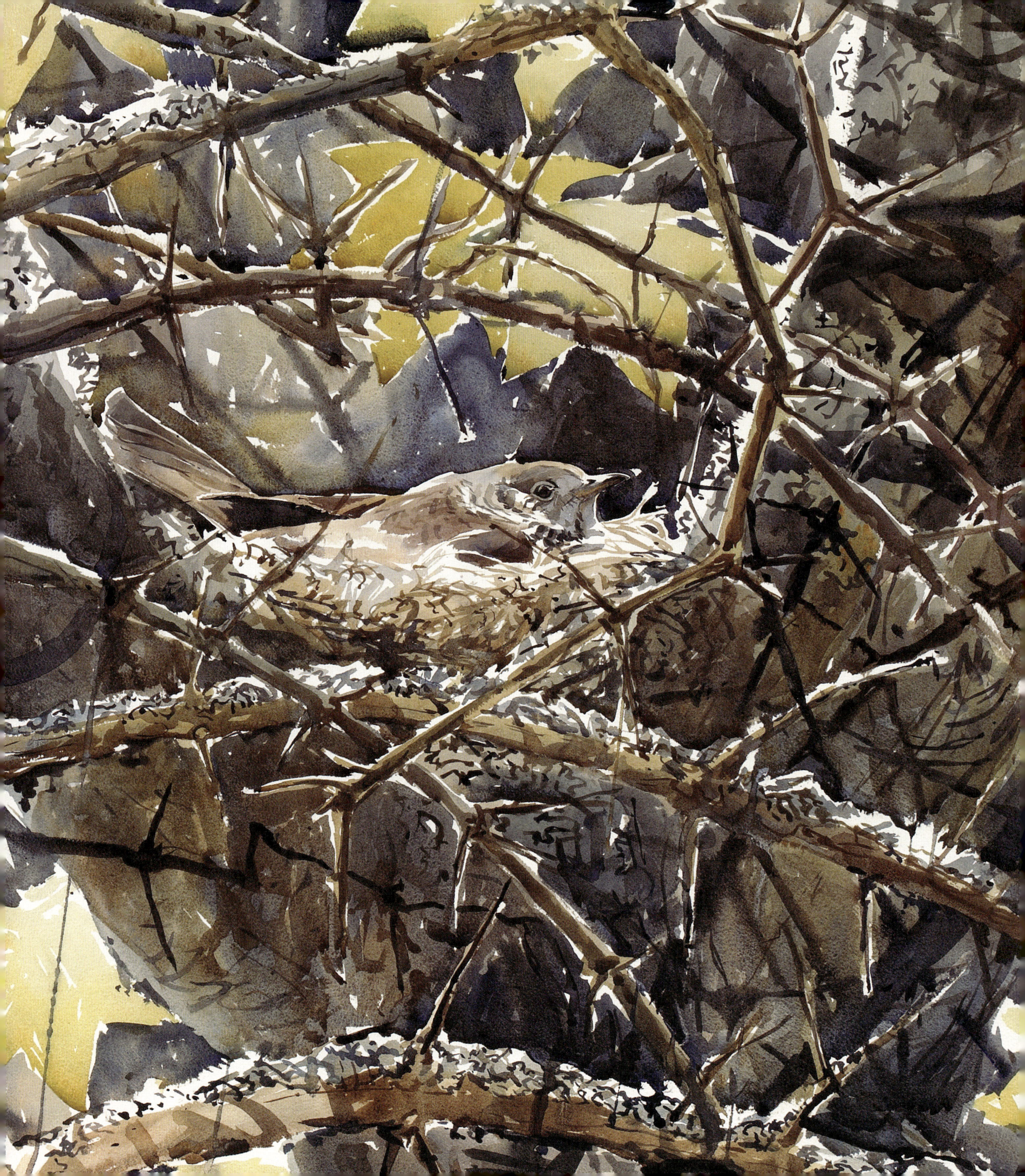

Incubating Mistle Thrush
(watercolour, 760mm x 560mm)

29th May 2006. Sitting Mistle Thrush, Fairlliehope wood, Carlops. Cool with moderate northerly and hail showers. Pair Spotted Flycatcher today but no sign definitely of Redstart. Tawny Owl box holding one young. Chaffinch and plenty of Curlew blasting from the hill.

Although I saw a fully fledged Mistle Thrush on 16th May whilst watching insects above the track from Lamancha to Kitleyknowe, this seemed early. More usual was what happened at Fairliehope, when the rattling of the parents coming in and out of the nest for food made it easy to locate a nest, situated some fifteen metres up in the fork of a Sycamore. Fighting off the incessant Midges, it was possible to sit and look into the nest from further up the slope in the wood. Working my way between trunks, I eventually secured a grandstand position.

The nest was made up of mostly of Lichen, entangled with the occasional strand of sheep wool and lined with Moss. In those first weeks the parents changed incubation shift several times daily, the new shift arriving with a raucous declaration in contrast to the silent sitter. On cooler days the sitting bird would be reluctant to move and the swap-over was postponed.

Throughout May and June, I religiously visited a small wood in the hills. The south-east facing wood, positioned on a steep slope, gets much of the day's sun – when it shines. Standing on the incline above the wood brings you on a level with many of the higher branches. Scots Pines predominate the entrance, giving a clear and airy feel to the relatively sparse canopy. All this makes the wood an ideal place for watching and observing. It was a small community in itself, and I got to know the routines of its inhabitants, though often the element of surprise would leave me speechless.

23rd June 2006. Despite the cool weather, woods full of life with successful broods. As I walked along the track leading in, my presence was greeted by an array of alarm calls silencing the higher notes of fledglings. Scrambling over a fallen Pine with cumbersome pack and equipment, Great Tits, Robin, Wren and at last, the male Redstart were keeping their distance but voicing their opinions. Had I walked into something or was I the cause of the commotion? A Kestrel flew out of the lower boughs – perhaps it was not just me. I sat some distance away as Blackbirds and Thrushes kept stirring up activity. Then, in among the panic, the male Redstart flew down among an adjoining fallen Pine and fed a lone youngster! Wonderful, proof of breeding, I thought, and proudly noted it on the painting. The youngster was hidden for most of the time but I was sure that I had seen enough of it to be confident. Only as I walked back through did it become clearer what had happened. The youngster flew out up into a Pine ten metres away, calling. It was then immediately fed by a Robin, and again and again with no sign of the Redstart. Rightly or wrongly ruling out the absurd possibility of hybridisation, I presumed that during the commotion and state of panic that had ensued, the Redstart had mistakenly fed the Robin fledgling! This seems to be the most logical solution, until next year when perhaps I may see a Robin with a black face and grey back! So much for my proof of Redstart breeding.

Sitting Mistle Thrush
(watercolour, 560mm x 380mm)

24th May 2006. Mistle Thrush on nest, Fairliehope, Carlops.Bitterly cold day, heavy rain and hail showers. Gusty south-west wind, more like winter!

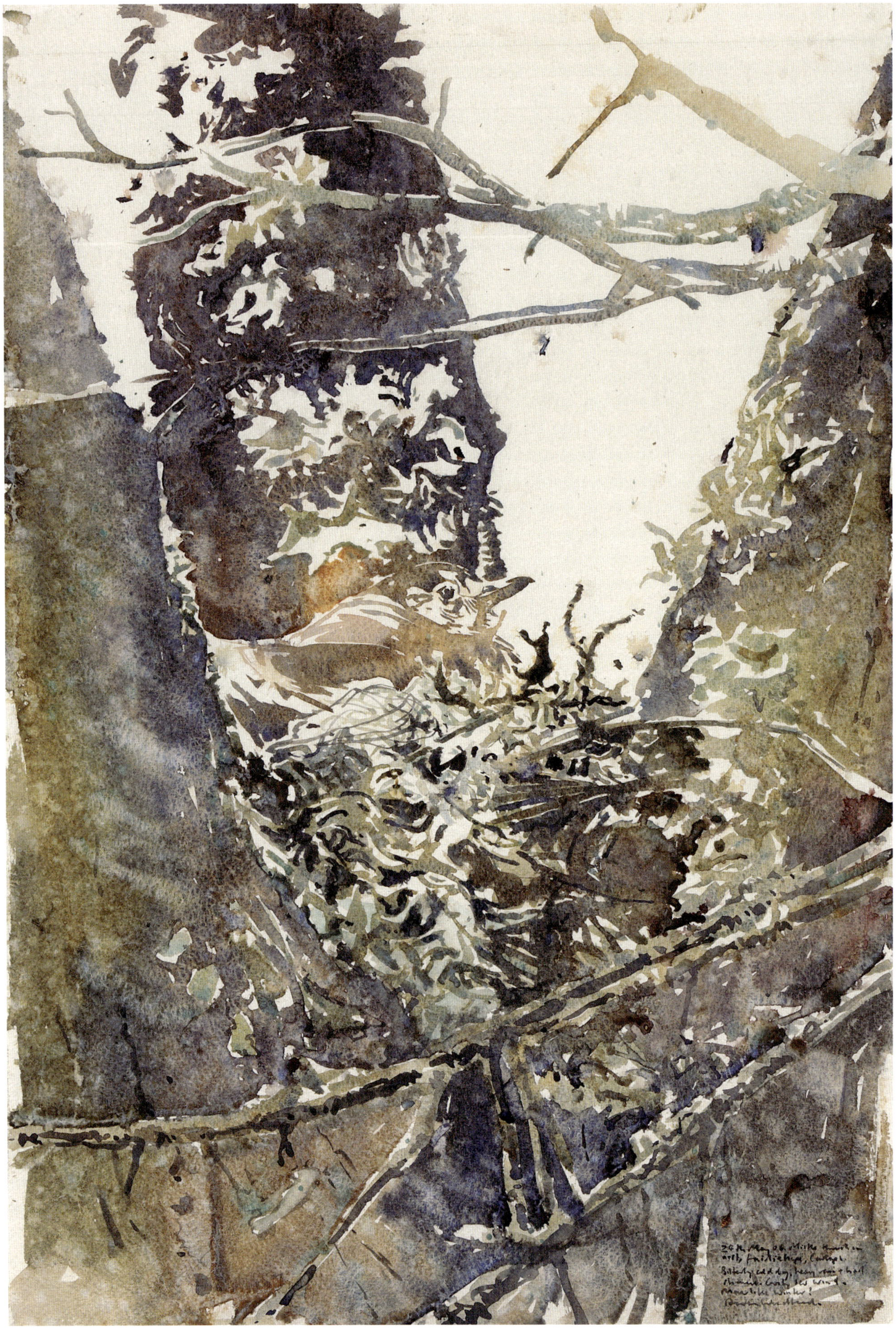

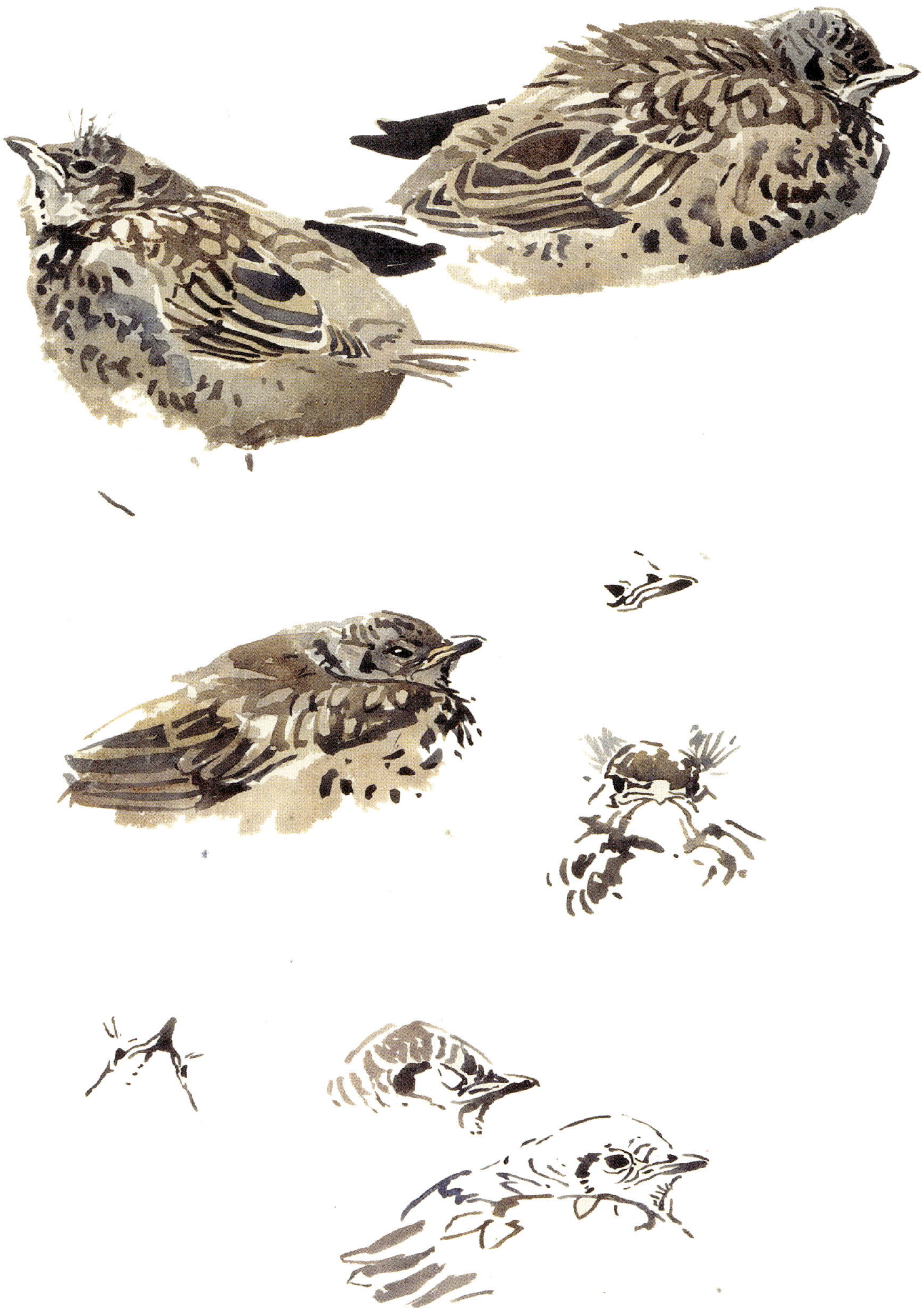

Mistle Thrush chicks, 23rd
June 2006.
(watercolour, 560mm x 380mm)

Bustling Mistle Thrush family
(watercolour, 560mm x 380mm)

23rd June 2006. Mistle Thrush nest, Fairliehope wood. Overcast and cool moderate breeze. Light showers. Not long to go for fledging. Already seen fledgling Redstart this morning.

The text on the image was written in reference to the event that I had witnessed moments earlier.

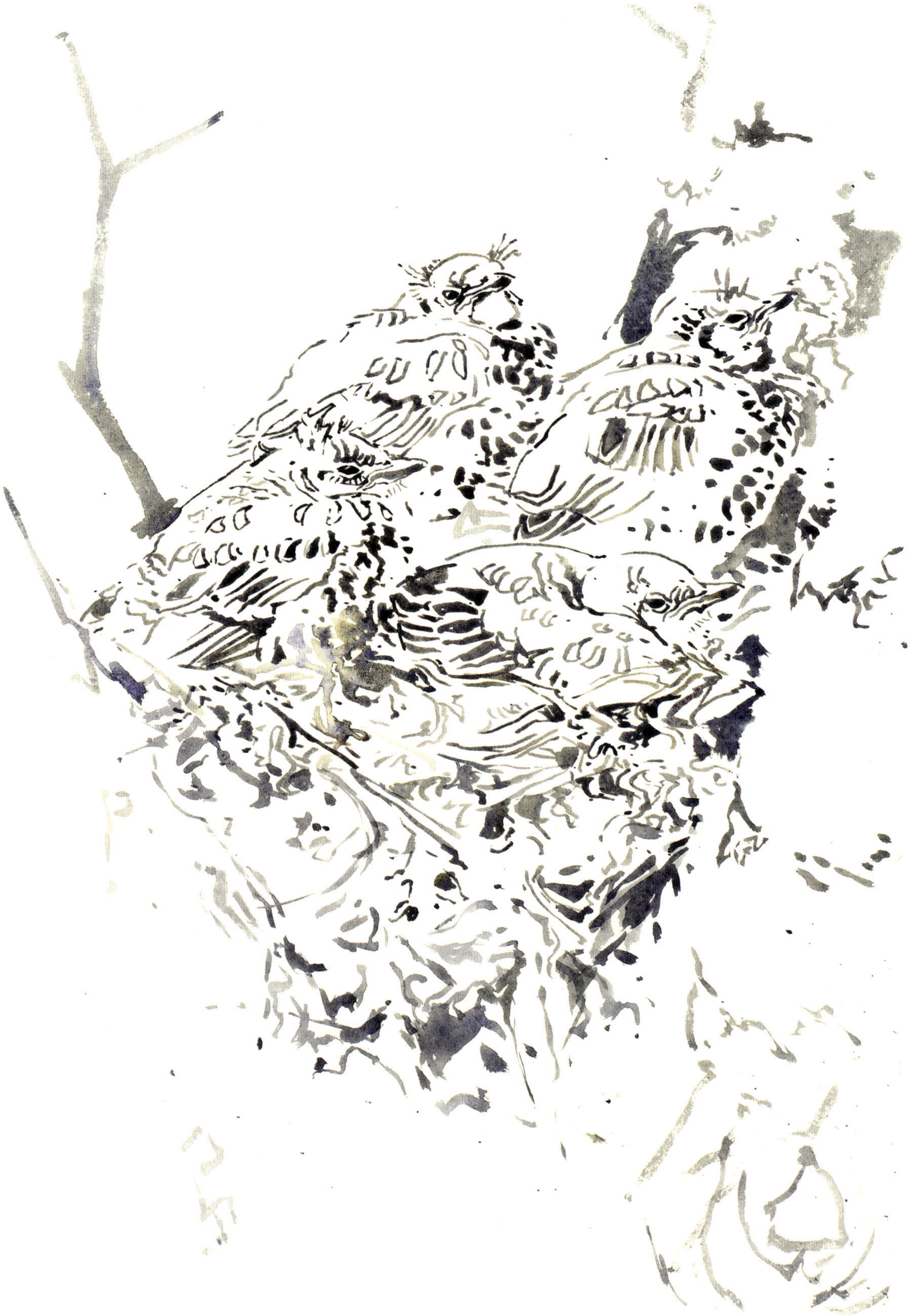

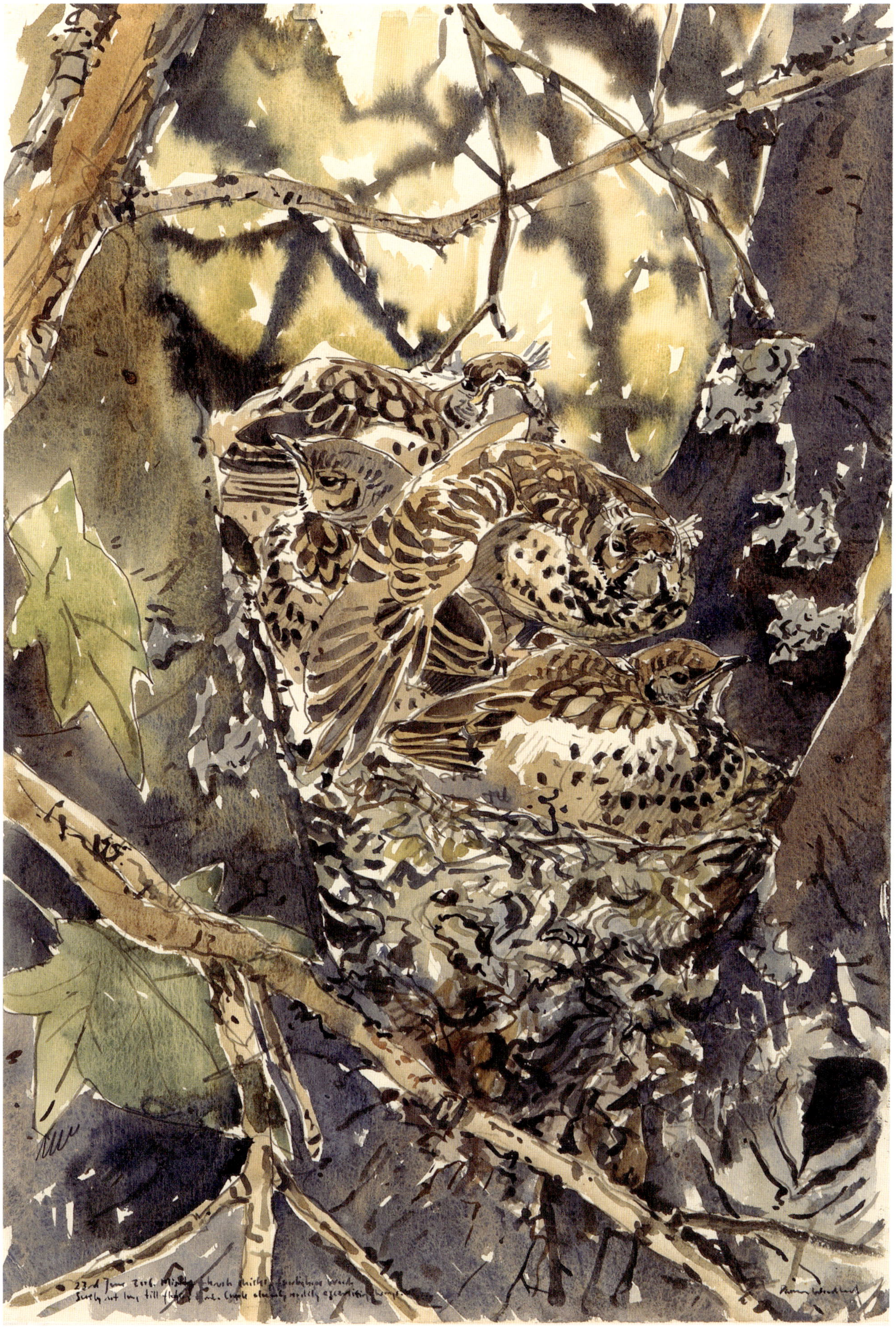

Young Thrushes
(watercolour and pencil, 560mm x 380mm)

23rd June 2006. Mistle Thrush chicks, Fairliehope wood. Surely not long till fledging time. Couple already readily exercising wings.

Tawny Owl and Chaffinches
(watercolour, 760mm x 560mm)

5th June 2006. Roosting adult Tawny Owl being mobbed by Chaffinch pair, Fairliehope woods, Carlops, 10 a.m.

A momentous day spent watching a roosting adult Tawny Owl at Fairliehope. I was heading towards the Sycamore when an adult Owl flew out of a row of Pines, across the edge of a tree in which some Thrushes were nesting and into the top section of a Fir. Instantly, the Thrushes gave chase, followed closely by local Blackbirds, Great Tits and Chaffinches intent on pestering the Owl. It was a great day – four paintings, all of them reproduced here. Such days are rare in the extreme, and it seemed propitious as the following day at 16:00, on the sixth of the sixth 2006, my first son, Corin, was born. The last image I painted that day (p. 47), is Corin's gift. Two paintings, both done in haste and displaying my usual confusion for dates, are labelled 6th rather than 5th June.

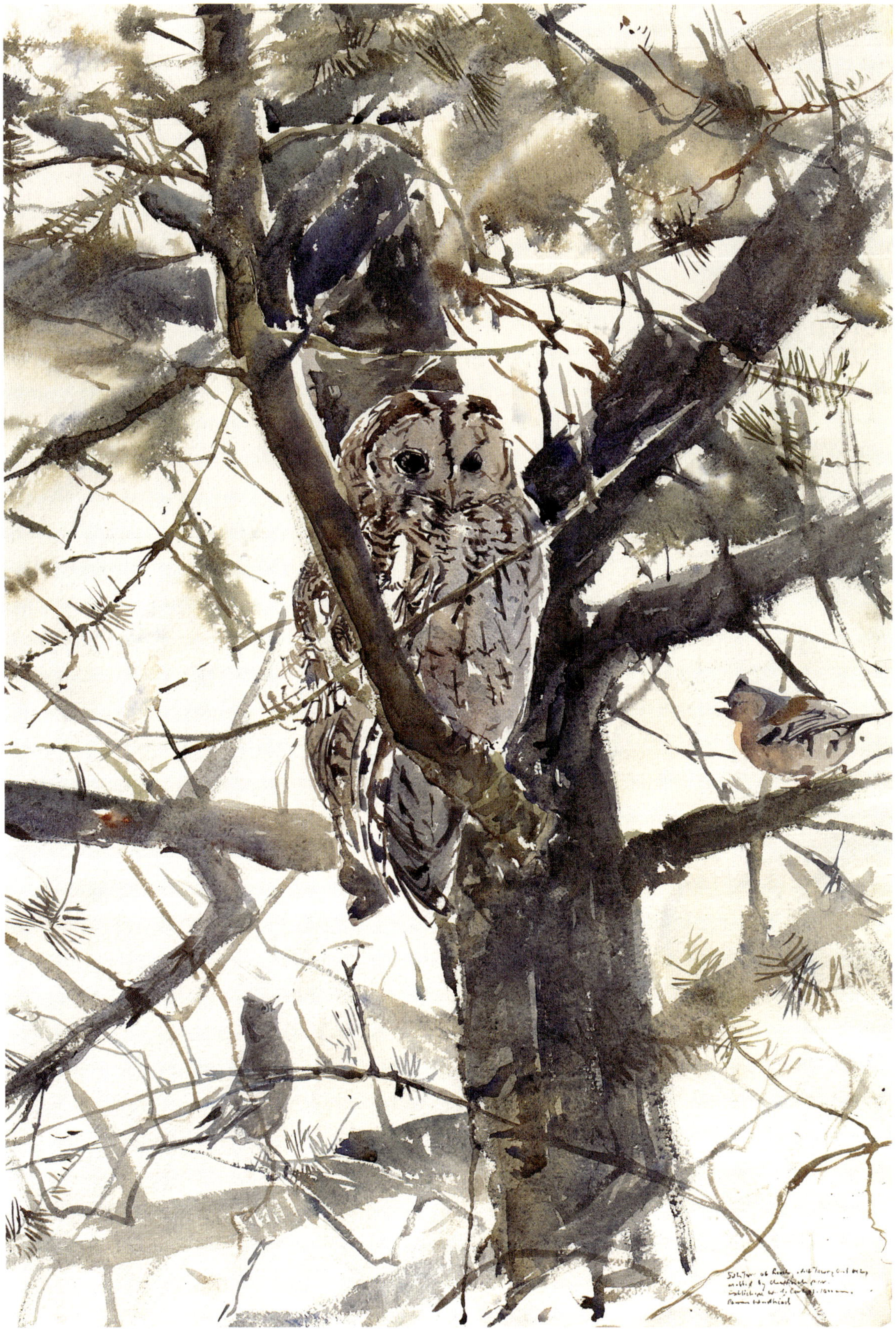

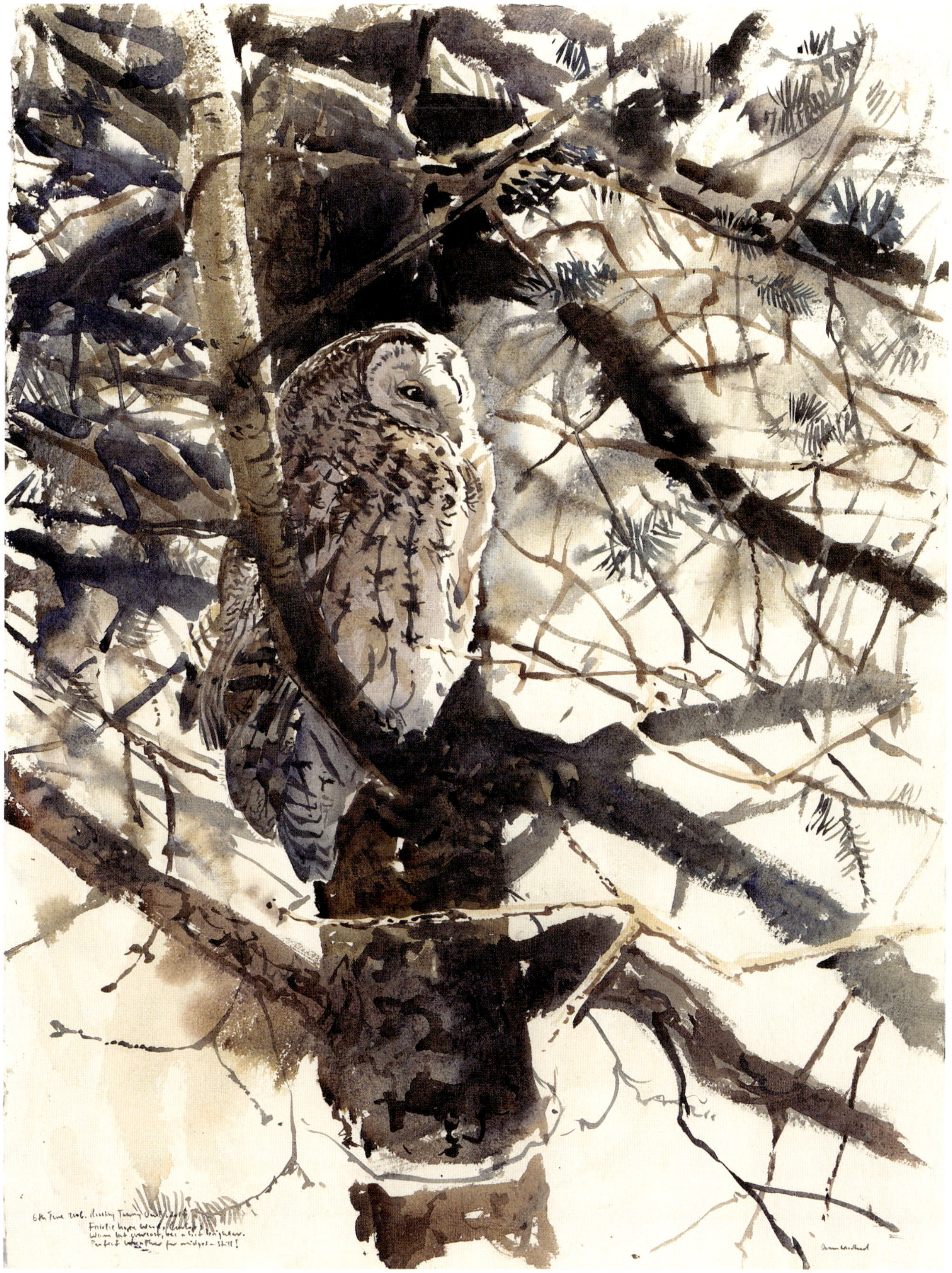

Adult Tawny Owl
(watercolour, 760mm x 560mm)

5th June 2006. Roosting Tawny Owl adult, Fairliehope woods, Carlops. Warm but overcast becoming a bit brighter. Perfect weather for midges – Still!

Adult Tawny Owl

(watercolour, 560mm x 380mm)

5th June 2006. Roosting Tawny Owl, Fairliehope wood. Warm but overcast, becoming bright too as sun burnt off cloud.

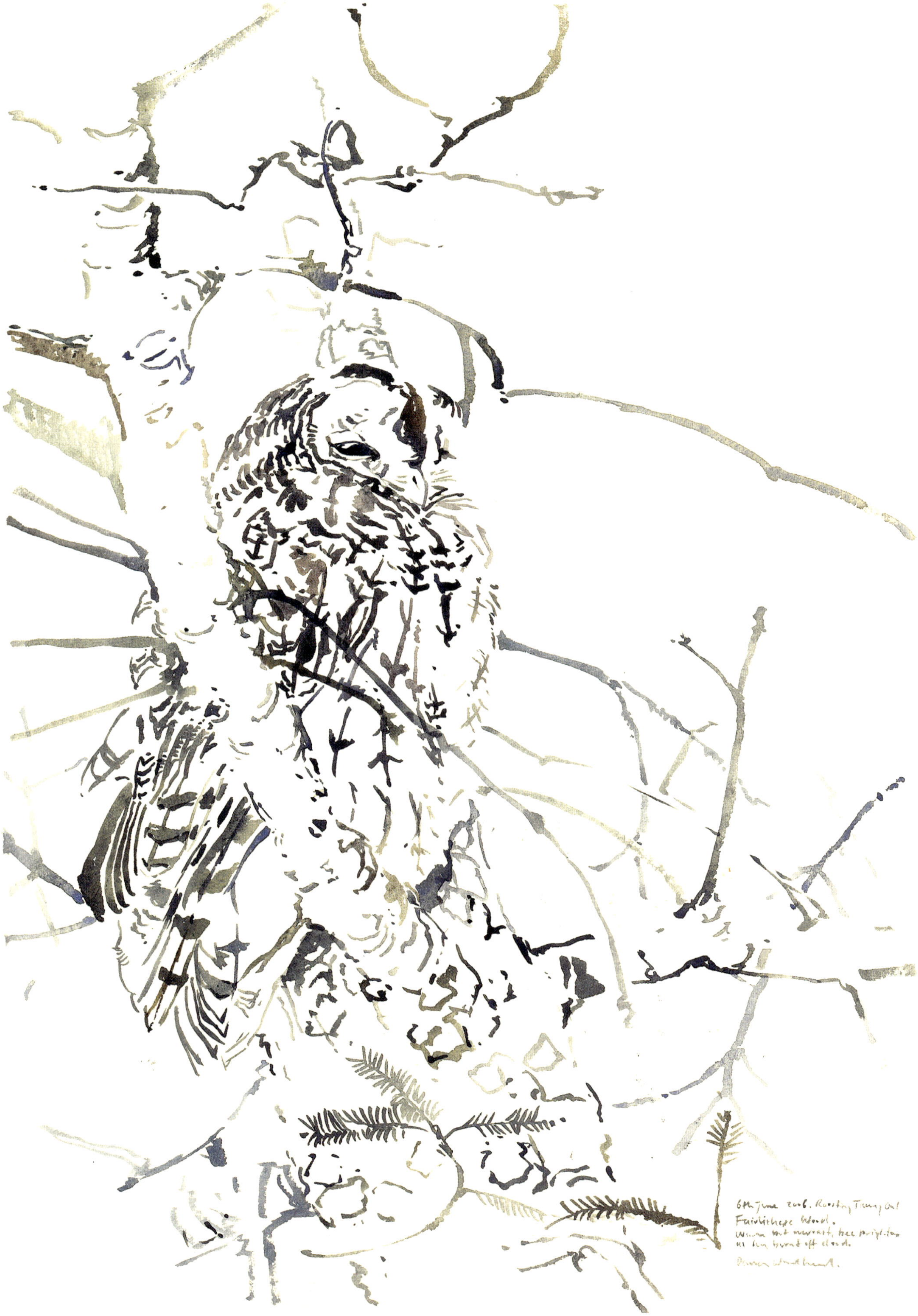

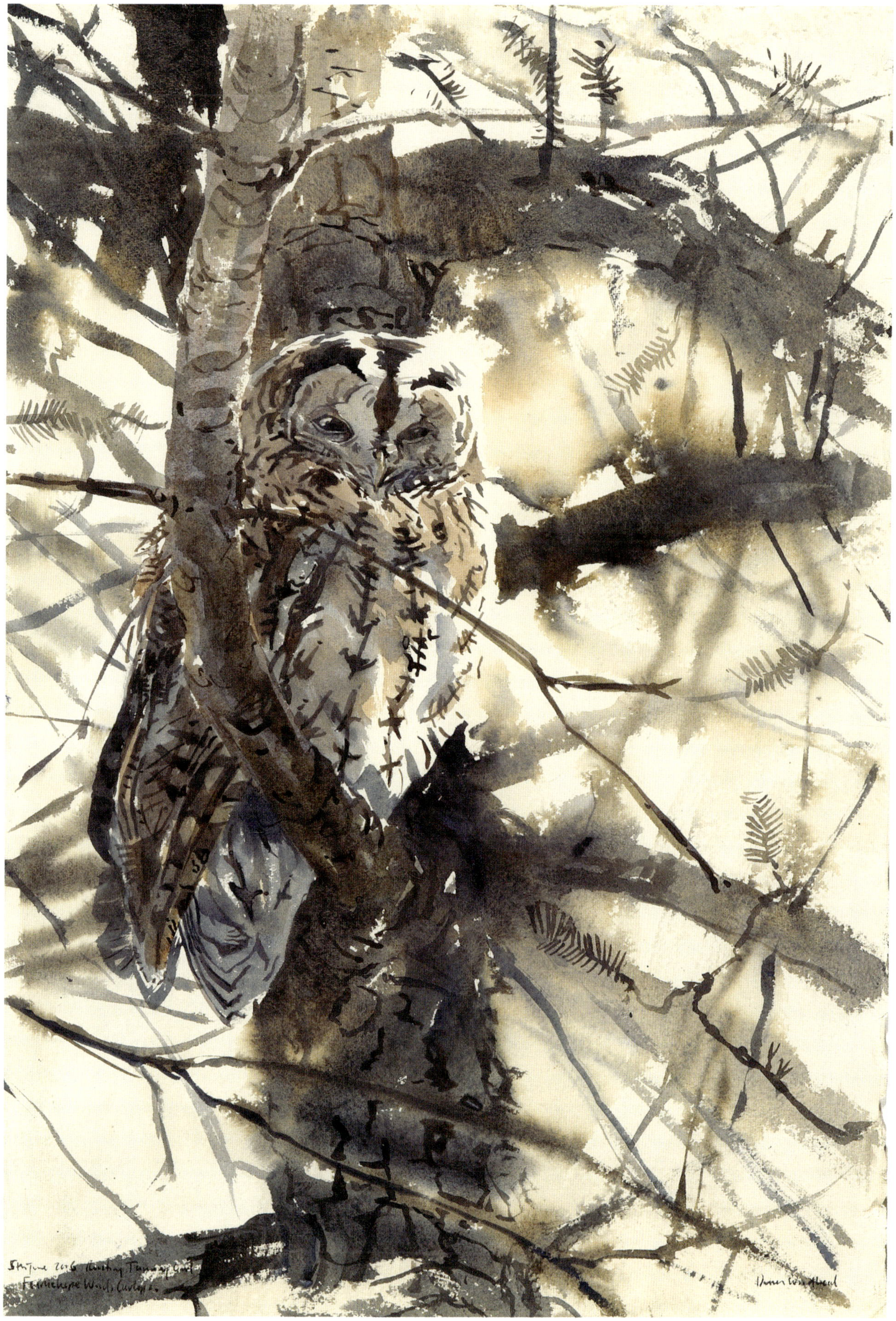

Corin's Owl
(watercolour, 560mm x 380mm)

5th June 2006. Roosting Tawny Owl, Fairliehope wood, Carlops.

I finally stopped working for the day as the sun moved round to the north-west and the light became too intense and blinding from behind. It had been a memorable day of far-reaching significance.

Beeches and Brambling at Amazondean
(watercolour, 560mm x 380mm)

Friday 10th November 2006. Beech wood and Brambling, very wet and windy, becoming total washout.

The first painting of the imposing tunnel of Beech trees that lead into Amazondean from Kitleyknowe. Weathered and formed with their moss-covered overlapping root systems and elegant trunks, they stand as majestic guardians to the dean. They appear to weep in rain, their pale dusty grey succumbing to bleeding drips of dark moisture. I tied my umbrella between two trunks and positioned myself on the steep slope below. As the rain and wind intensified, I slid several times uncontrollably down, leaving the trial of getting into position again a challenge. A group of Brambling called from above; I could not see them yet their nasal 'squeaks' were just audible against the wind-bent rattling branches. The area of sienna rich leaves against the sleek sculptured forms becoming impossible to protect against the elements.

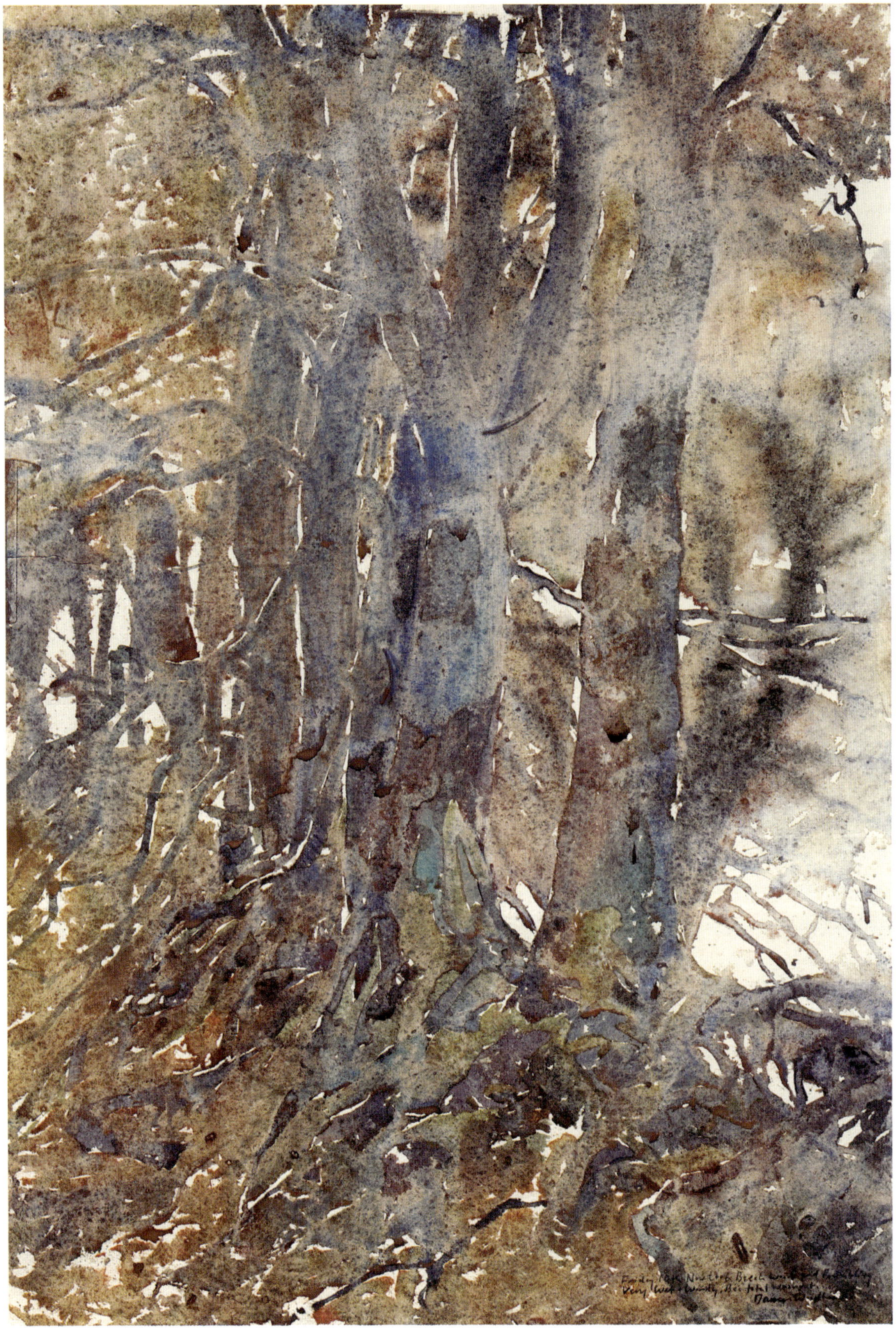

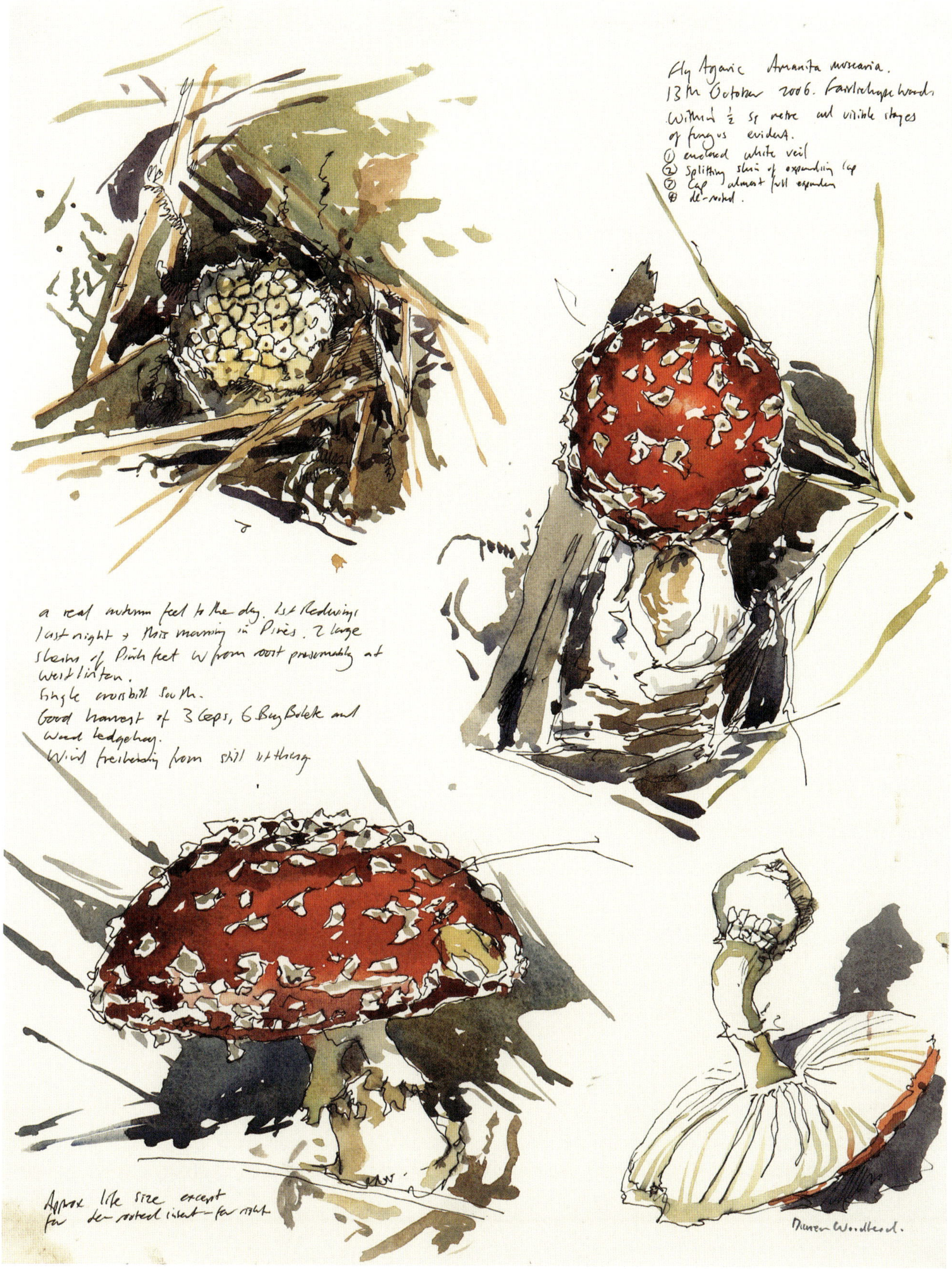

Fly Agaric
(watercolour and pen, 380mm x 280mm)

13th October 2006. *Amanita muscaria*, Fairliehope woods. Within half a square metre all visible stages of fungus evident. 1. Enclosed white veil; 2. Splitting skin of expanding cap; 3. Cap almost fully expanded; 4. De-rooted. A real autumn feel to the day. First Redwings last night and this morning in Pines. Two large skeins of Pinkfeet west from roost presumably at West Linton. Single Crossbill south. Good harvest of three Ceps, six Bay Bolete and Woodland Hedgehog. Wind freshening from still first thing. Approximately life-size except for de-rooted insert far right.

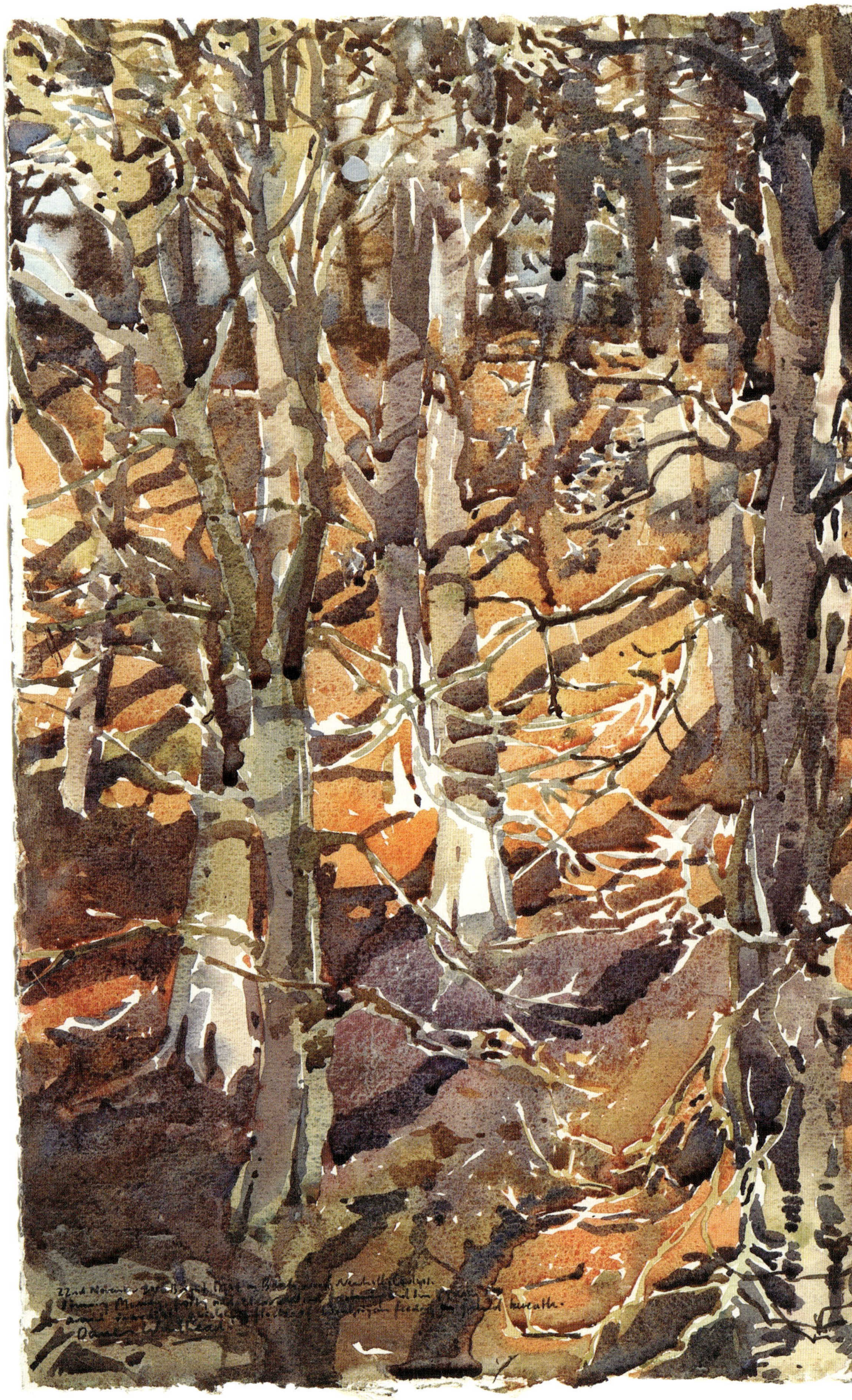

November Beeches
(watercolour, 440mm x 285mm)

22nd November 2006. Bright light in Beechwood, Newhall/ Carlops. Stunning morning, frosty and clear. Wind freshening and sun progressing around incredibly quickly, flock of Woodpigeon feeding on ground beneath.

The colours during the first autumn of my residency were extreme, and the season was rich with a mass of fruits of the forest. Beneath the trees laden with berries was a woodland floor alive with a rainbow of colour and a dazzling show of shapes and forms of different fungi. Previously, I had not been captivated by fungi, but then again, I had never seen before the variety and intensity I was witnessing now. A good morning out with Mike Jones of Fairliehope started the ball rolling, learning different families and groups, and it was this beginning of something new that I found so compelling. That first year sparked off a child-like curiosity, and the remaining part of the autumn was concentrated on developing this knowledge.

Fungi form the basis for woodland life, playing a vital role in the ecosystem by breaking down all organic matter and providing fertile layers. The fungi that we see are the fruit bodies and the reproductive systems that spread spores; beneath this is the organism itself, the mycelium. This net, made up of tiny threads, sits either underground or within wood. Occasionally, when thick enough, the mycelium can be seen; it is the violet carpet that often sits neatly beneath a Wood Blewitt, for example.

Not being used to observing and gathering fungi from the forest floor I hadn't up till then appreciated the beauty of their fruiting form and their role in the environment – not forgetting their culinary value! The whole experience of mycology can involve all the senses, stimulating sight, touch, smell and taste. I will never forget tasting milk from the first bounty of Milkcaps or finding my first yolk-yellow Chanterelles embedded in lush deep-green moss. The exquisite shape of a Chanterelle makes it almost too good to consider eating, as does the flash of deep violet blue that hits you as you turn over a neatly pale-rimmed Wood Blewitt. The whole unexpectedness and surprise of the day's find can make the silent hunt addictive.

Autumn Bridge, Amazondean
(watercolour, 560mm x 380mm)

Friday 17th November 2006. Bridge over Esk at Kitleyknowe. Still colours of Beech despite recent winds.

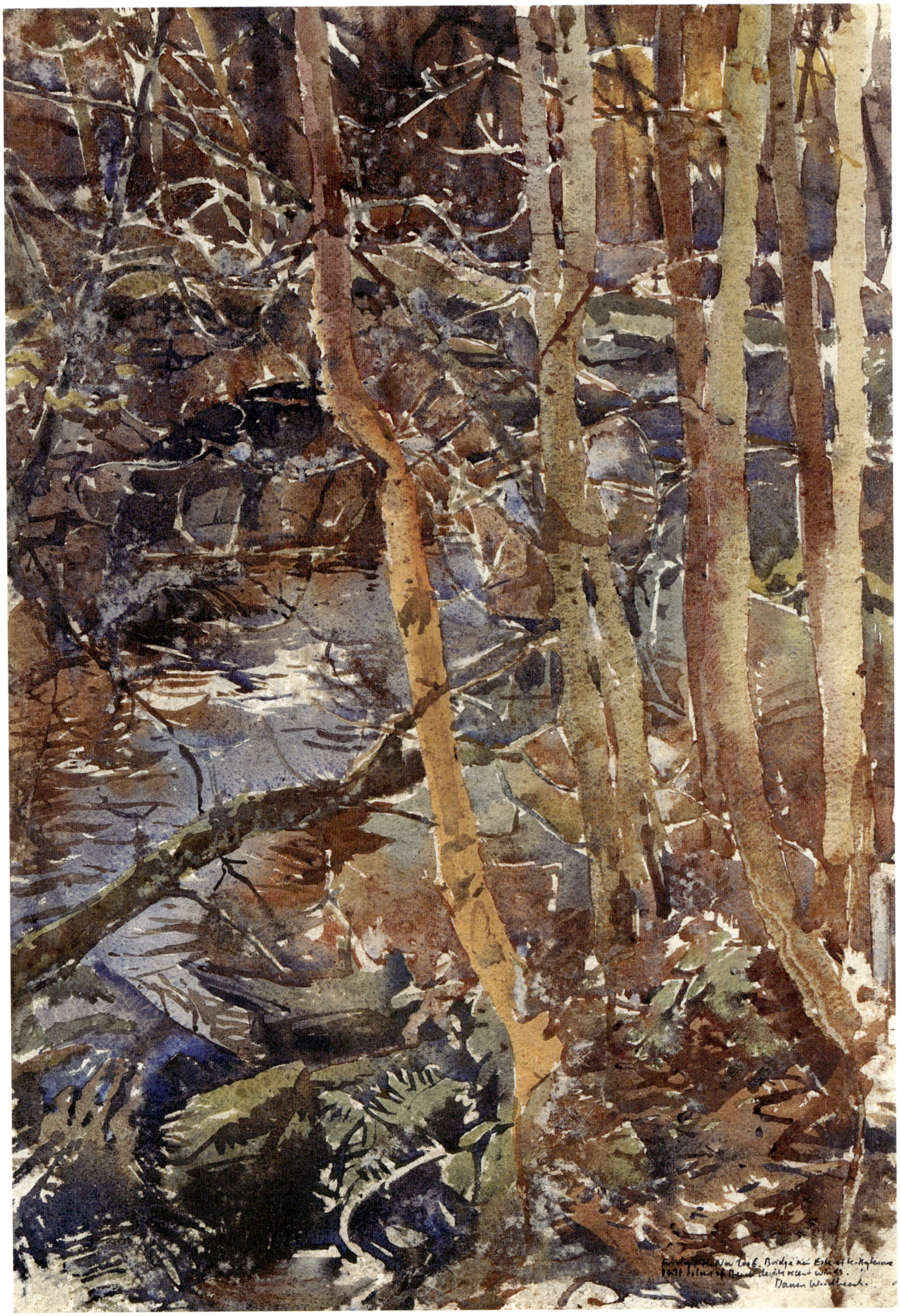

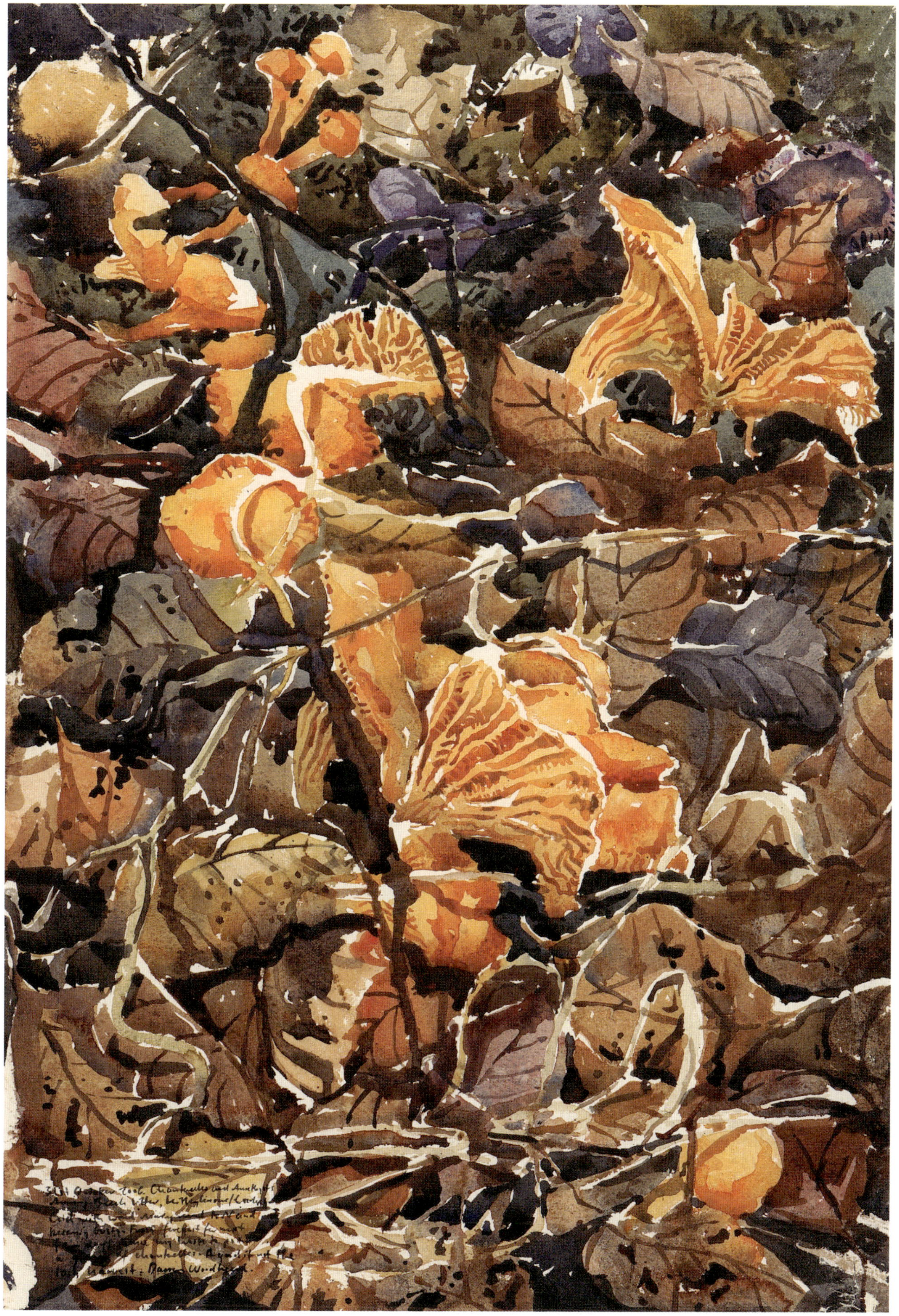

Hallowe'en Chanterelles
(watercolour, 560mm x 380mm)

31st October 2006. Chanterelles and Amethysts among Beech litter, Kitleyknowe/Carlops. Cold with wind moving round to north and becoming gusty. Frost forecast for next few days hence my haste to paint a group of Chanterelles. A good if not the last harvest.

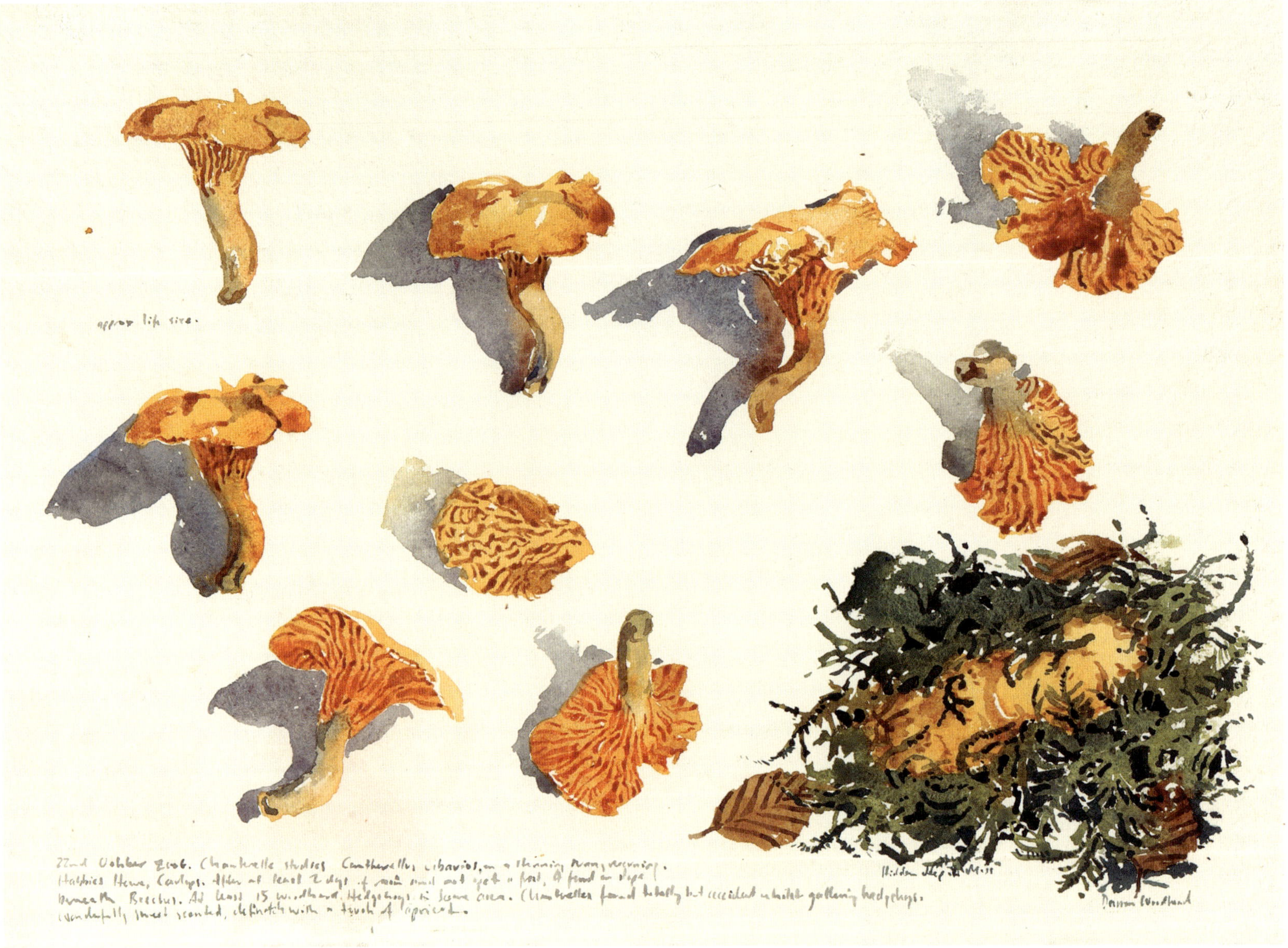

First Chanterelles

(watercolour, 280 mm x 380 mm)

22nd October 2006. *Cantherellus cibarius* on a stunning morning, Habbies Howe, Carlops. After at least two days of rain and not yet a frost, four found on slope beneath Beeches. At least fifteen Woodland Hedgehog in same area. Chanterelles found totally by accident whilst gathering Hedgehogs. Wonderfully sweet scented, definitely with a touch of Apricot. Approximately life size.

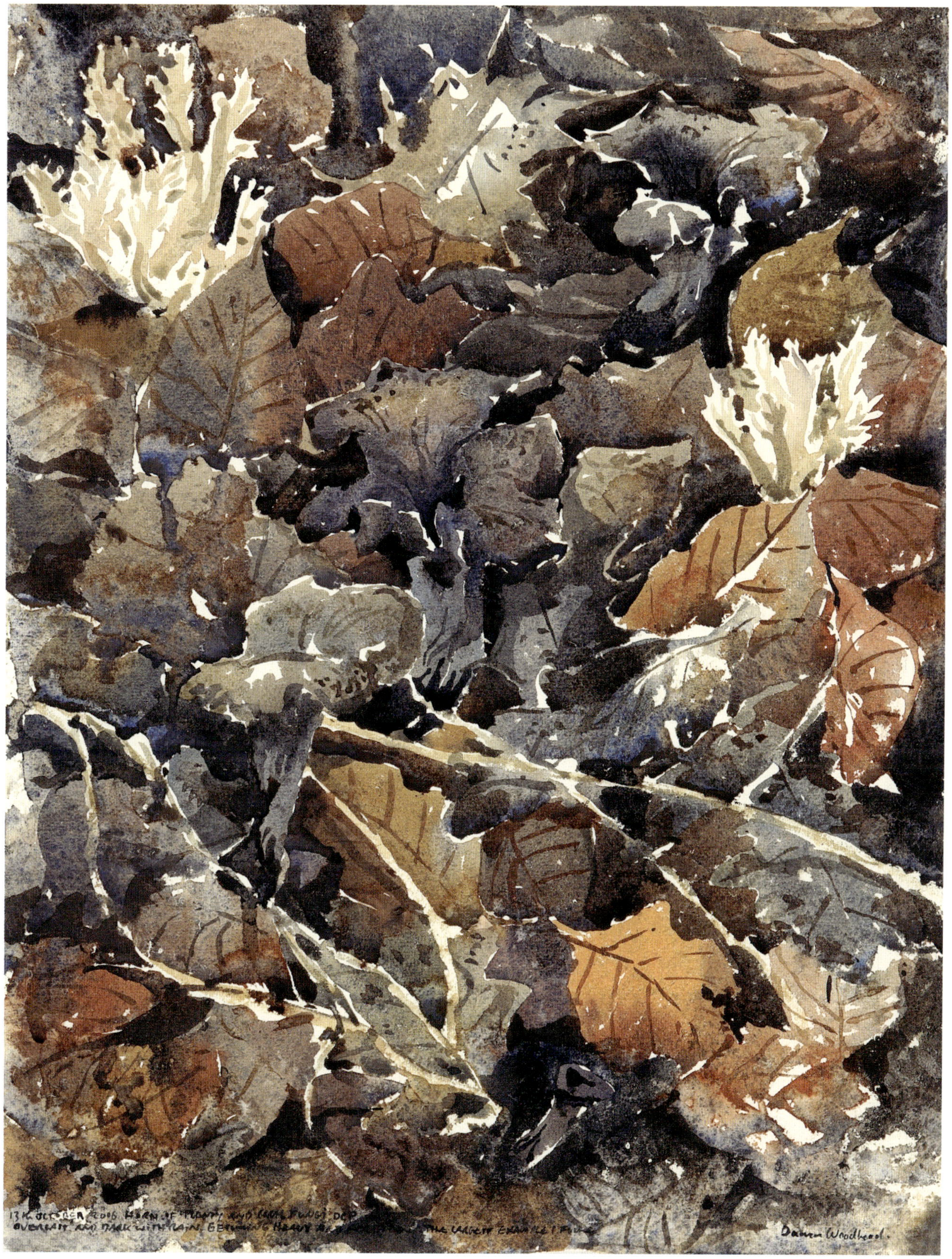

Horn of Plenty and Coral Fungi
(watercolour, 380 mm x 280mm)

13th October 2006,Overcast and dark, with rain becoming heavy and persistent. The largest example I found.

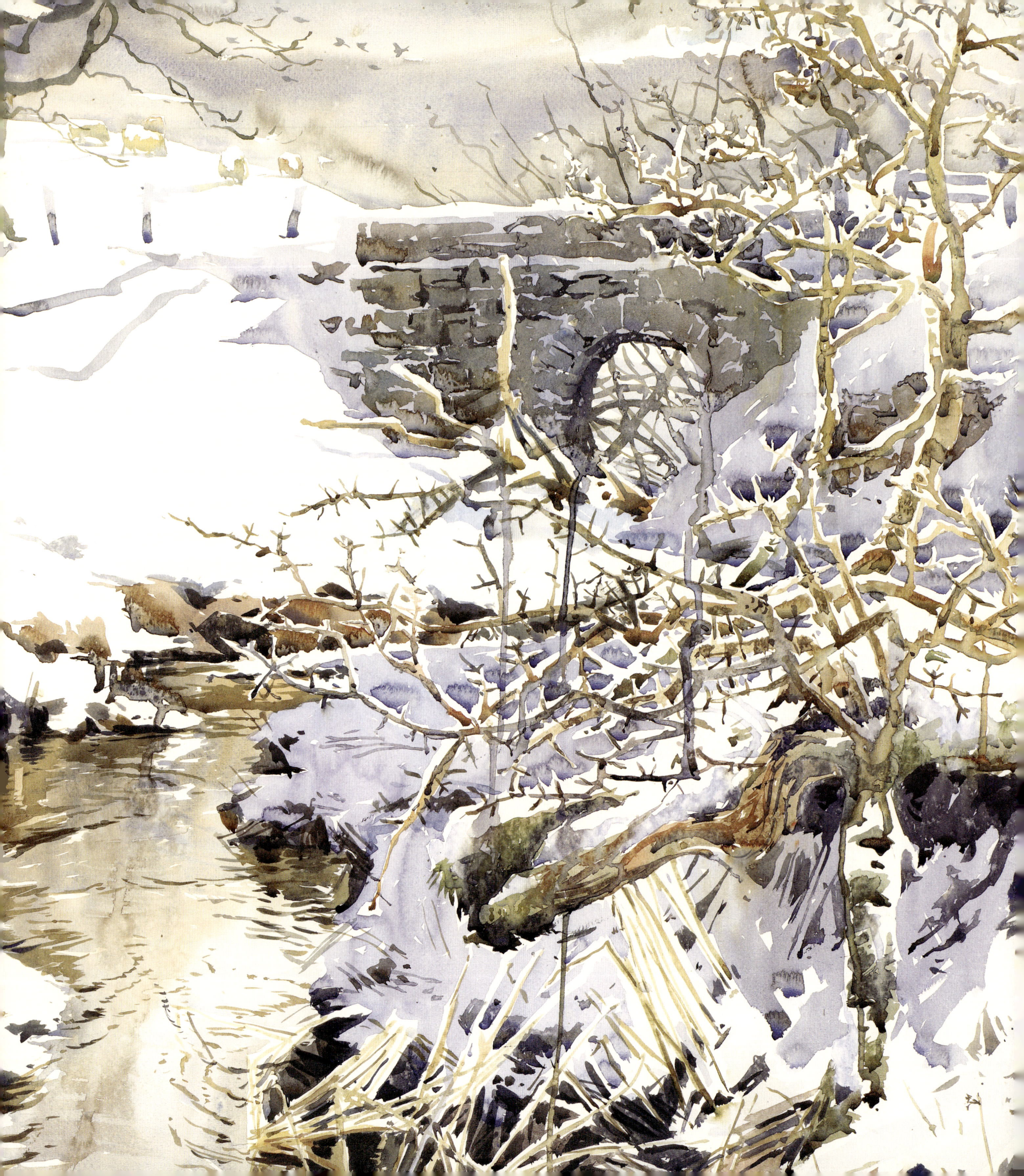

2007
The Labyrinth of the Dean

Snow, Sheep and Brambling, Kitleybrigg
(watercolour, 760mm x 560mm)

12th March 2007. Fall of snow at Kitleyknowe, Carlops. Cold with snow showers until lunch, with gusting northerly wind. Brambling in Beeches, Dipper singing and Peregrine pair low over fields.

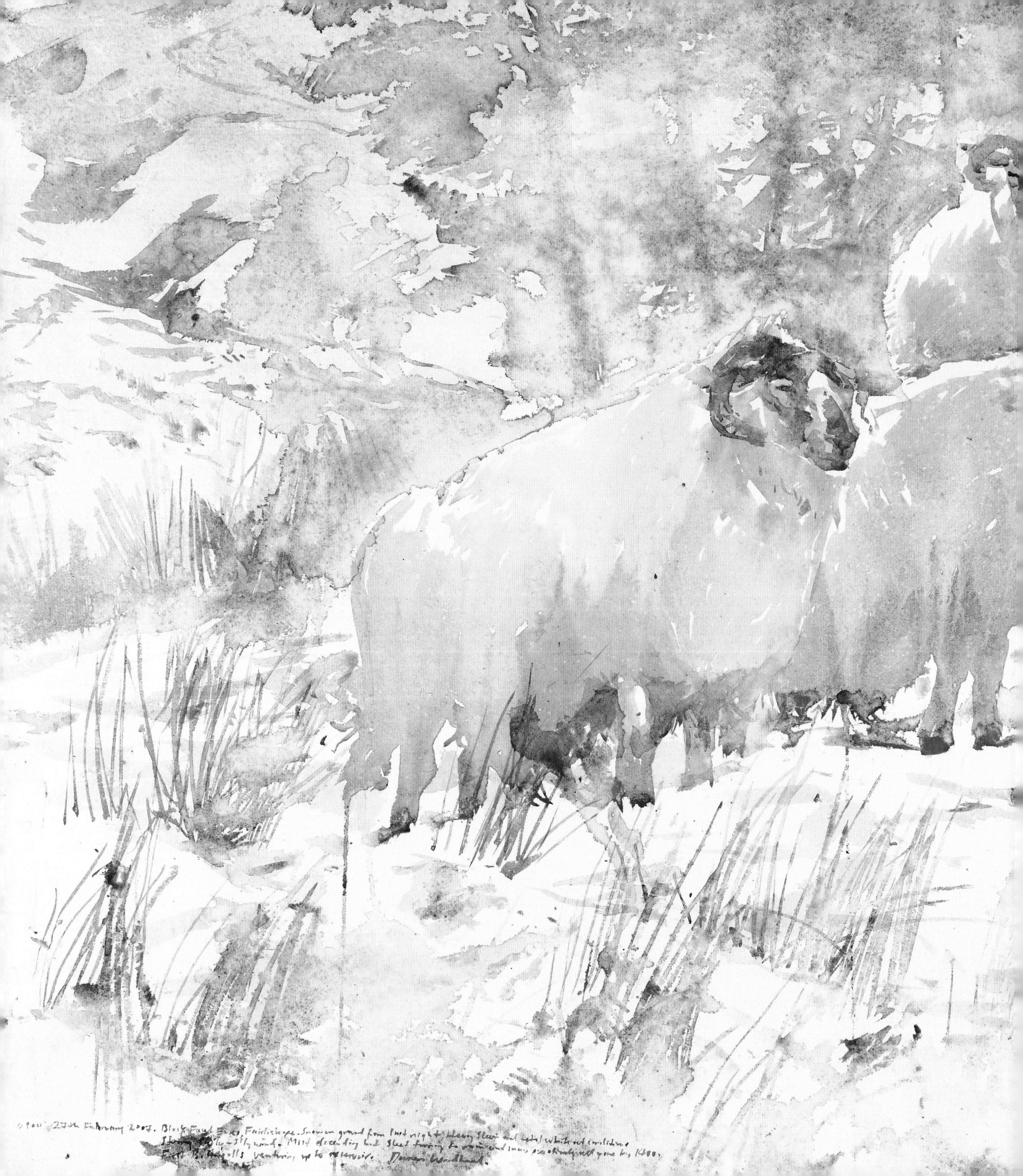
27th February 2007. Black Faced Ewes, Fairlishope. Snow on ground from last night. Heavy sleet and total white out conditions.
Mist descending but sleet turning to rain and snow practically all gone by 1400.
venturing up to reservoir.

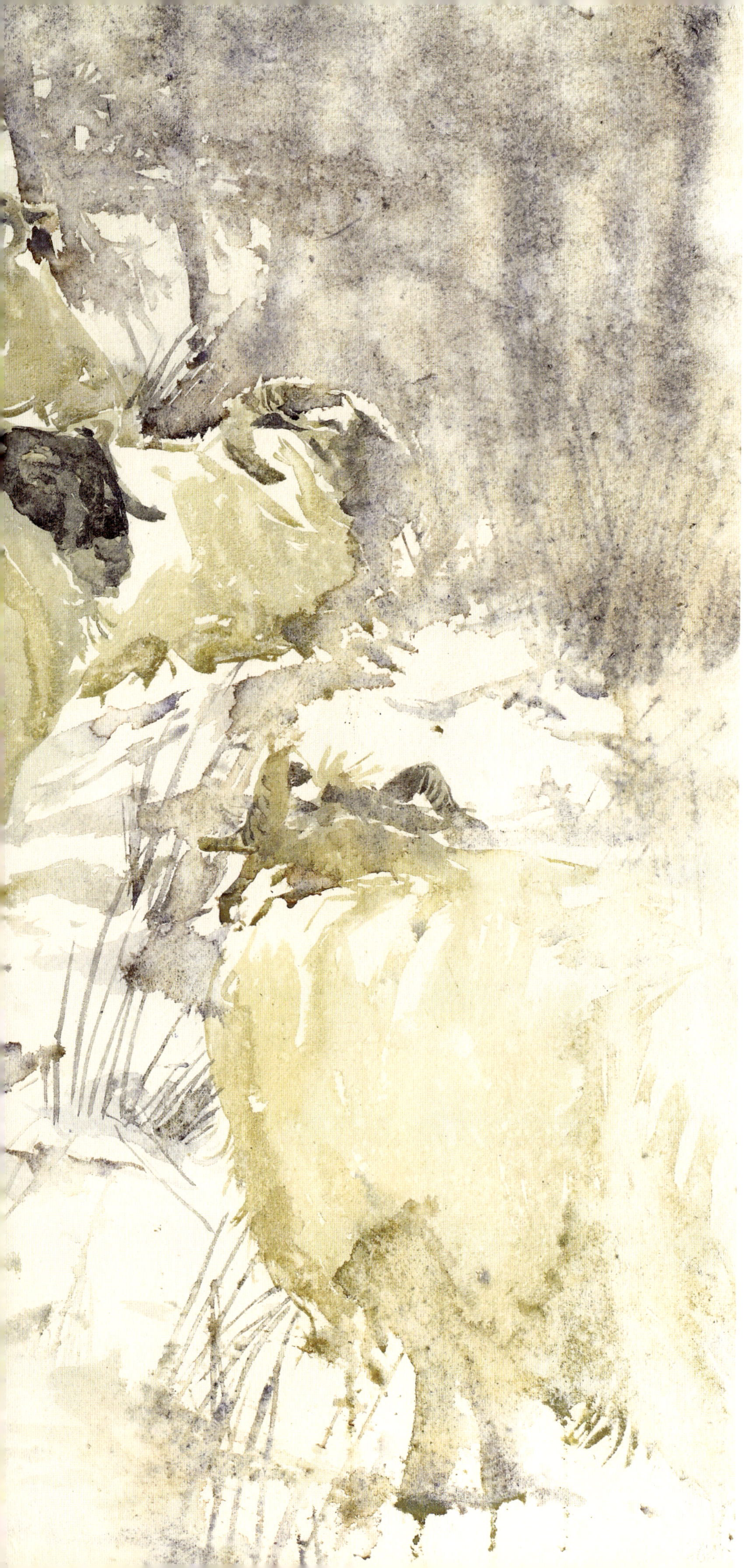

Ewes in snow
(watercolour, 560mm x 760mm)

27th February 2007 09:00. Black-faced ewes, Fairliehope. Snow on ground from last night, heavy sleet and total white-out conditions. Strong south-westerly to southerly wind. Mist descending but sleet turning to rain and snow practically all gone by 14:00. First Black-headed Gulls venturing up to reservoir.

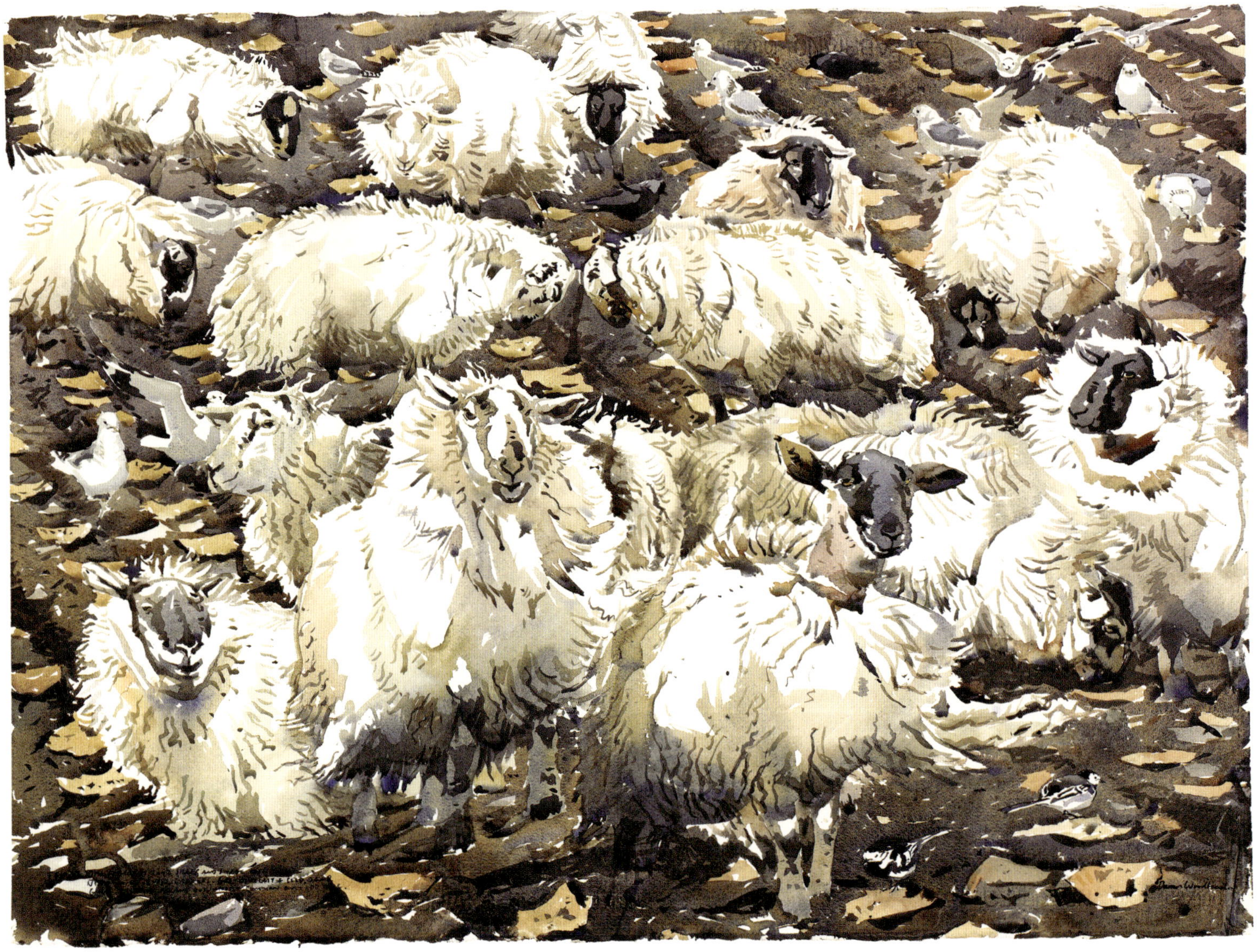

Sheep among swede tops
(watercolour, 560mm x 760mm)

Friday, 16th February 2007. Nine Mile Burn, Carlops. Grey, overcast, cold and damp. Gulls drifting in and out, mostly Common but odd Black-headed Gull.

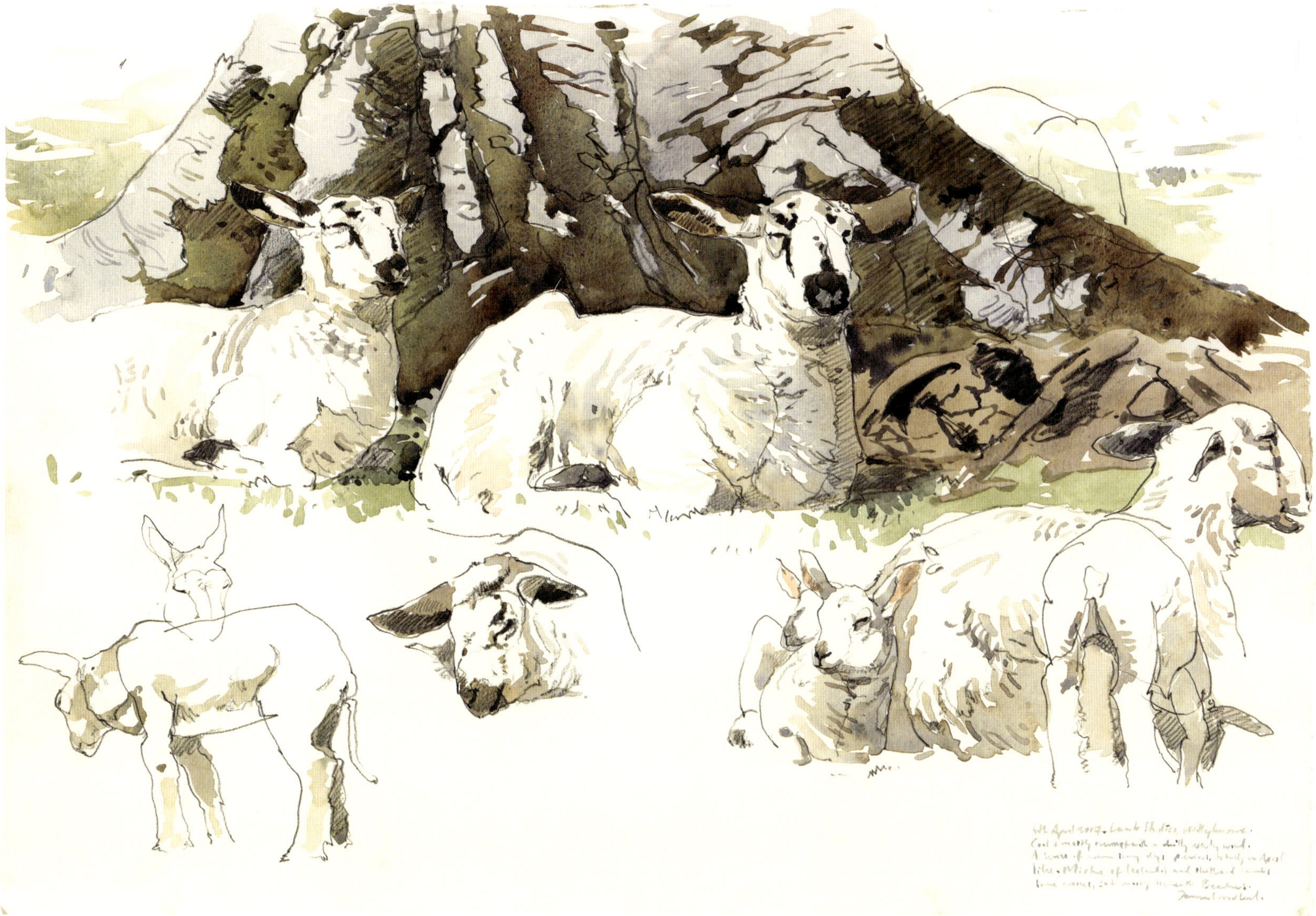

First Lambs of the year

(watercolour and pencil, 420mm x 594mm)

6th April 2007, Lamb studies Kitleyknowe. Cool and overcast with chilly north-westerly wind. A series of warm sunny days previous, totally un-April-like. Mixture of Icelandic and Shetland lambs some crosses, sat mostly beneath Beeches.

Black-faced Lambs, Spittal Farm,
April 2007.
(watercolour, 560mm x 760mm)

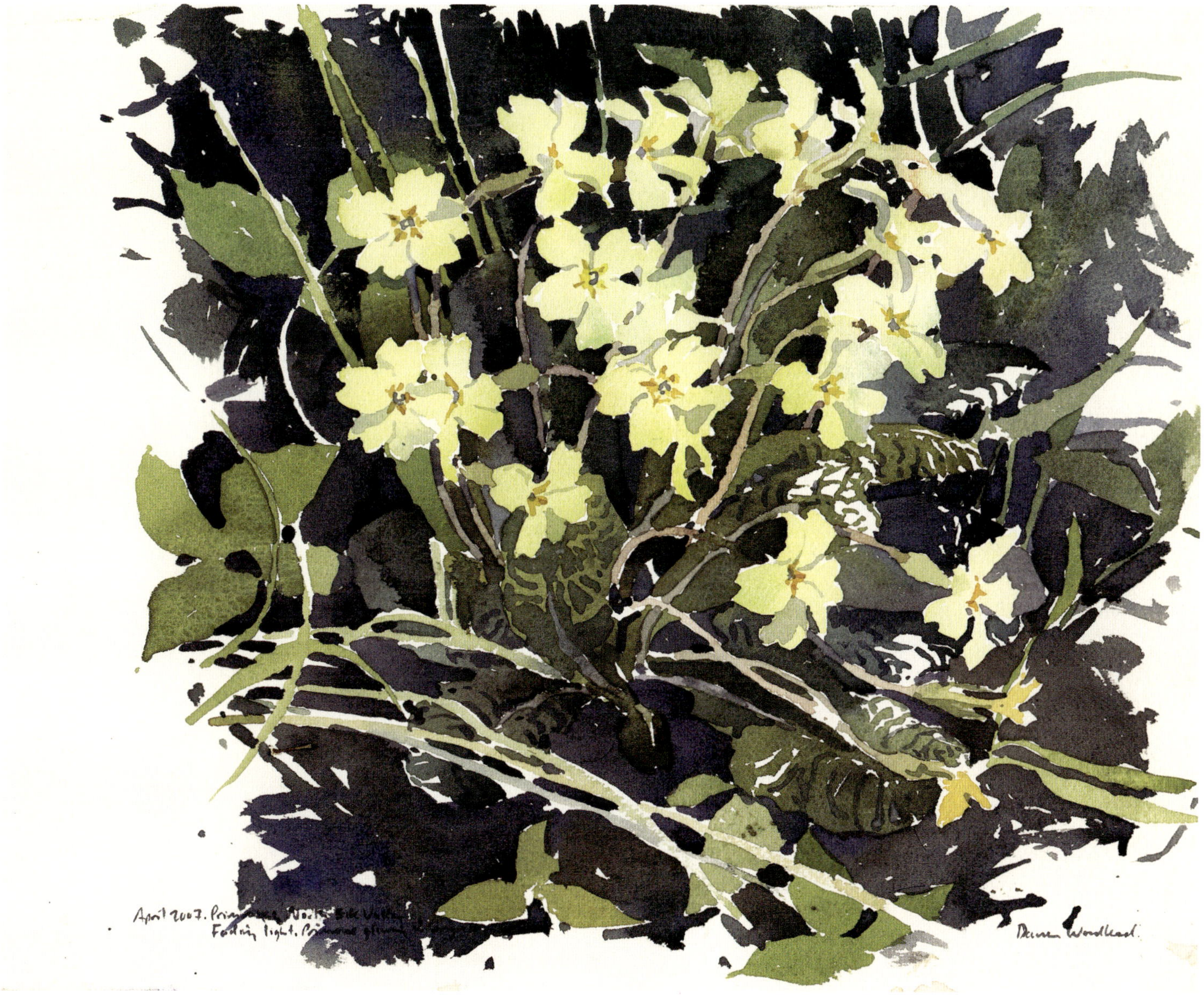

Primroses, North Esk valley
(watercolour, 280mm x 380mm)

April 2007. Fading light, Primroses glowing in the progressing darkness.

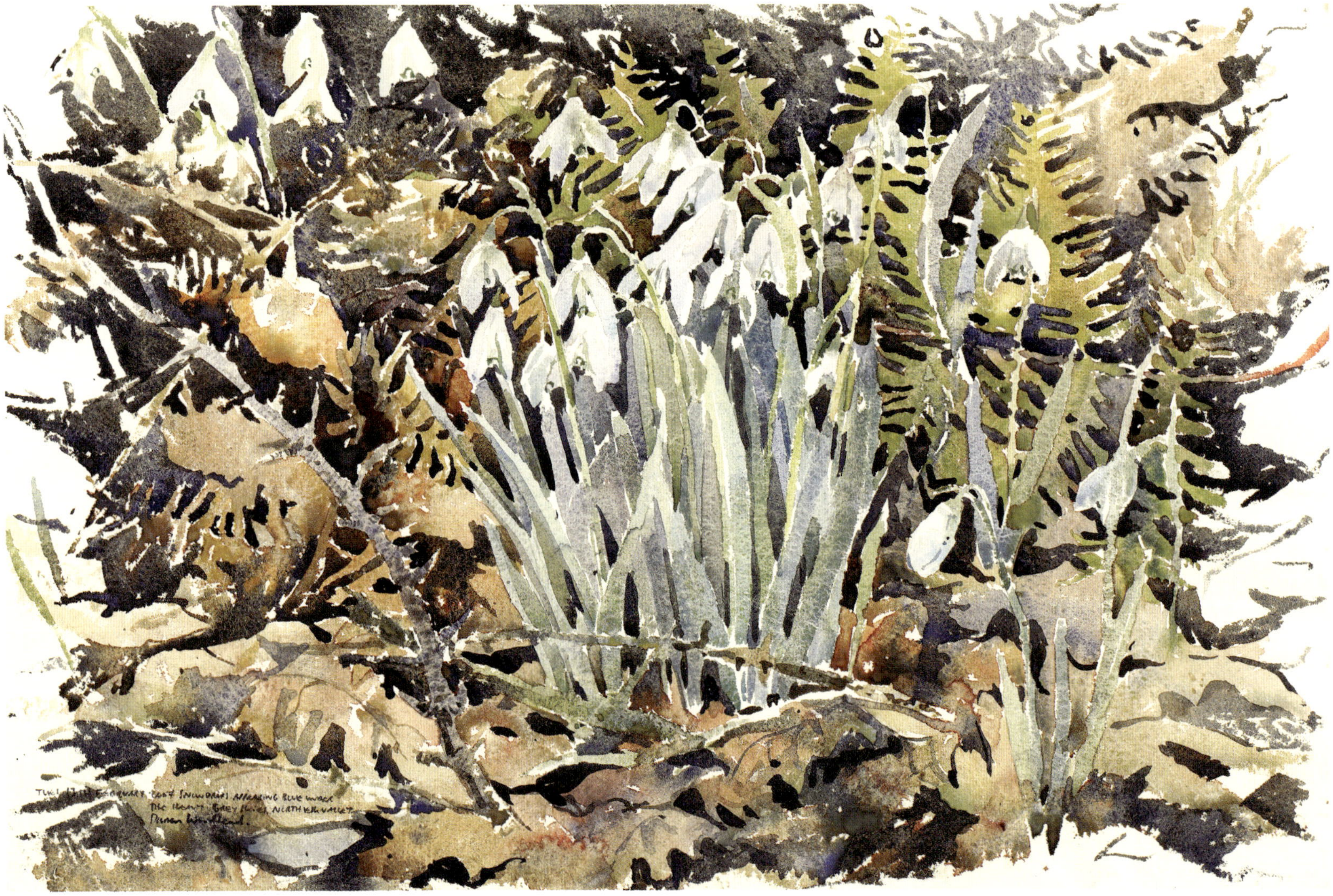

Snowdrops
(watercolour, 380mm x 560mm)

Tuesday, 13th February 2007.
Snowdrops appearing blue under
heavy grey skies, North Esk valley.

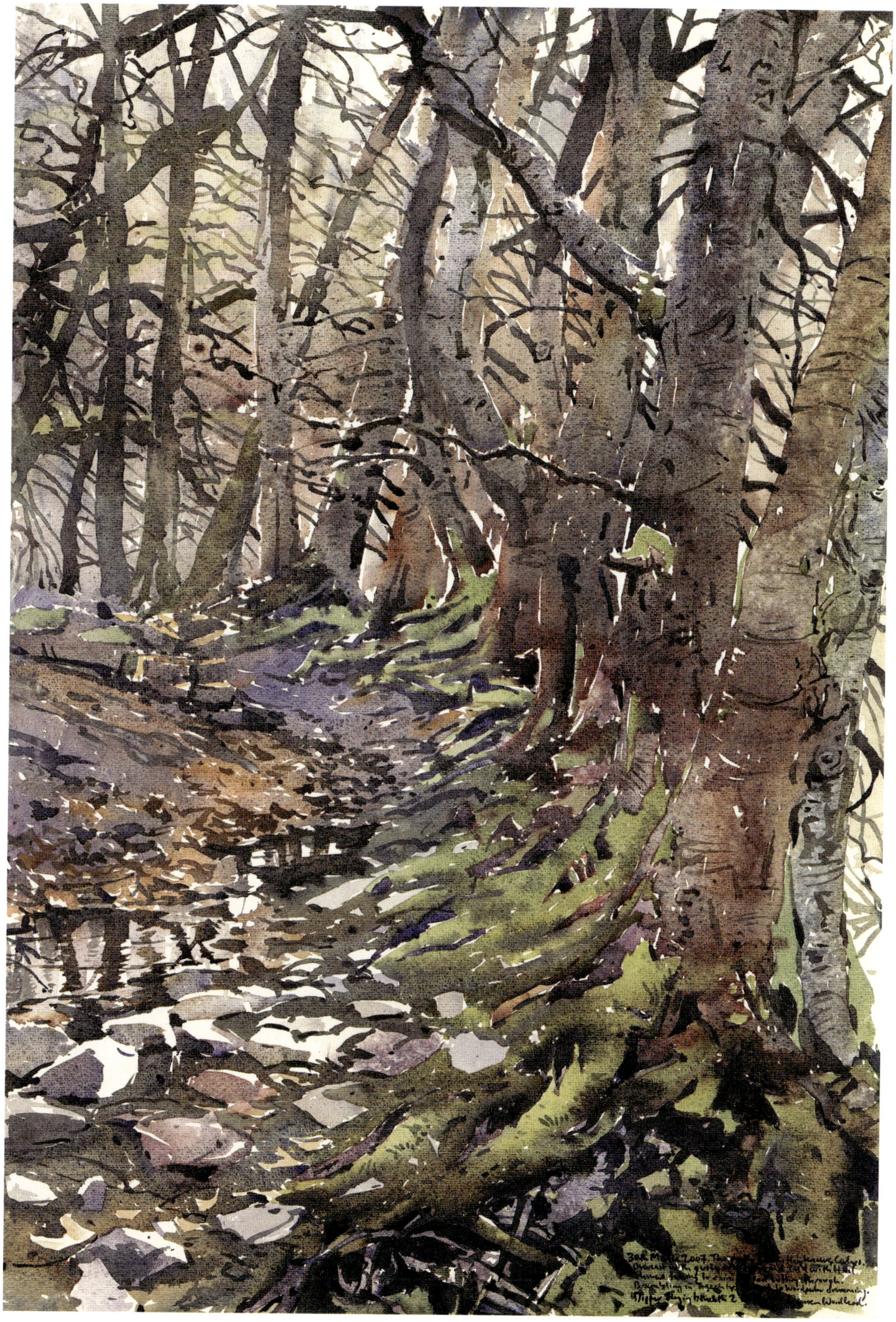

Towards the Dean
(watercolour, 560mm x 380mm)

30th March 2007. The path from Kitleyknowe, Carlops. Overcast with gusty north-westerly wind, cold with hail showers turning to rain, and a wind that cut right through. Brambling in Beech tops, Great-spotted Woodpecker drumming. Dipper singing beneath two bridges.

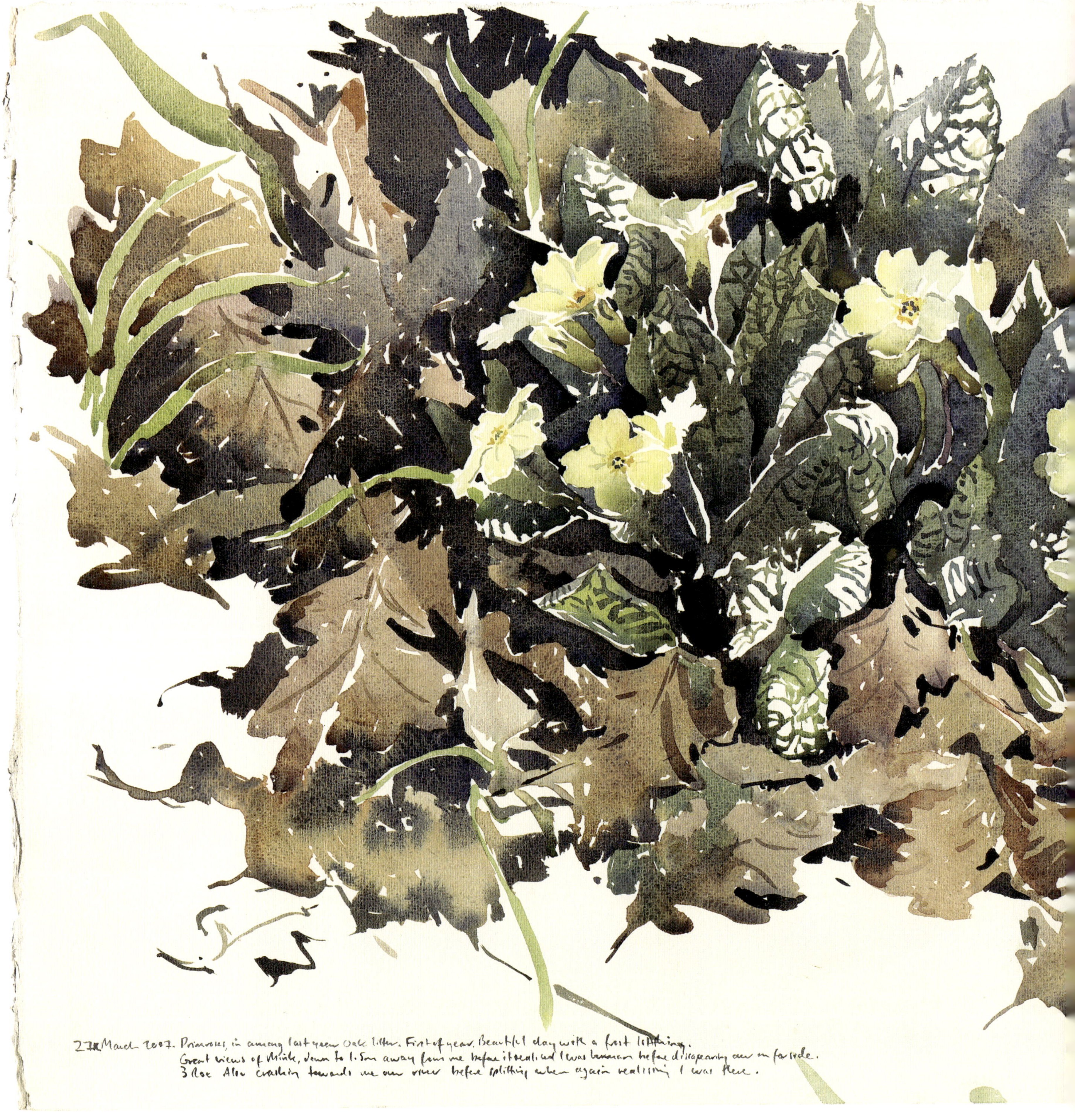
27th March 2007. Primroses, in among last years Oak litter. First of year. Beautiful day with a frost lifting.
Great views of Mink, down to 1.5m away from me before it realised I was human before disappearing over on far side.
3 Roe Also crashing towards me over river before splitting when again realising I was there.

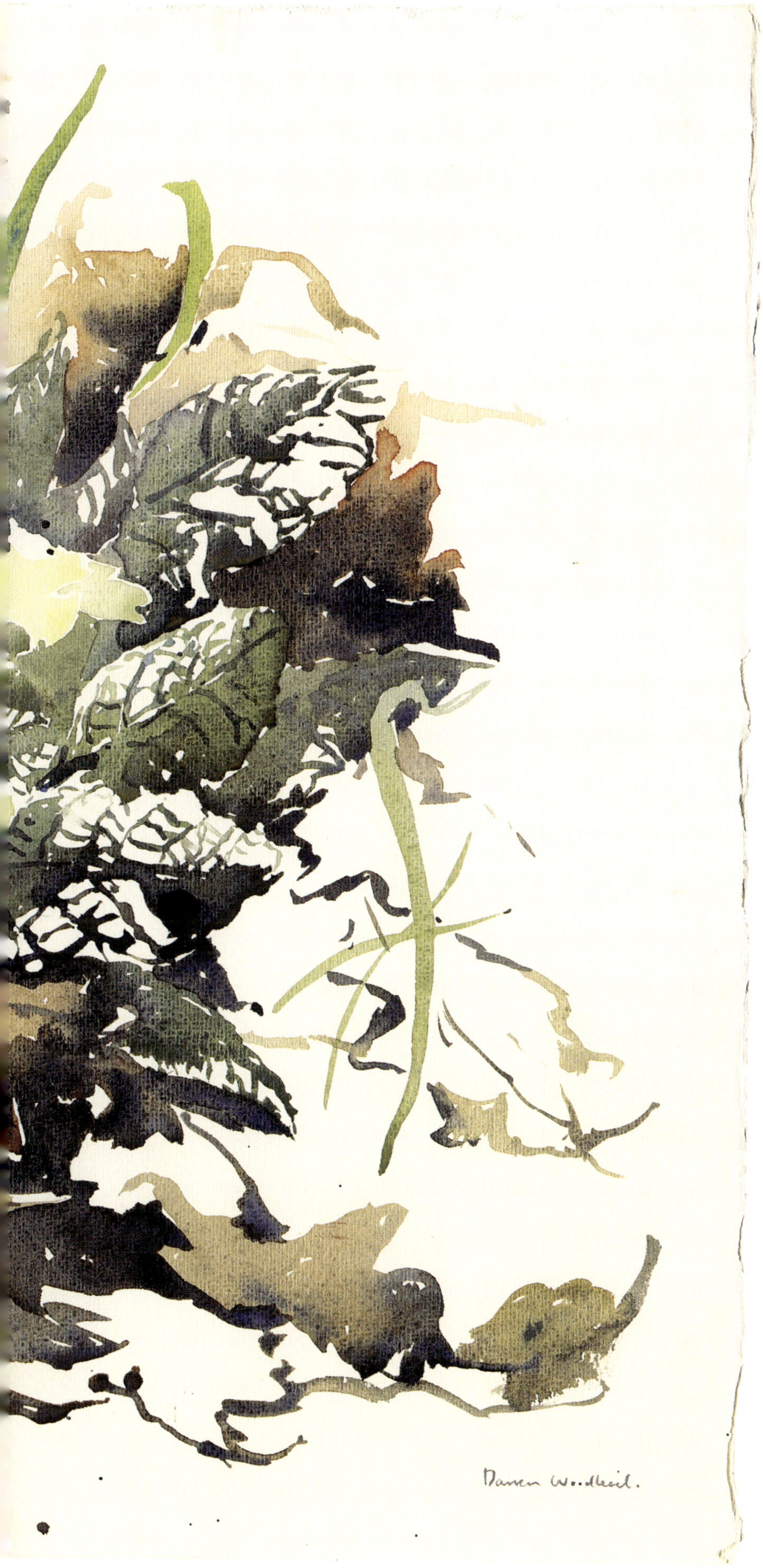

Primroses

(watercolour, 380mm x 560mm)

27th March 2007. Primroses in among last year's Oak litter. First of year. Beautiful day with frost first thing. Great views of Mink, down to one and a half metres away from me before it realised I was human and disappearing over onto far side. Three Roe also crashing towards me over the river before splitting when again realising I was there.

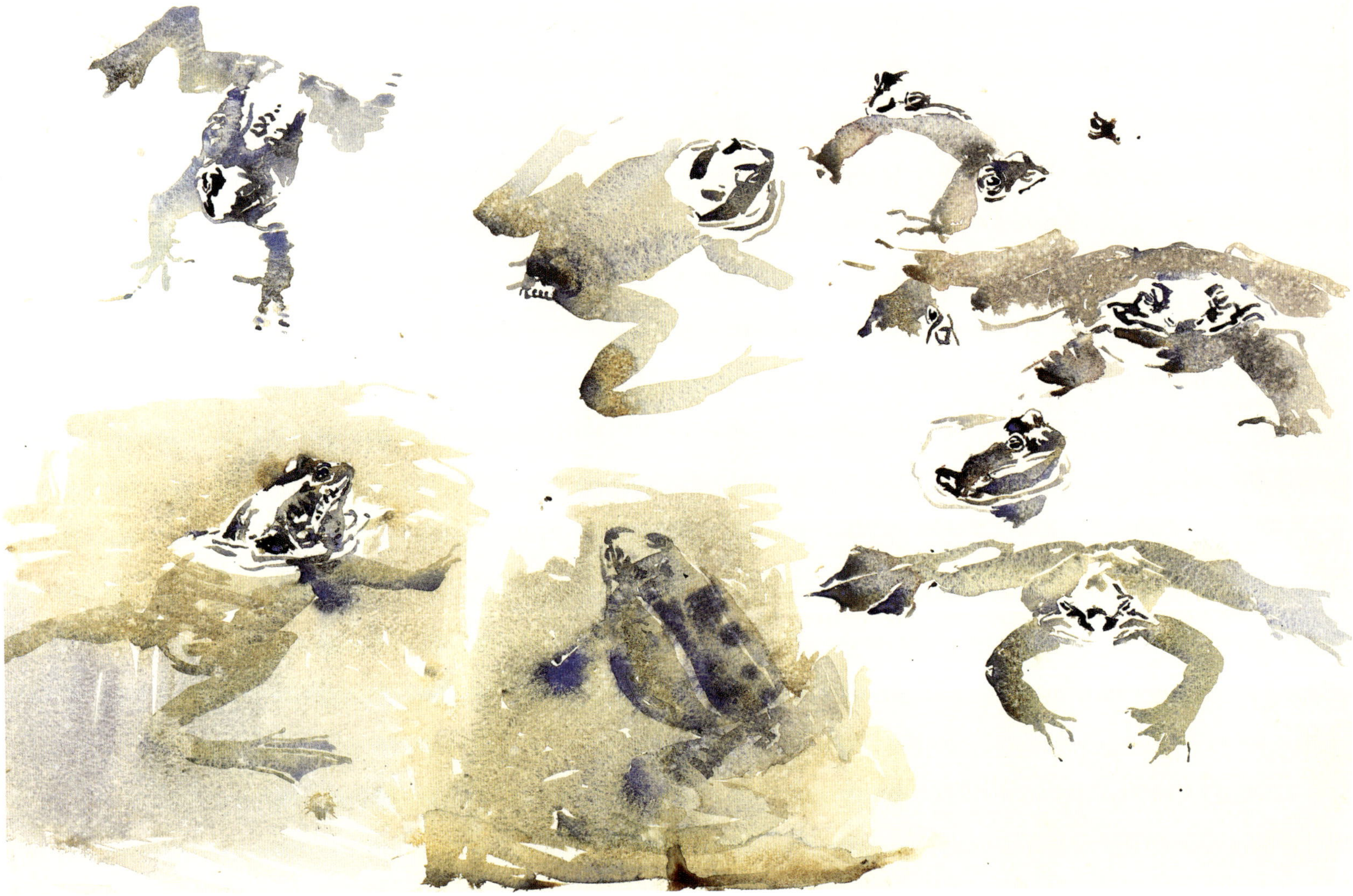

Common Frogs
(watercolour, 380mm x 560mm)

March 2007. Newhall pond.
Overcast with heavy rain.

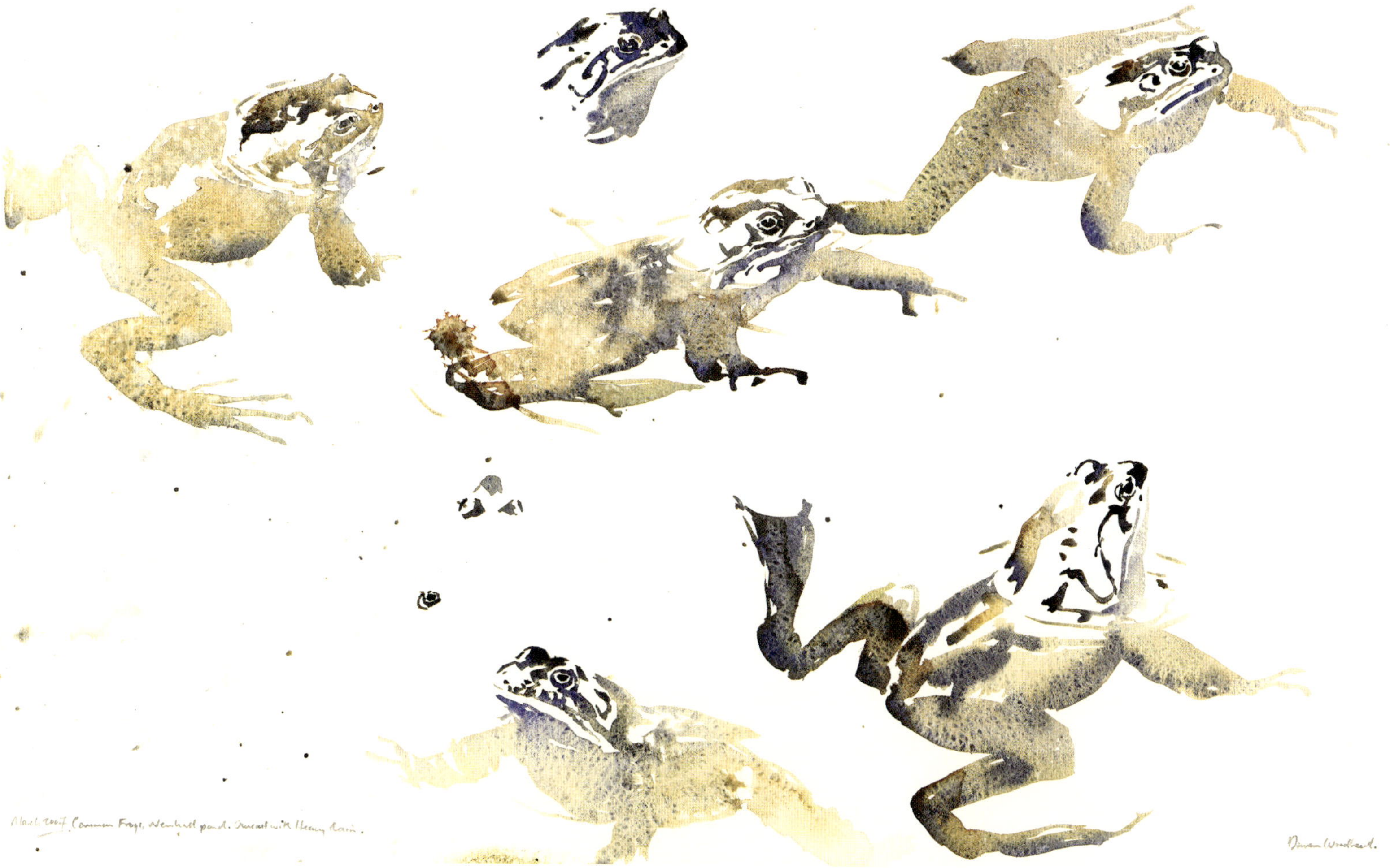
Common Frogs, pond. Overcast with Heavy Rain.

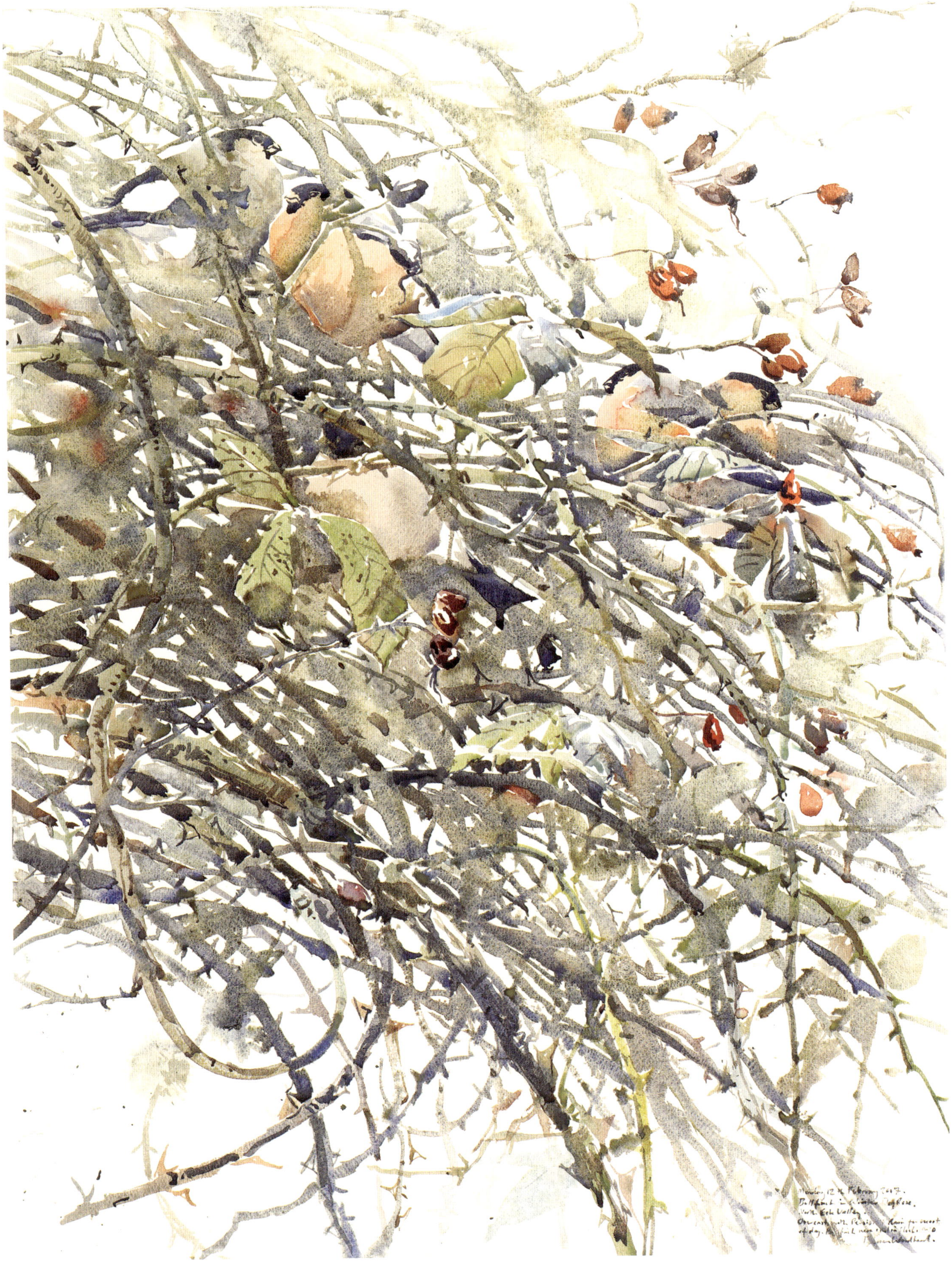
Monday 12 th February 2007.
North Esk Valley.

Bullfinch in winter Dog Rose
(watercolour, 760mm x 560mm)

Monday, 12th February 2007. North Esk Valley. Overcast, with persistent rain for most of day. Bullfinch here still in flock of nine to ten birds.

Before 2007, I had never really had the chance to observe Bullfinches closely. By pure accident, in December 2006, I stumbled across a near perfect spot for observing them whilst out with Sula. After the Christmas break, on 2nd January, I found them feeding mainly on the ground on small fallen fruit and sycamore-type seeds. The area, about eighty square metres, was bordered by tall mature deciduous trees on three sides with a selection of small shrubs and bushes between. A track split the area in two and it became obvious that this formed a border for two distinct troops or 'bellows' of Bullfinch. Although the numbers varied, both groups held on average nine or ten birds with roughly an equal number of males and females.

My first sightings were intermittent. The finches disappeared between feeding for lengthy periods, or kept very low to begin with, feeding mainly on the ground or hidden in bushes. I gradually became familiar with them, following them as they fed in their separate areas. Although often within sight of each other, I never saw any crossing of boundaries. I tried to spend at least two days a week working on them, until late spring, when the leafing trees hid much of their activity.

Their diet consisted of seeds and berries, foraged from the ground. This was particularly true of group A, while group B also fed on dried dock stems. They were not shy, often coming within a few metres to preen and wing stretch. Wind throughout the first part of January was a hindrance and continued to make the birds very hard to find at times, as they chose to remain within the shelter of cover, and the clattering of bare branches easily drowned their delicate calls. After 15th January, I found myself working mostly with group B, when I located the hedge of Dog Rose where they sat feeding. This allowed me to work on them most of the day as they fed and rested.

26th January 2007. Attention has switched from the ground seeds to the newly emerging buds, with Blue Tit and Siskin also enjoying the new feast. Many singing interludes by the males when solitary, a mixture of soft 'peu' and 'pu' notes with slightly more musical short notes and the occasional twitter.

The onset of spring and the emergence of buds meant a change in diet, and they were now spending more time in bare trees, inevitably ending with breaks in their favourite Dog Rose. Familiarity with them meant I could confidently increase paper size and work on more ambitious compositions.

12th February 2007. Thinking big now, trying to combat that boundary of white. From mid March, the Bullfinch gorged on Blossom. The whole group would acrobatically tear into branches adorned with white, creating snow-like showers of plucked petals which drifted in the wind, all this accompanied by the drones of queen Bumble Bees and the tunes of newly arriving Chiffchaff.

Robin and Bullfinch in Dogrose
(watercolour, 560mm x 380mm)

6th March 2007. Singing Robin with Bullfinch pair behind. Bright and clear morning with moderate to fresh south-westerly, making it cool. More cloud p.m. Bullfinch pair really close, with male occasionally dipping head to female. Robin standing on my sketchbook, River Esk valley.

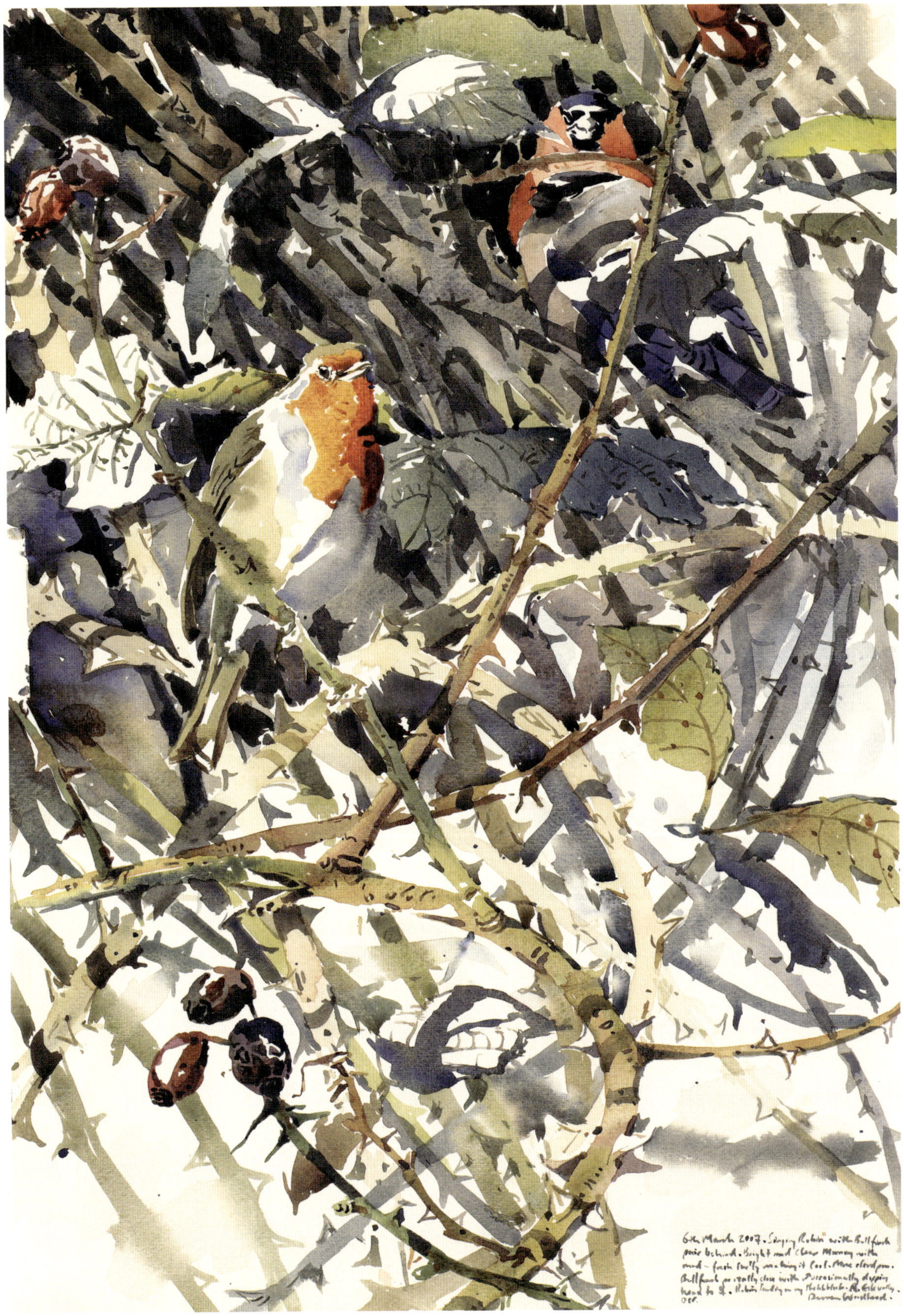

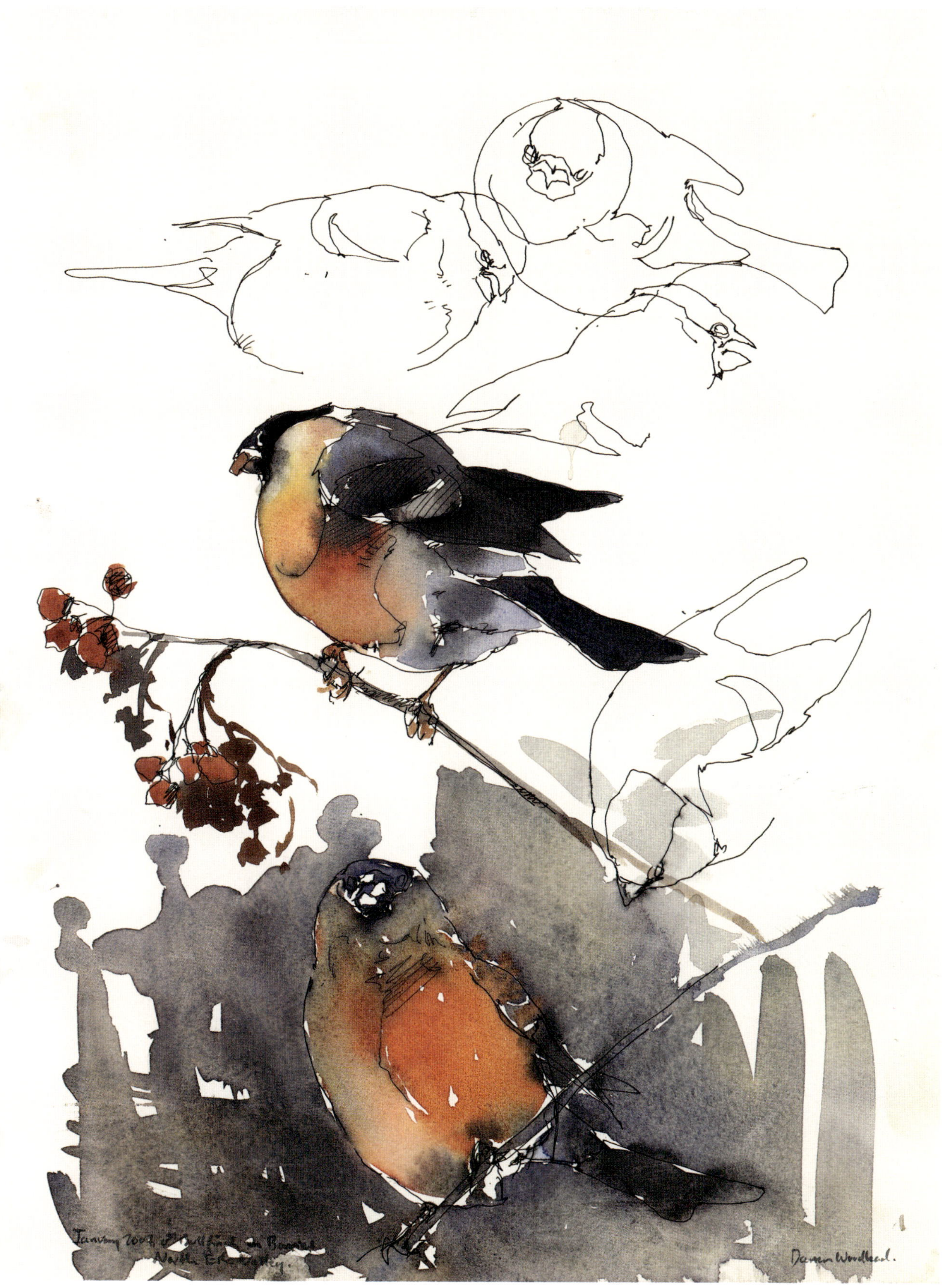

Male Bullfinch
(watecolour and pen, 380mm x 280mm)

January 2007. Male Bullfinch on Berries, North Esk valley.

Bullfinch on newly emerging buds
(watercolour, 560mm x 380mm)

13th March 2007. Feeding Bullfinch in glorious spring morning sunshine, North Esk Valley. Cool, with moderate south-westerly becoming showery mid afternoon.

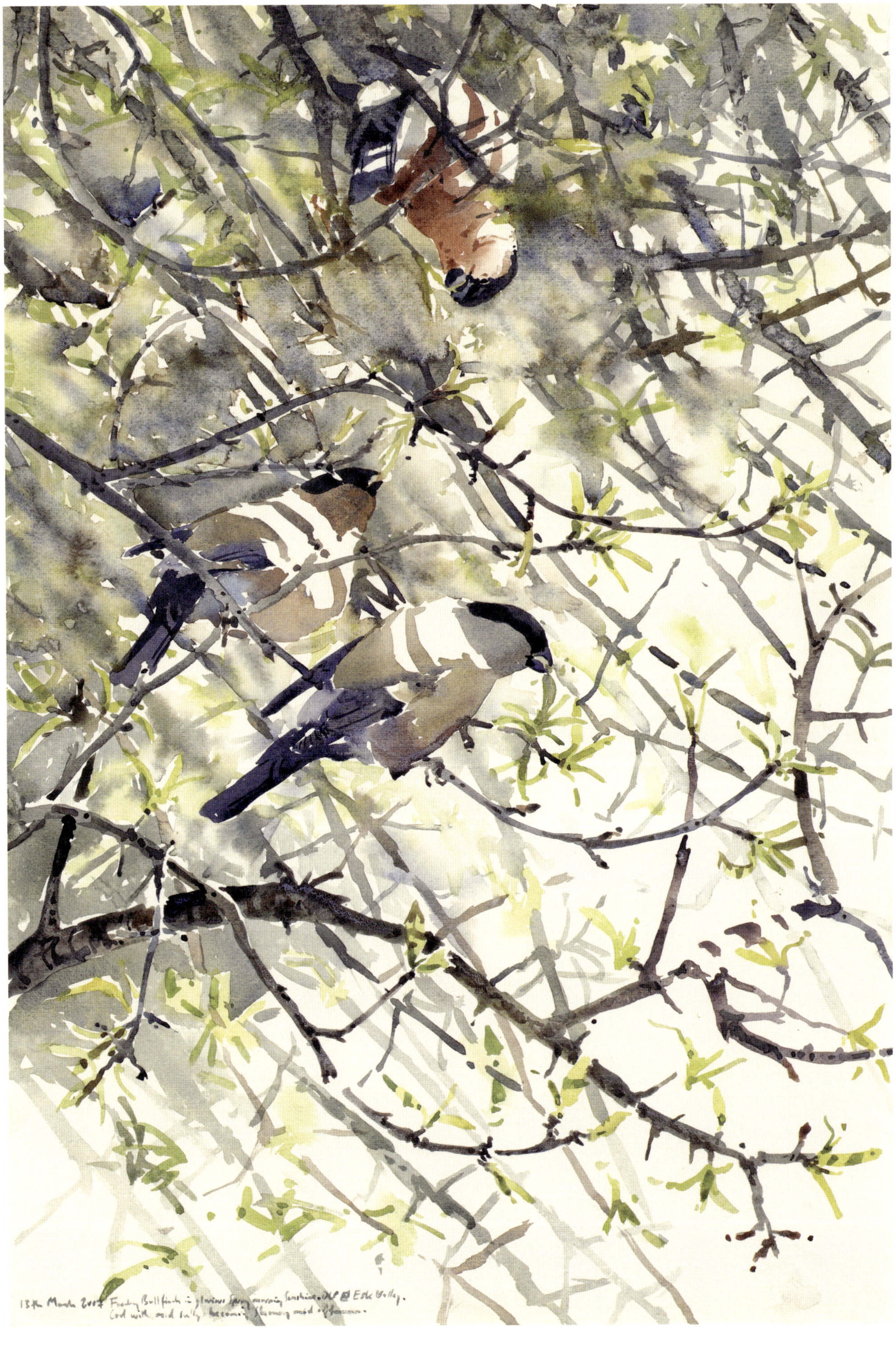

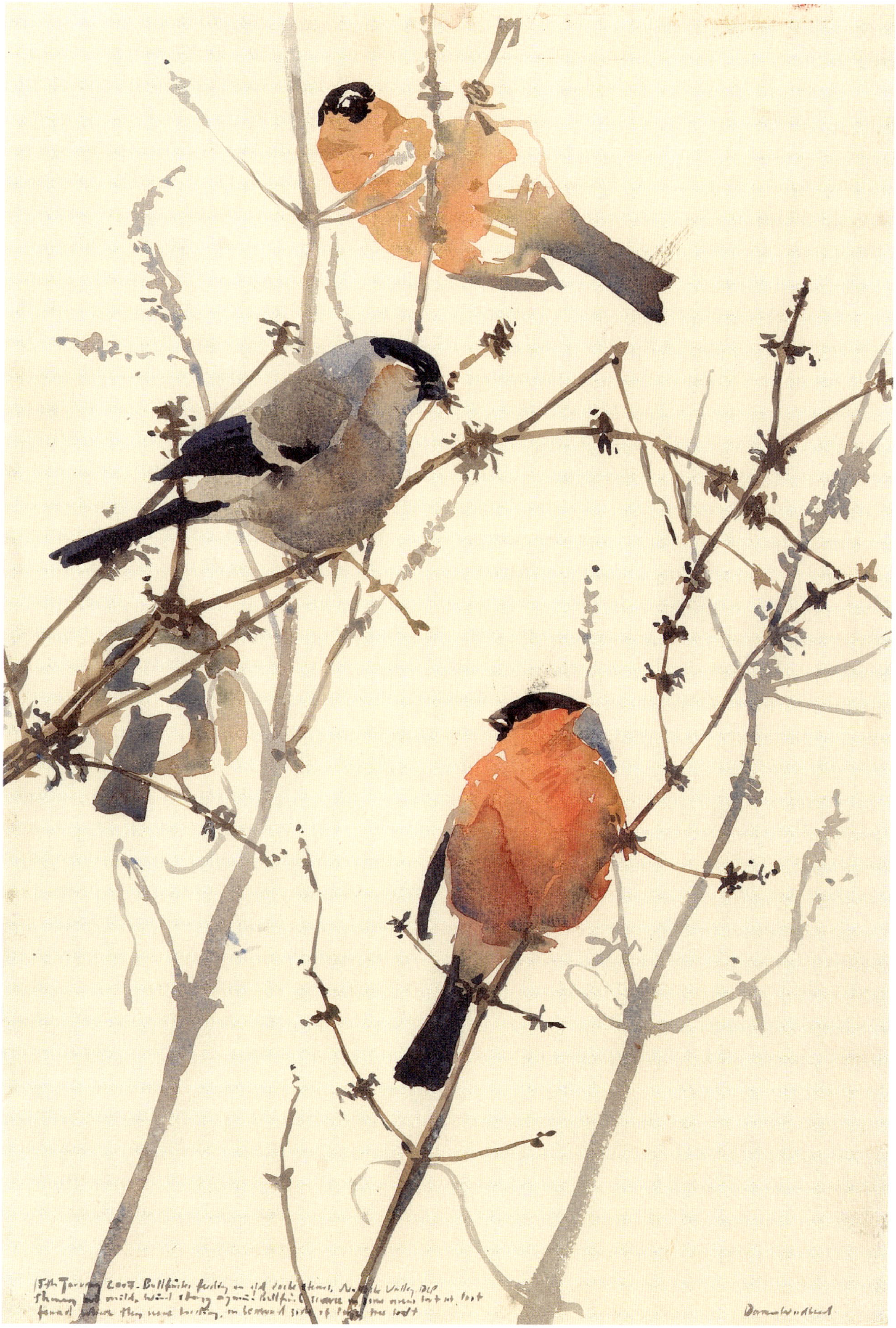

Bullfinch on Docks
(watercolour, 560mm x 380mm)

15th January 2007. Bullfinch feeding on old dock stems, North Esk valley. Showery but mild, wind strong again! Bullfinch scarce in usual areas but at last found where they were feeding on leeward side of large trees.

Singing male Bullfinch
(watercolour, 580mm x 380mm)

9th February 2007. North Esk valley. Late afternoon, light shower.

A lone male Bullfinch sings from the thin branches towards the top of a bare tree between the showers. Its shallow crest and head are raised slightly as it warbles a shy, soft song, a mixture of its normal call and finch-like twittering.

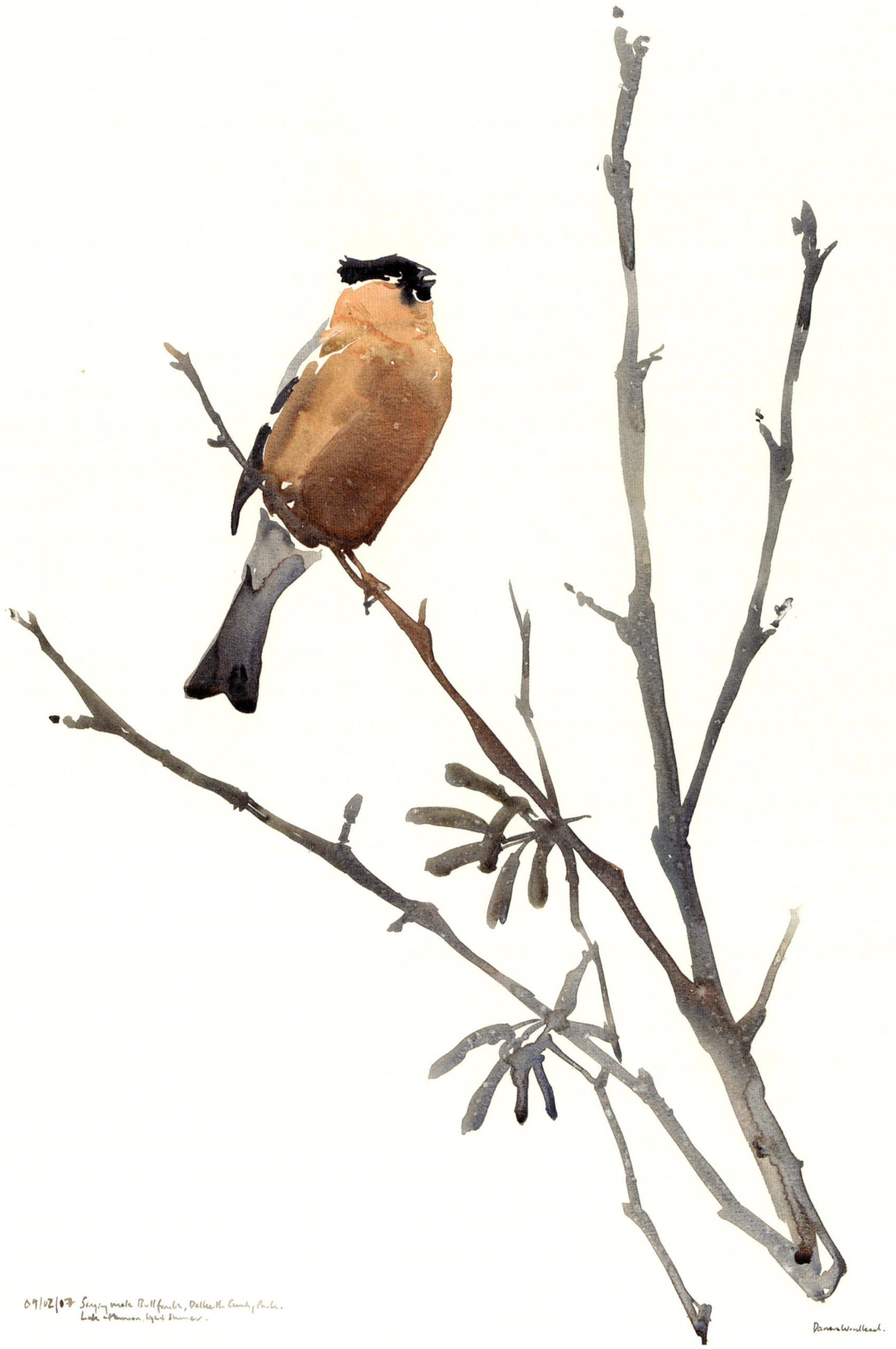

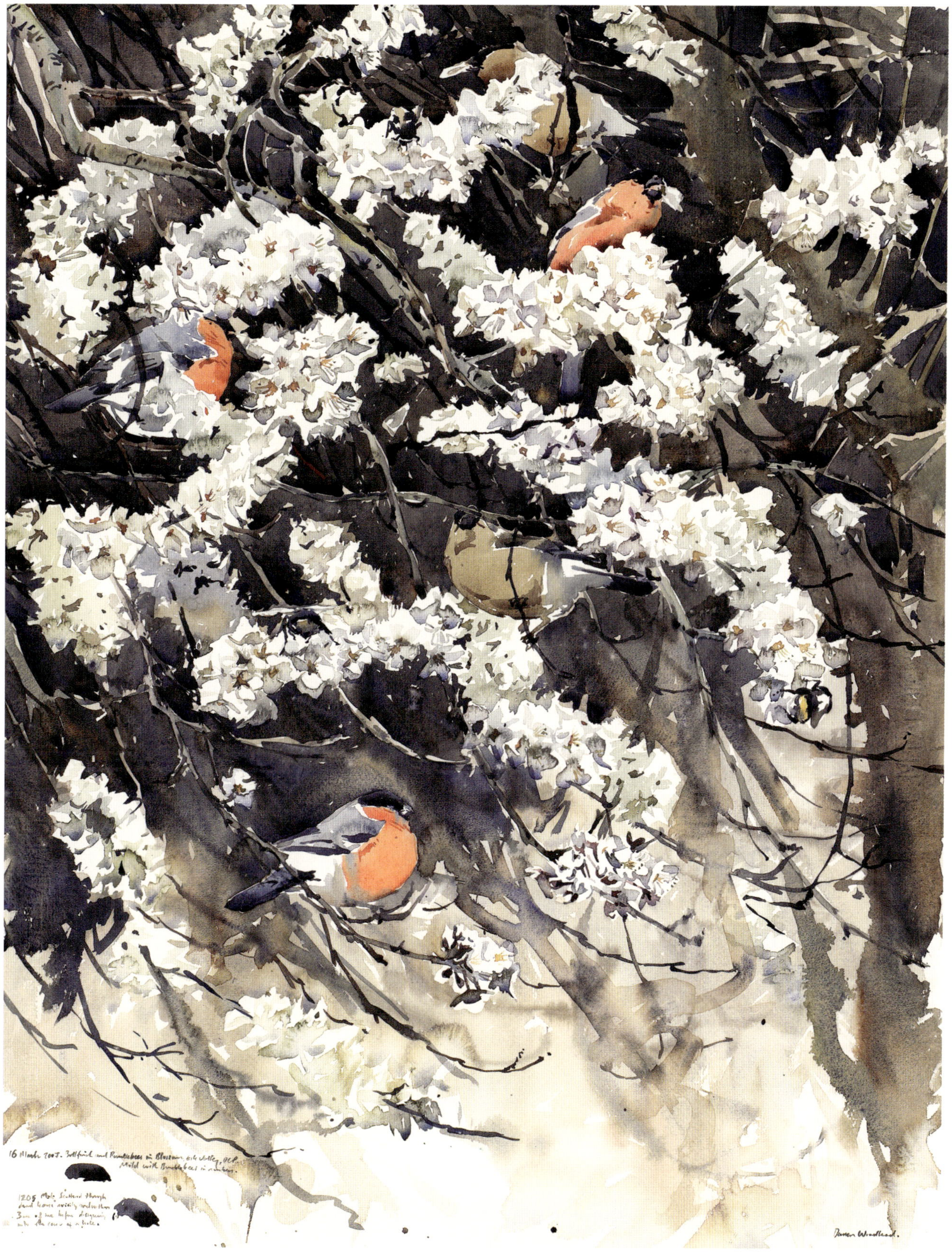

Bullfinch and Bumblebees in Blossom
(watercolour, 760mm x 560mm)

16th March 2007. Esk Valley. Mild, with Bumblebees in numbers. 12:05 Mole scuttled through dead leaves and within three feet of me before disappearing into cover of a hole.

Three Tawny Owlets,
18th May 2007
(watercolour, 560mm x 380mm)

A wonderful opportunity to draw three Owlets that had been found a couple of days earlier, nestled together on the ground. Being temporarily homed in a large owl box, the female continued to feed them, often spending the day alongside if not in the box. The comfort was not to last long, however, remains of one found taken by a Fox. A second disappeared shortly after, but hopefully to the relative safety of the trees, as Owl chicks have a natural ability to climb. Then only the third remained.

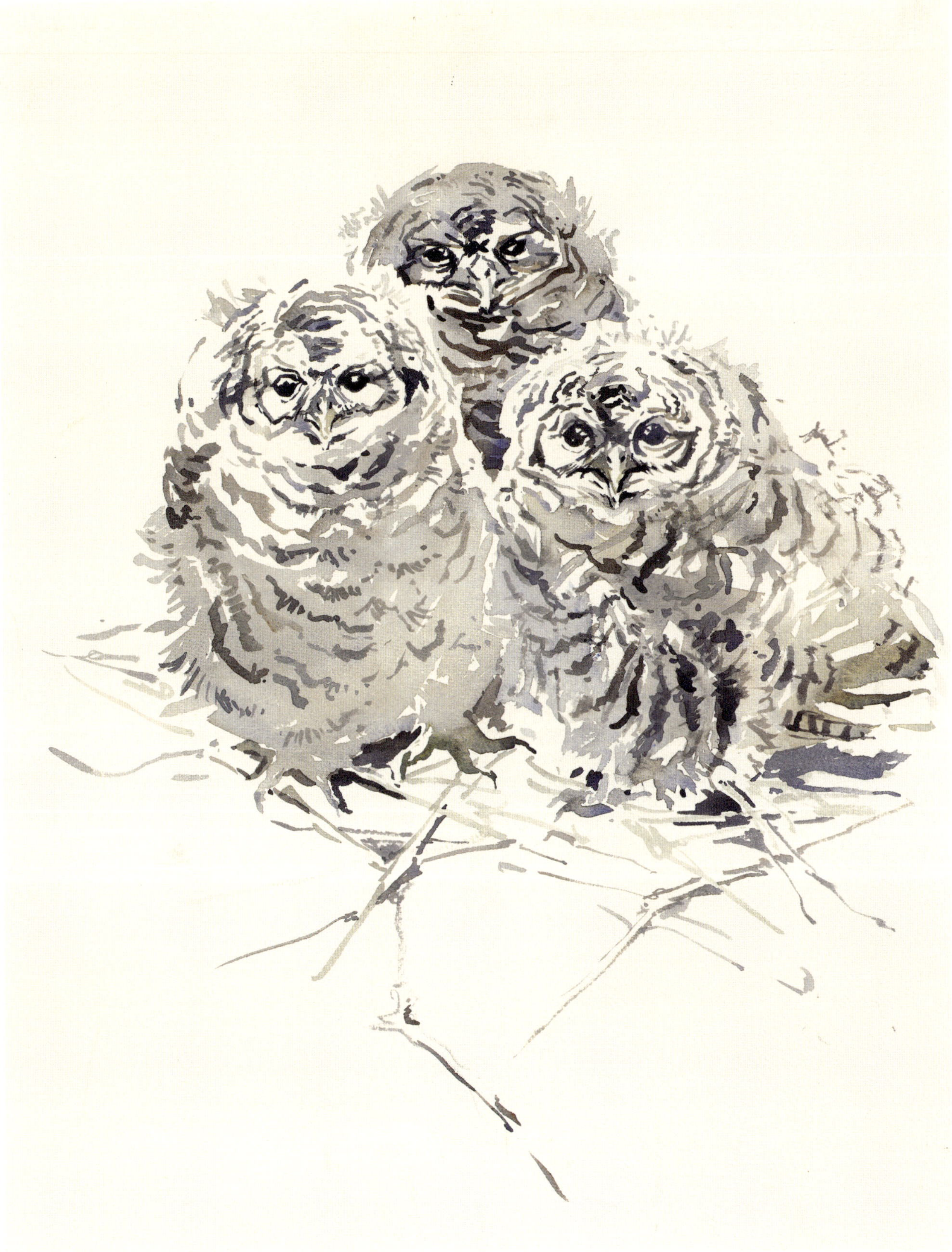

Single Owlet
(watercolour, 560mm x 380mm)

23rd May 2007. Tawny Owl chick.
The only one left out of the three.

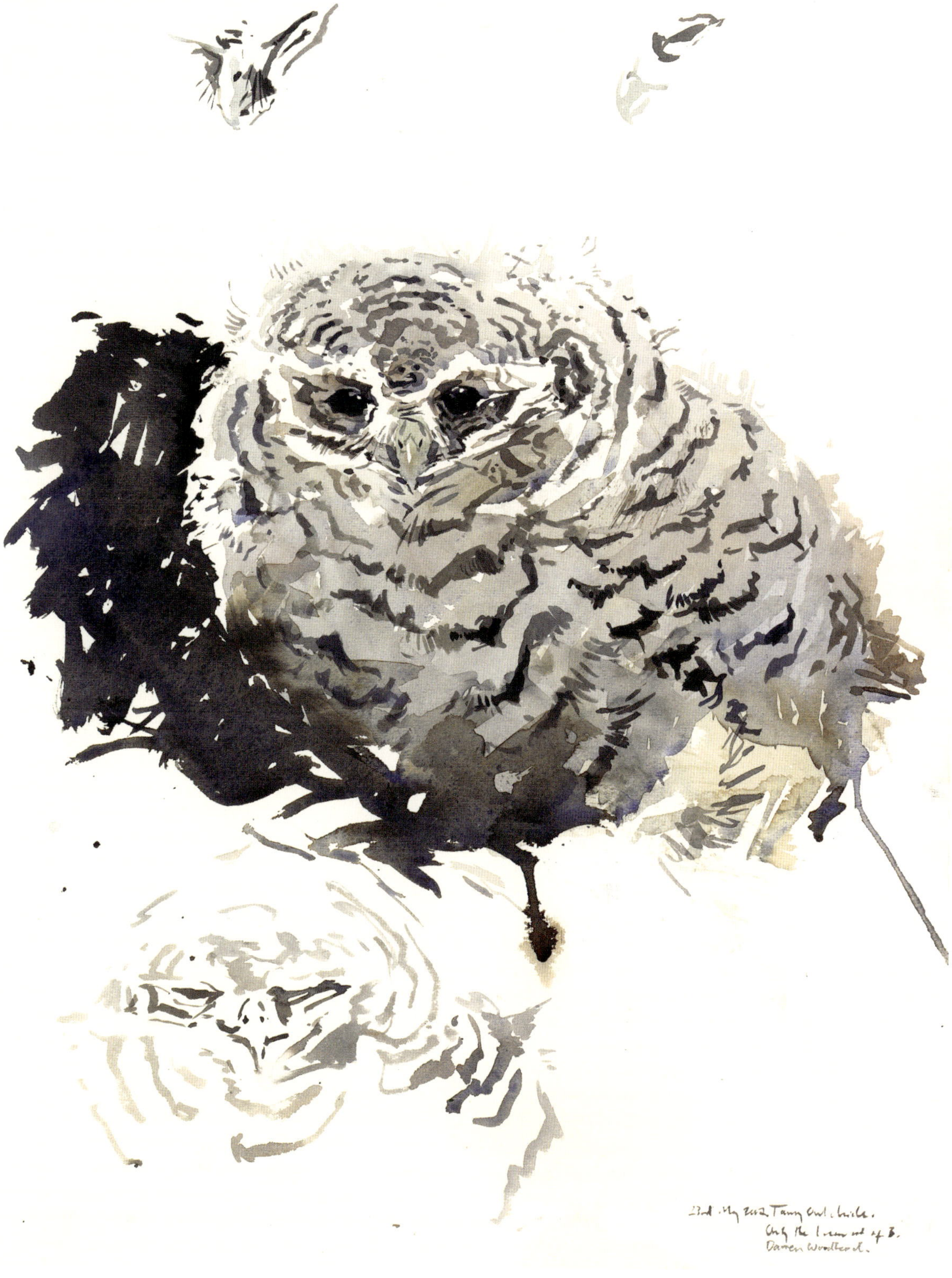

Calling newly fledged Mistle Thrush
(watercolour, 560mm x 380mm)

13th June 2007. Fairliehope Wood, Carlops. Overcast and humid after a couple of wet days. Thrushes fledging at least two weeks earlier than last year. Spotted Flycatchers out today as well as Pied Wagtails by Fairliehope House. Midges horrendous! Bottom of page littered with black carcasses! A product of the same parents of last year, this time fledging nearly three weeks earlier.

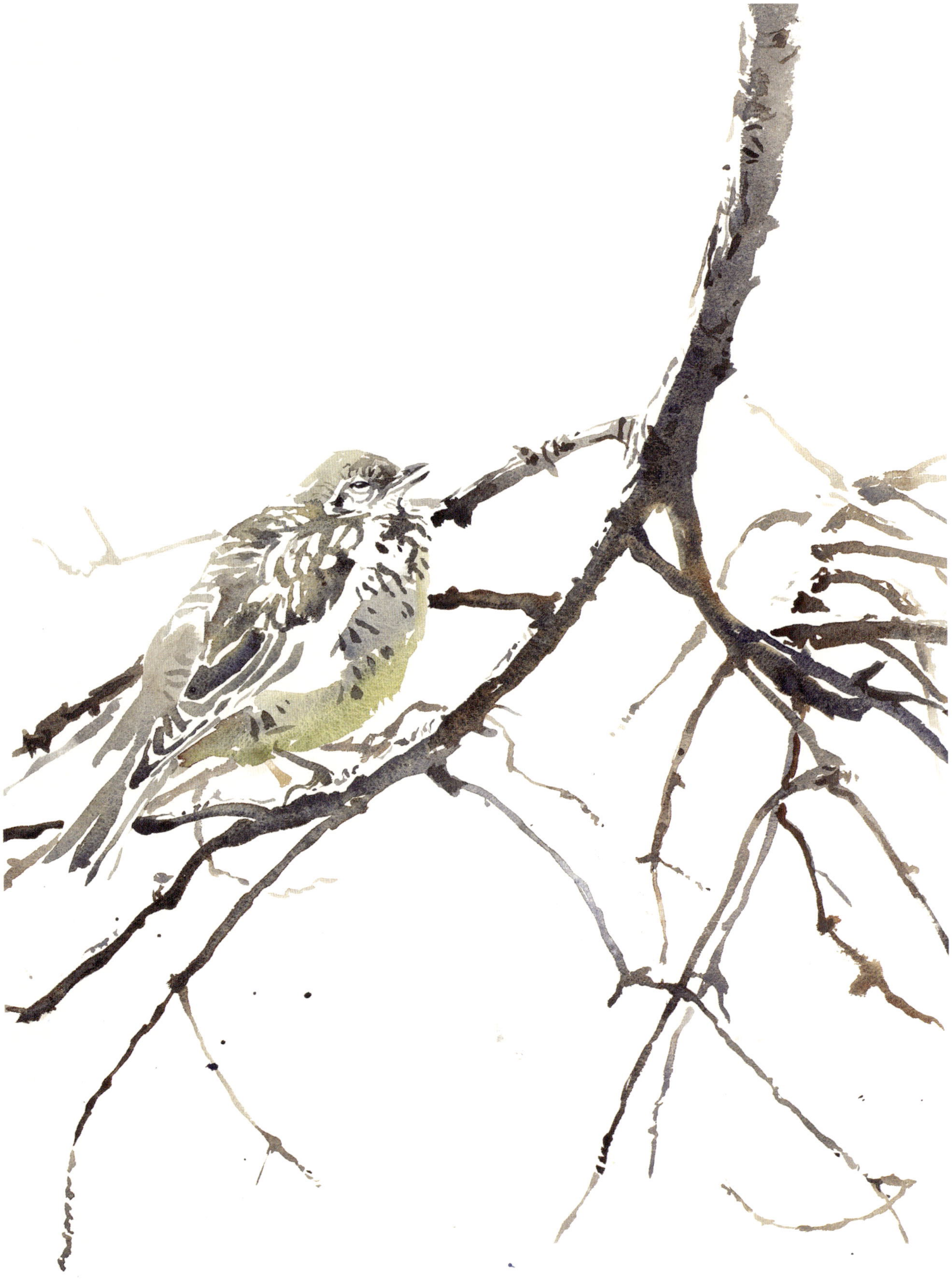

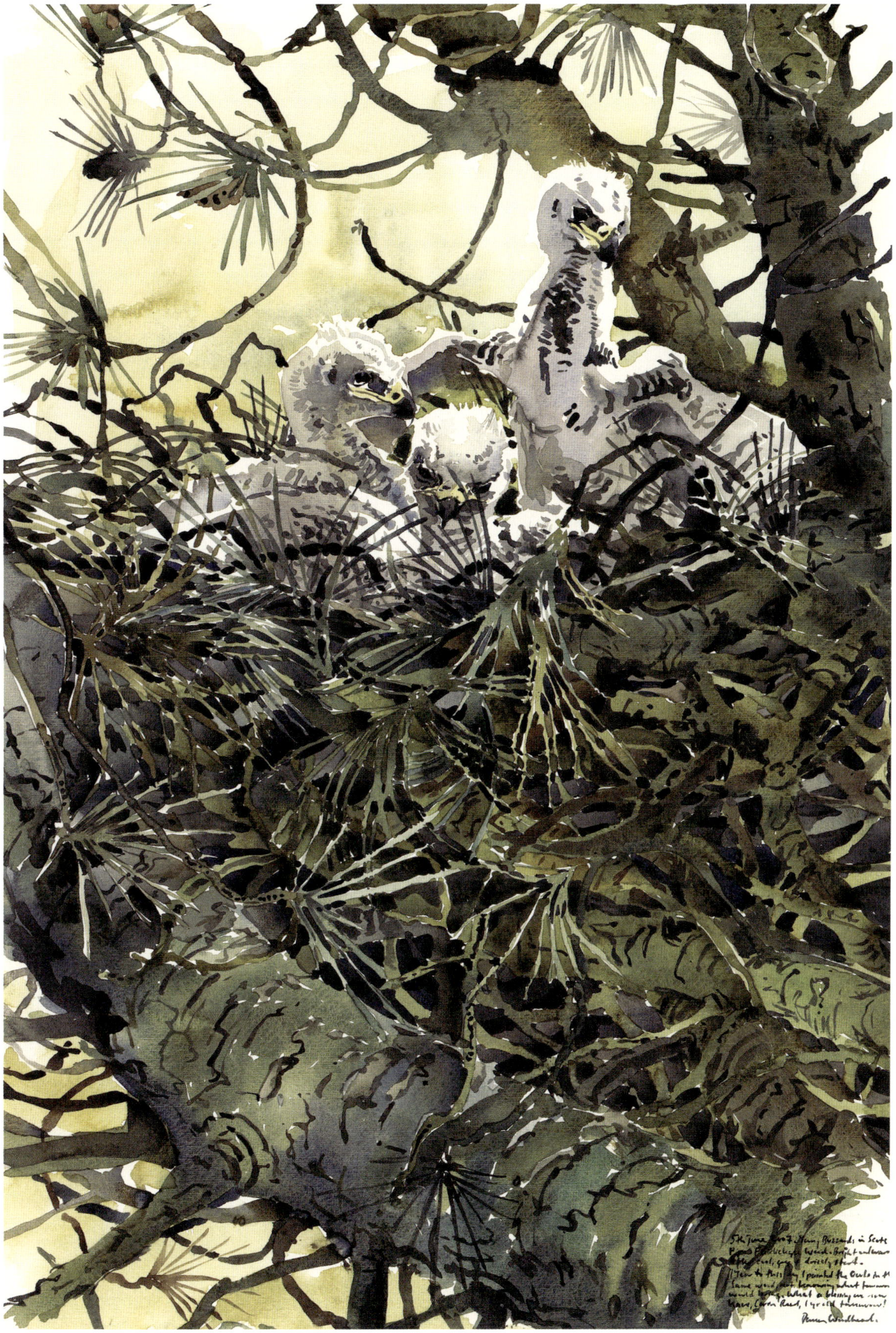

Buzzard nest
(watercolour, 560mm x 380mm)

5th June 2007. Young Buzzards in Scots Pine. Fairliehope wood. Bright and warm after cool, grey and drizzly start. One year to this day I painted the Owls in same wood not knowing what tomorrow would bring. What a blessing we now have, Corin Reed, one year old tomorrow.

On the outskirts of the wood, a Buzzard's nest sits high in the Pines, enjoying an unending view down the valley. Three clumsy, downed chicks are visible with golden yellow gapes and just a hint of the darker feathers to come. It is hard to imagine how in just over three weeks, they go from this early stage to fully winged predators on the verge of taking to the skies.

Buzzard chicks
(watercolour, 560mm x 380mm)

13th June 2007. Fairliehope wood. Overcast and cool wind freshening. Maybe only two now. One seemed to pick at something resembling a bird's wing.

With only the two visible, I had my fears for the third chick, especially as I noted one of the chicks picking and pulling at something resembling a wing in the cup of the nest below. My suspicions were confirmed later.

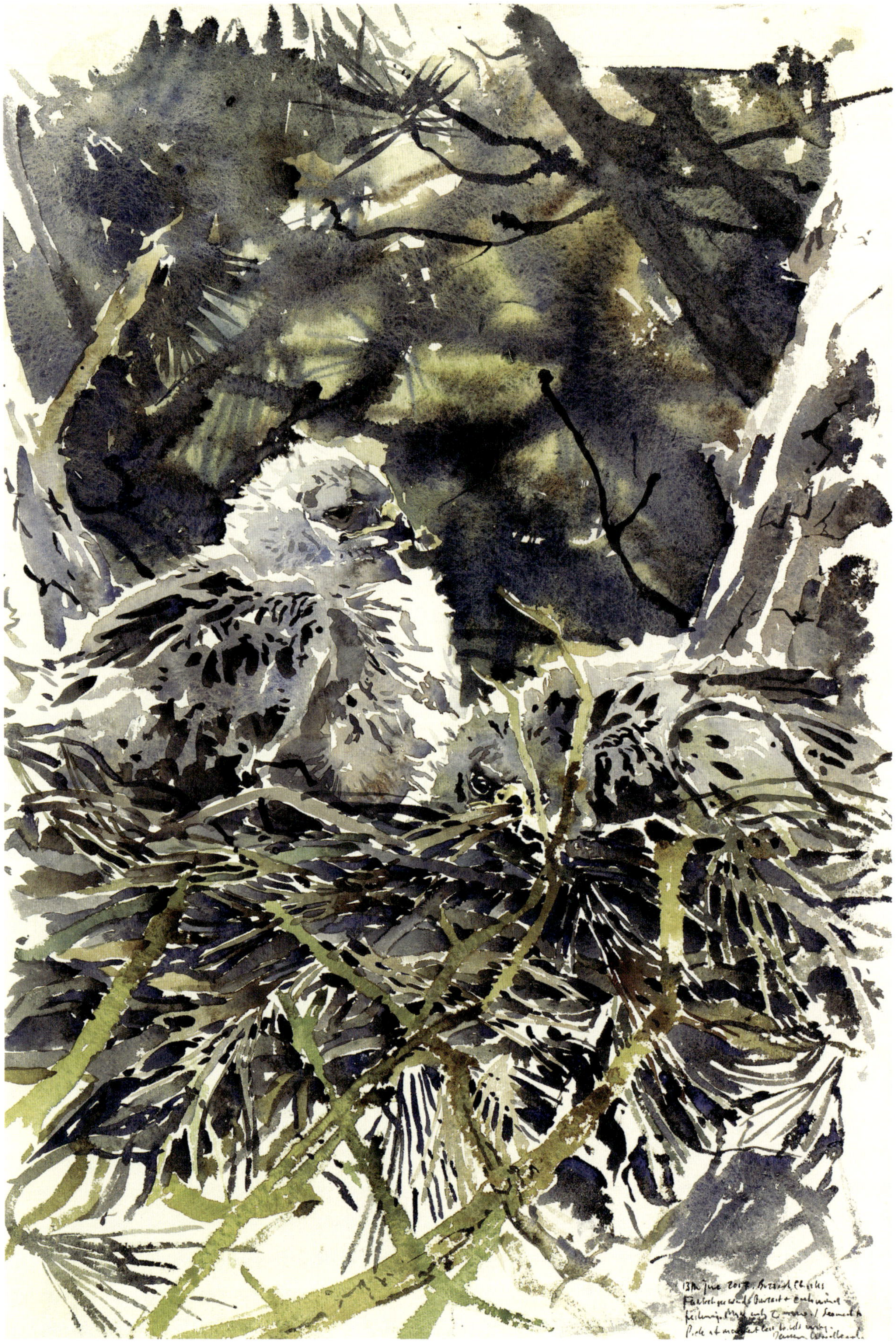

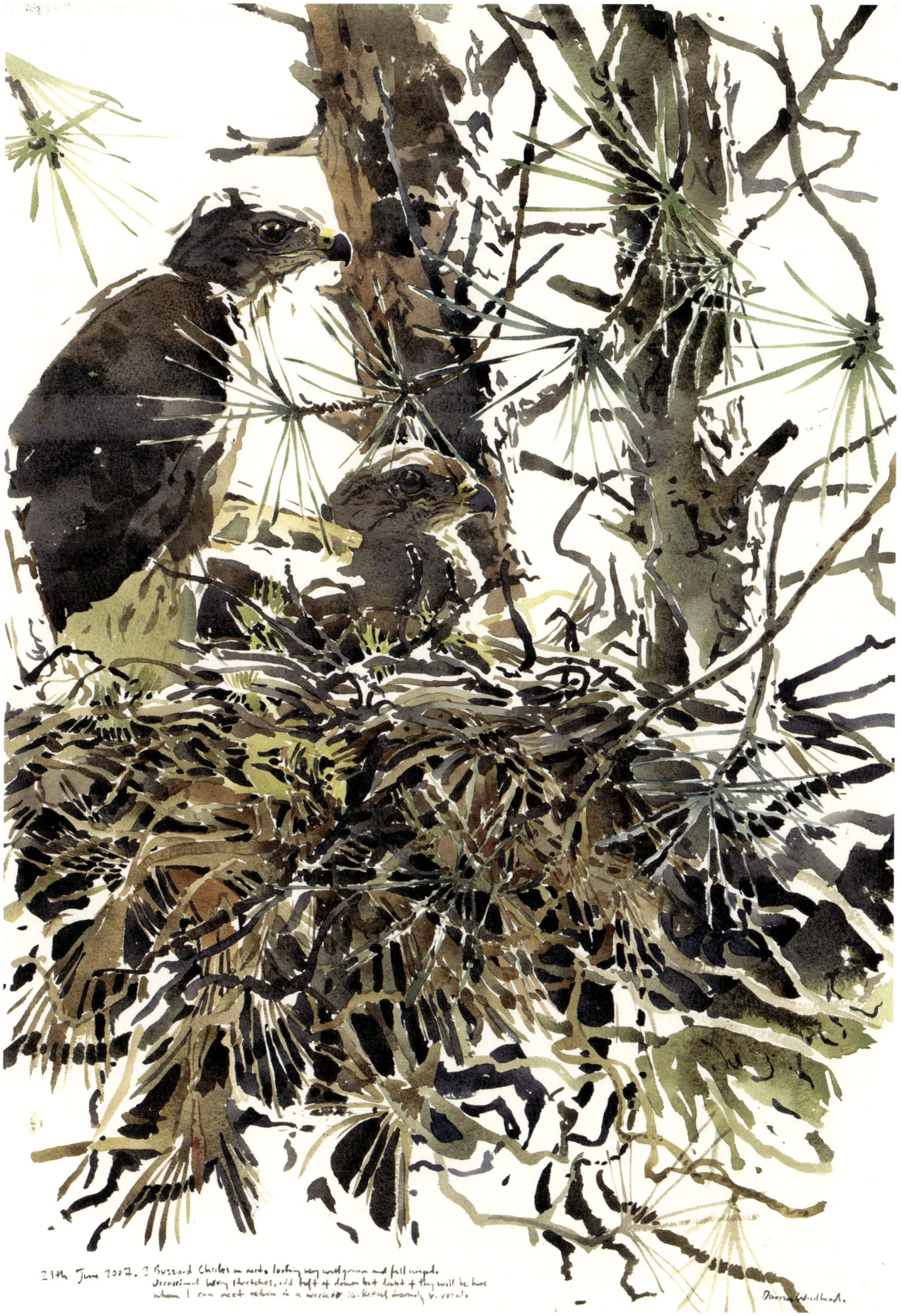

Young Buzzards
(watercolour, 560mm x 380mm)

29th June 2007. Two Buzzard chicks on nest and looking very well-grown and full-winged. Occasional wing stretches, odd tuft of down but doubt if they will be here when I can next return in a week or so. Kestrel family very vocal.

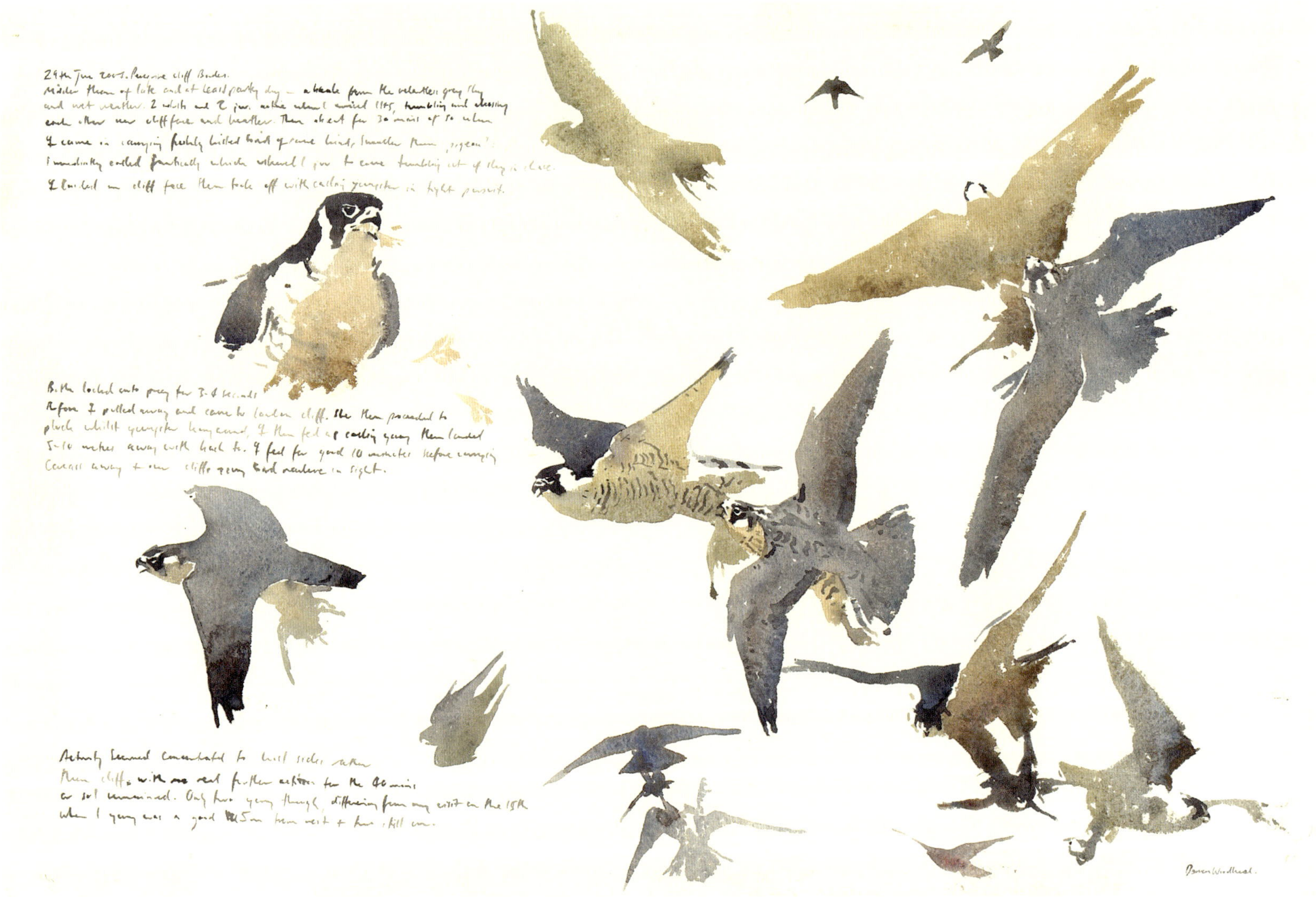

Young Peregrine
(watercolour, 560mm x 380mm)

14th June 2007. Fledged Peregrine chick sitting two metres or so above nest. Still two others in nest with spangled down still on heads. Both parents present, female vocal at first but then eventually calm. This is a month earlier than drawings I made last year. Overcast with gusting east wind. Becoming wet. Newly fledged Wheatear alongside. Borders.

Although I was unaware what happened to the pair that successfully moved location last year, certainly one of the Peregrine families was enjoying buoyant success. Three healthy youngsters watched the world attentively, and were soon to grace the skies.

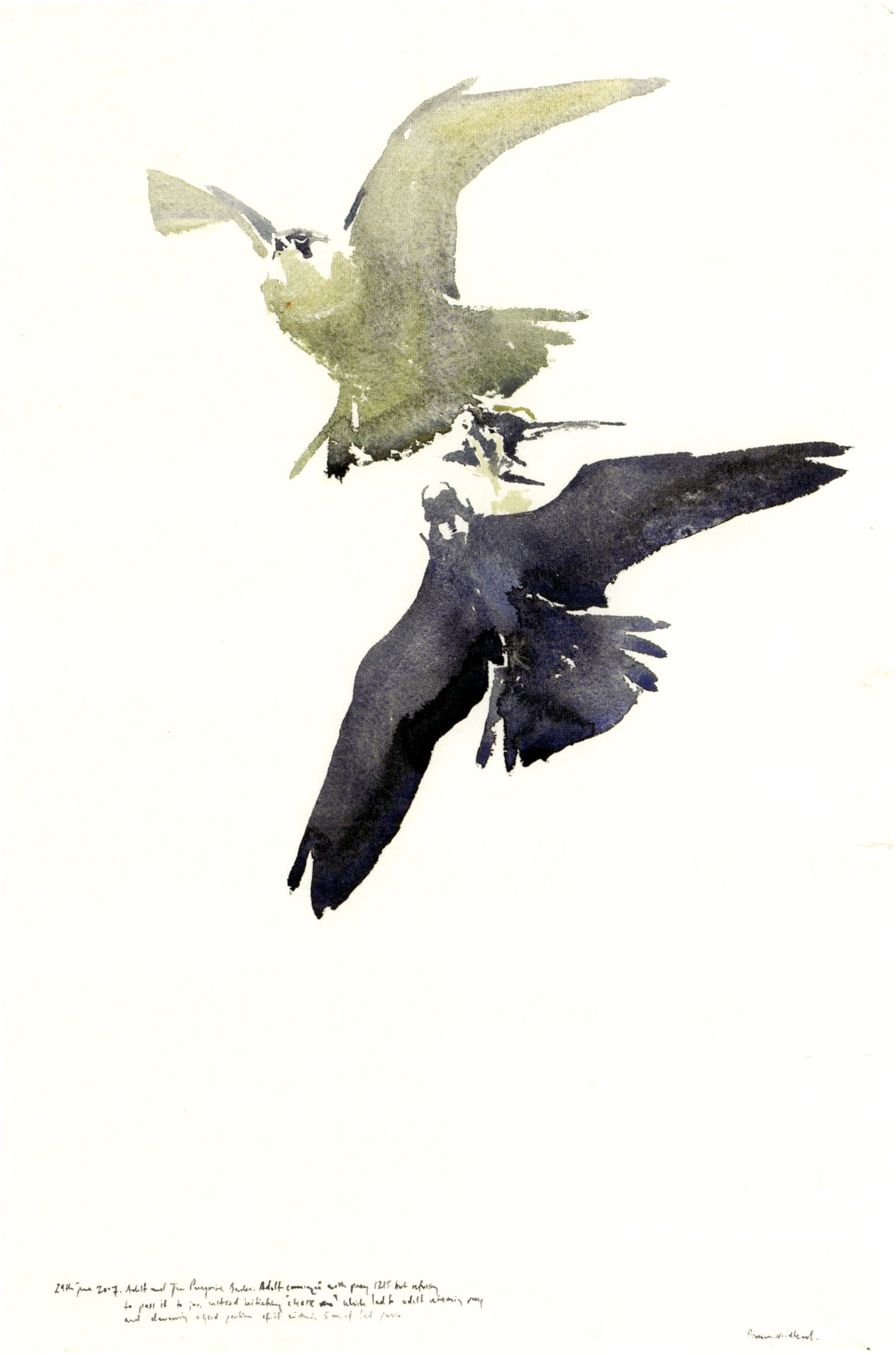

The learning curve
(watercolour, 560mm x 380mm)

29th June 2007. Adult and juvenile Peregrine, Borders. Adult coming in with prey 12:15 but refusing to pass it to juvenile, instead initiating 'chase me' which led to adult retaining prey and downing a good portion of it within five metres of sat juvenile.

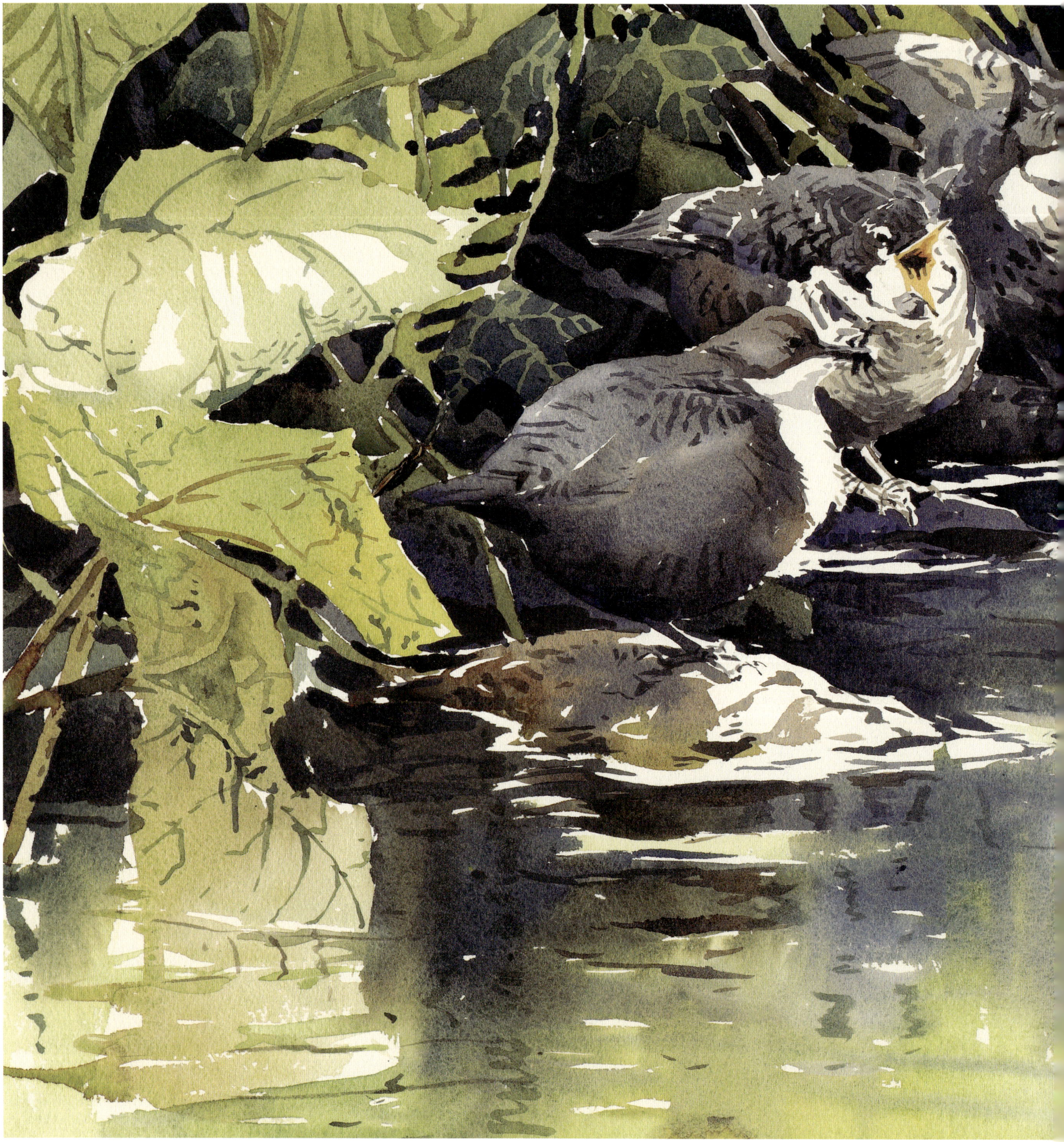

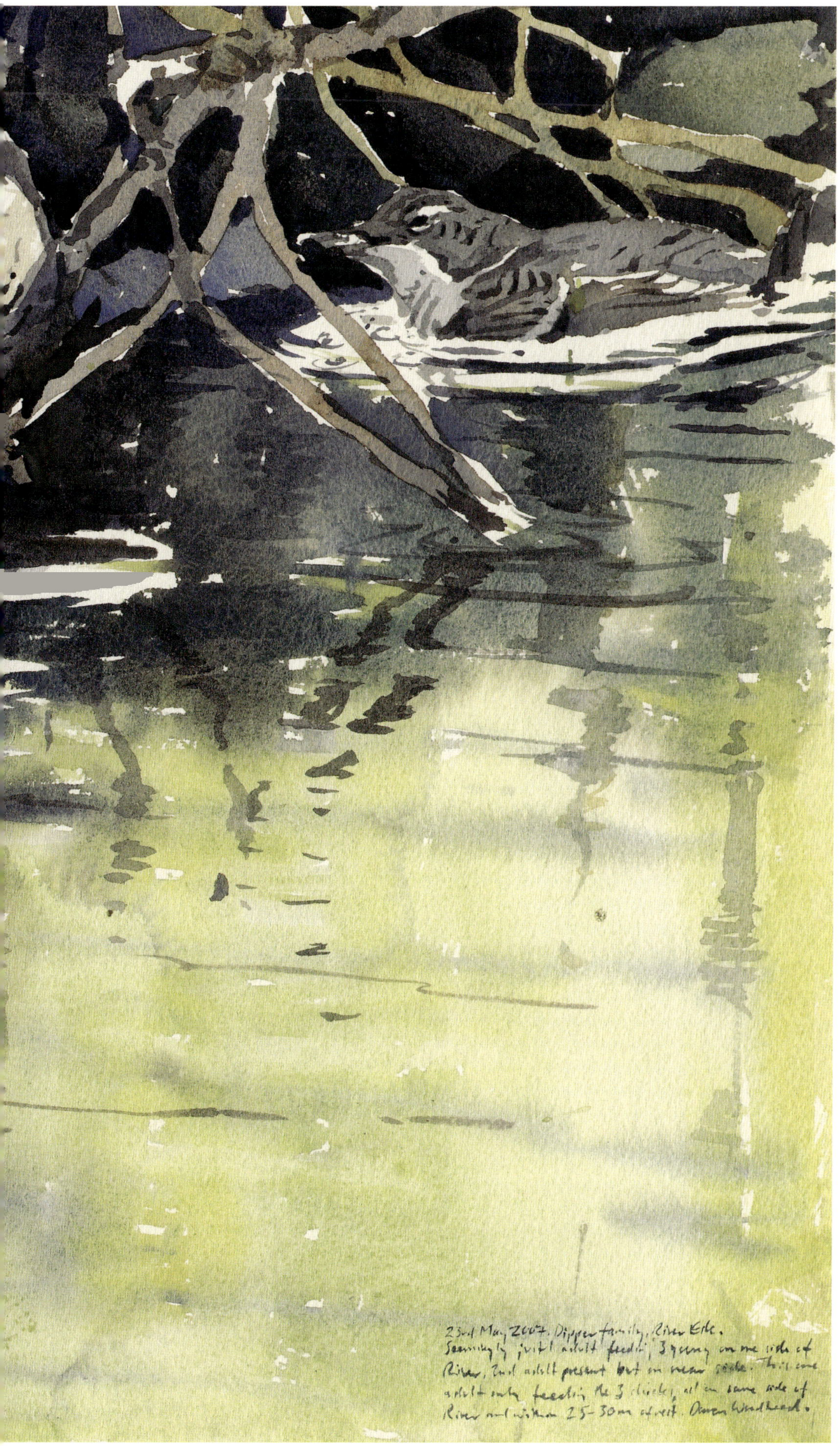

Dipper family, River Esk
(watercolour, 285mm x 440mm)

23rd May 2007. Seemingly just one adult feeding three young on the side of river, second adult present but on near side. This one adult feeding the three chicks all on same side of river and within twenty-five to thirty metres of nest.

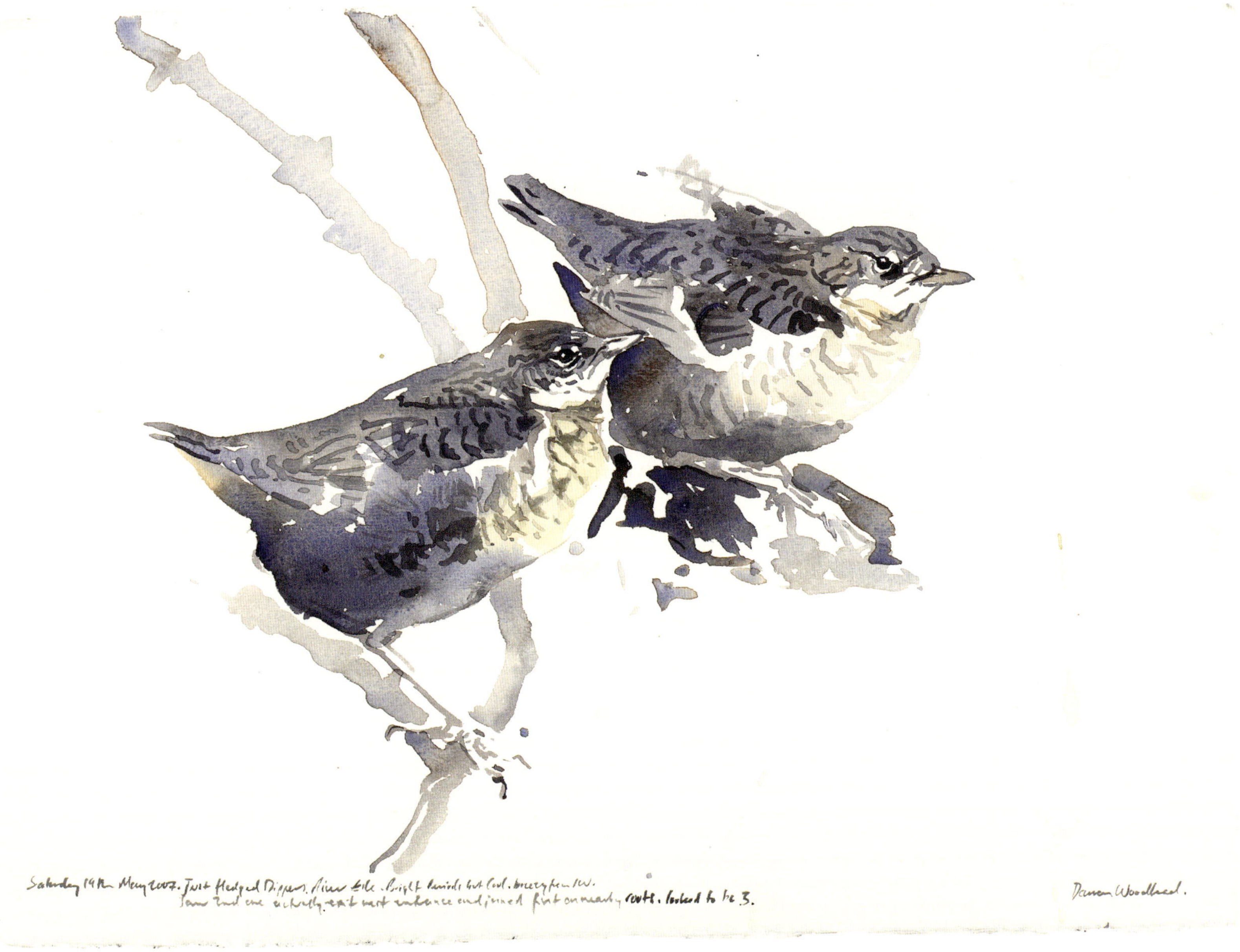

Fledgling Dippers *(watercolour, 280mm x 380mm)*

Saturday, 19th May 2007. Just-fledged Dippers, River Esk. Bright periods but cool, breezy from south-west. Saw second one actually exit nest entrance and joined first on nearby roots. Looked to be three.

Young Dipper Study
(watercolour, 240mm x 320mm)

8th June 2007. Young Dipper, River Esk. A strange feeling to the day today. After a run of several cool and humid, grey drizzly days, this afternoon became warm and summery. Only one adult Dipper alongside one young this afternoon, and further upstream to where I drew week before last. Barely a breath of wind, insects out in abundance, river with thousands of golden stars darting over centre. Adult seemingly unimpressed by close proximity of young. At one point looked almost as if adult looking for new nest site by flying up under overhanging branches and plants, but then adopting a pointed aggressive stance aimed at juvenile before chasing it downstream. Is this the beginning of its independence?

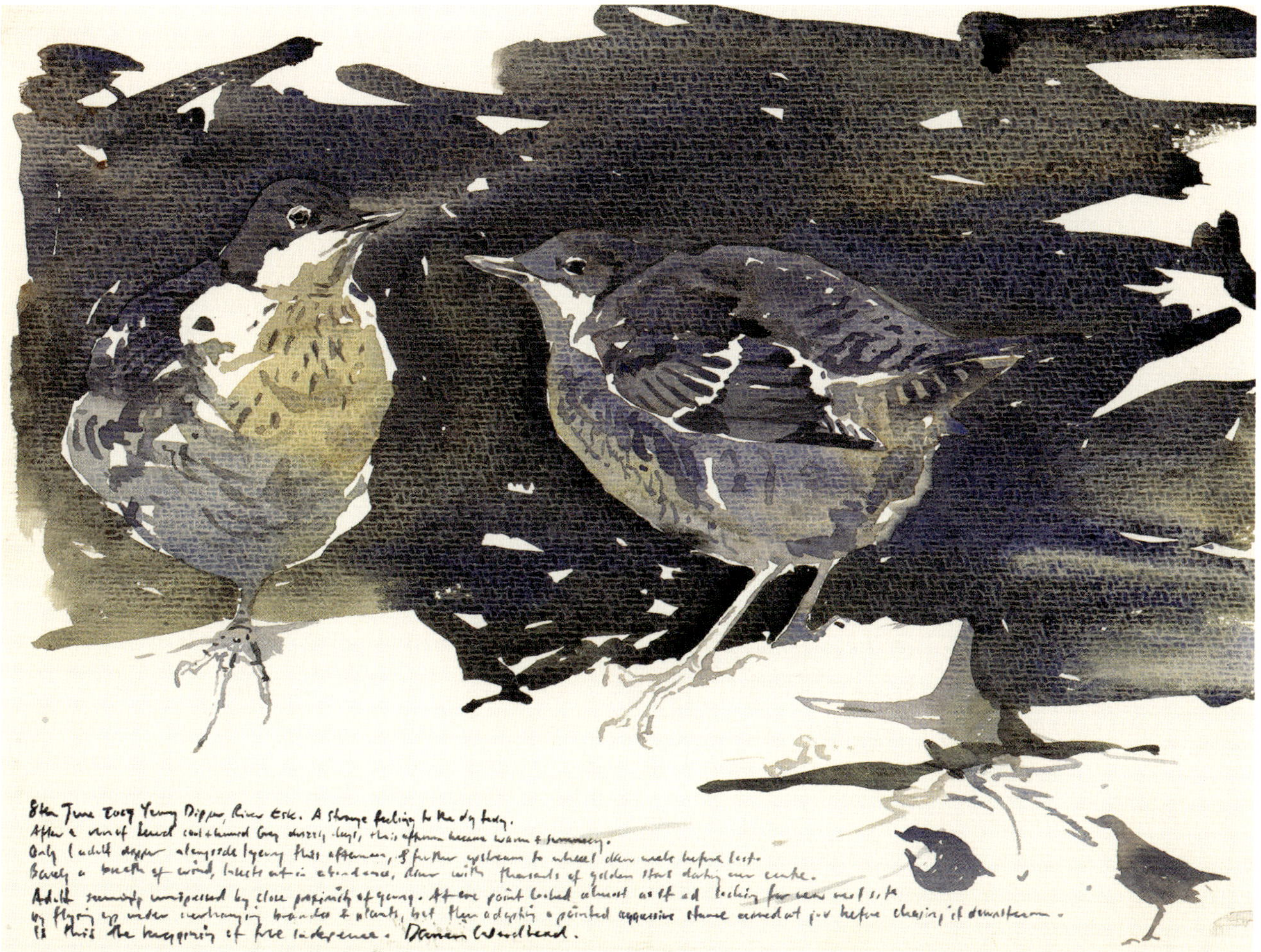

Dippers are the life and soul of the river. I spent time watching a pair from March onwards, early enough to enjoy their lively spring courtship flights through the trees and over the river. This gave way to the restlessness of nest-building, then the lull of incubation. A loud 'stip' announced any return or departure. The bonding between Dippers is unending. Throughout the incubation period, they would sing to each other, pass food to each other and delicately touch bills. Much time was also given to bouts of mutual preening. Comically, I watched one become frustrated trying to break off a section of Beech leaf, only to for its partner to pick up, tear off a part, then hand it back.

The intensity of feeding the young gradually picked up pace as a louder and more demanding din erupted from the bank opposite. As I arrived on the bank that day, I could not believe my eyes as I saw one chick bobbing on a stone immediately beneath the nest. As I watched, amazed, a second chick hopped out of the moss-tunnelled exit and began bobbing alongside on an emerging root. I had been lucky enough to see one actually fledge; I scribbled away on the scraps of paper that I had with me. The next couple of weeks were going to be busy.

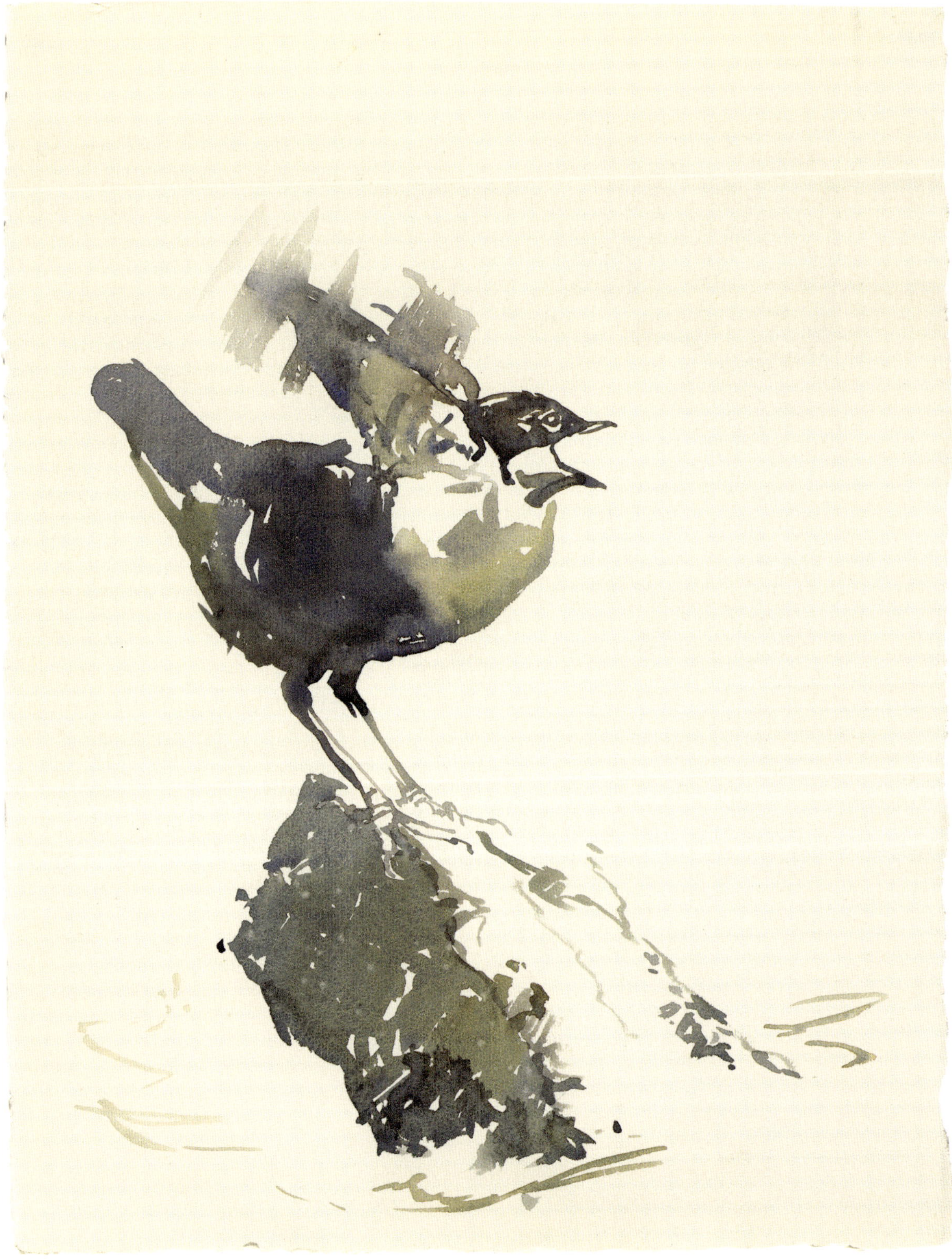

Begging young Dipper, River Esk, 4th June 2007.
(watercolour, 380mm x 280mm)

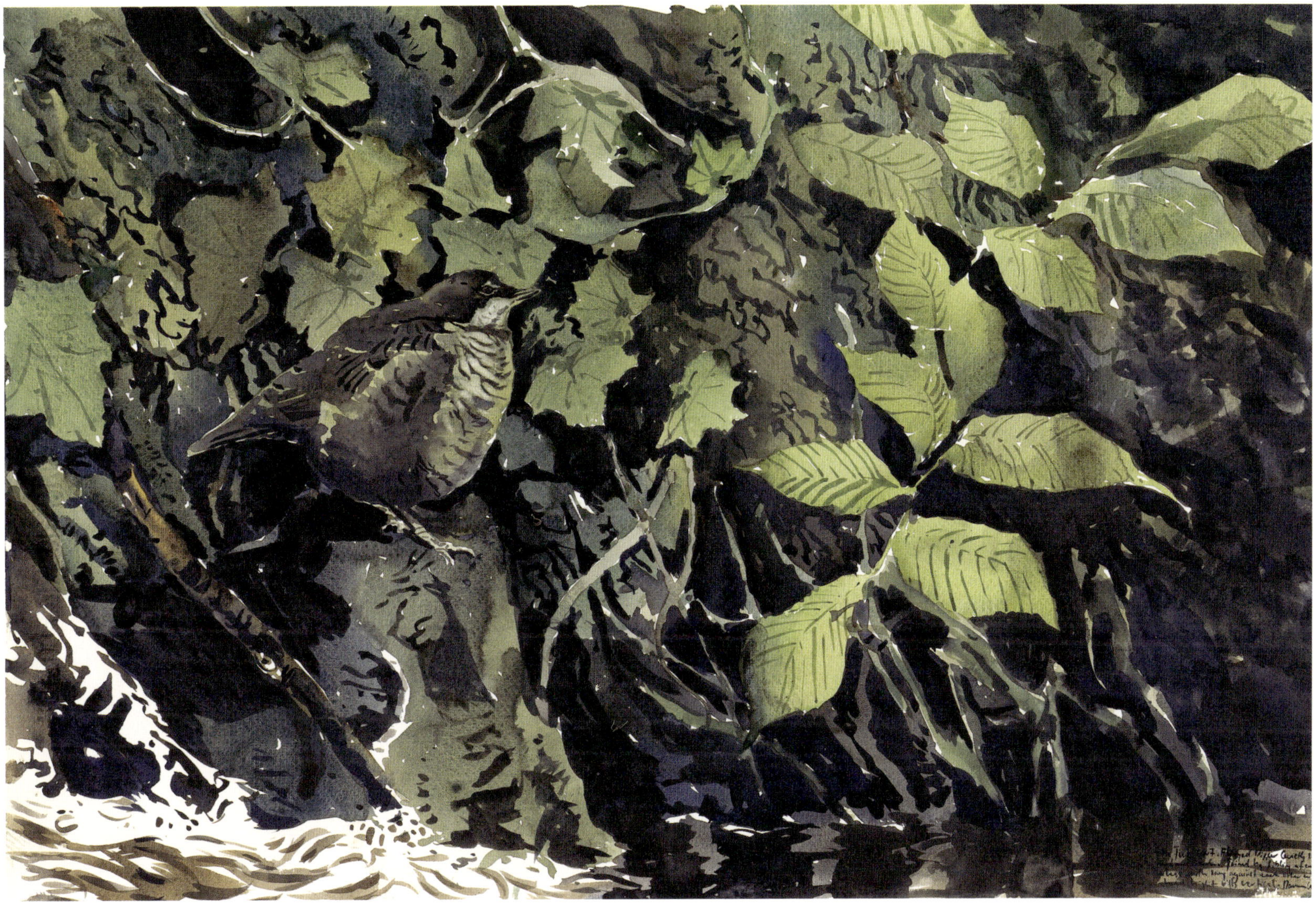

Singing Young Dipper
(watercolour, 380mm x 560mm)

4th June 2007. Fledged Dipper quietly singing from shadowed Beech. Joined by sibling at one point, when both sang against each other with heads held high and bills vertical.

Seemingly almost 100 per cent independent now, this was also the first time I saw an adult chasing a juvenile away despite the young bird's half-hearted begging. From then on it became harder to find any Dippers as the youngsters began slowly dispersing away from the nest area.

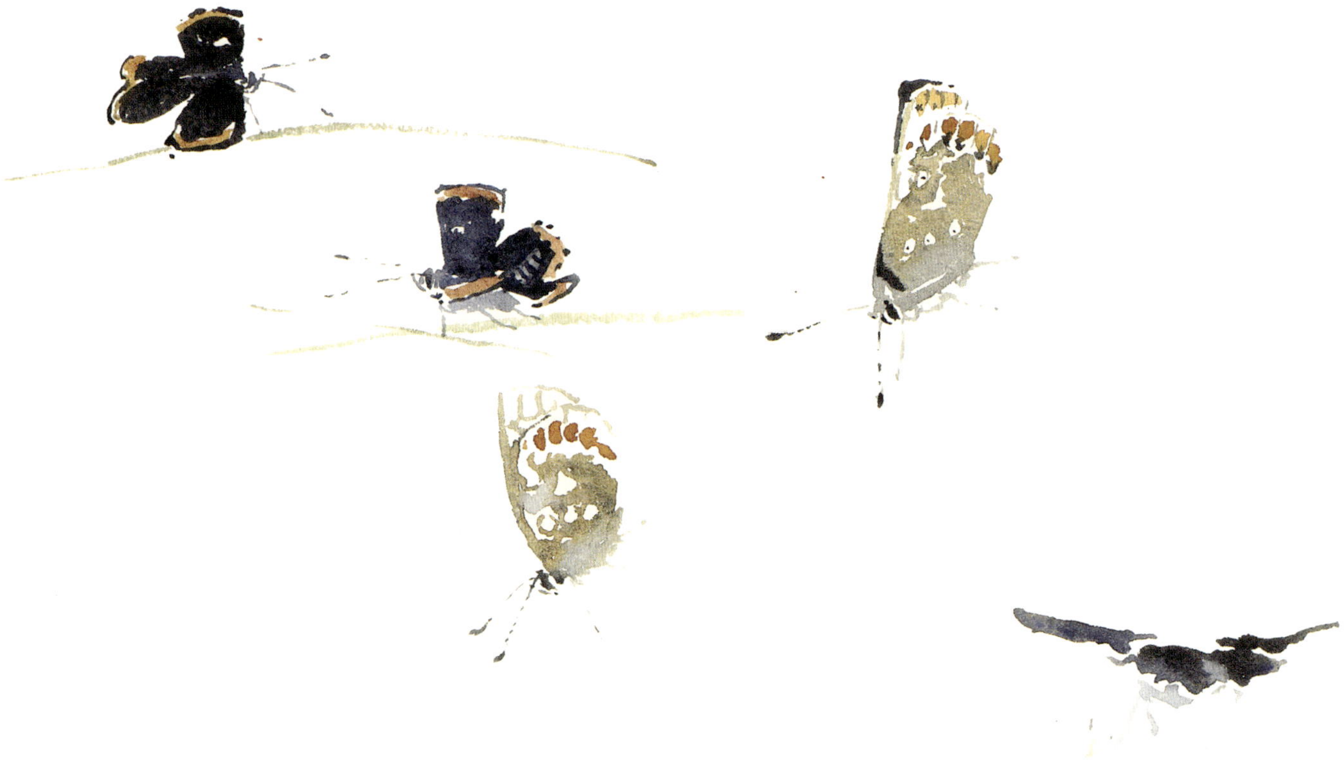

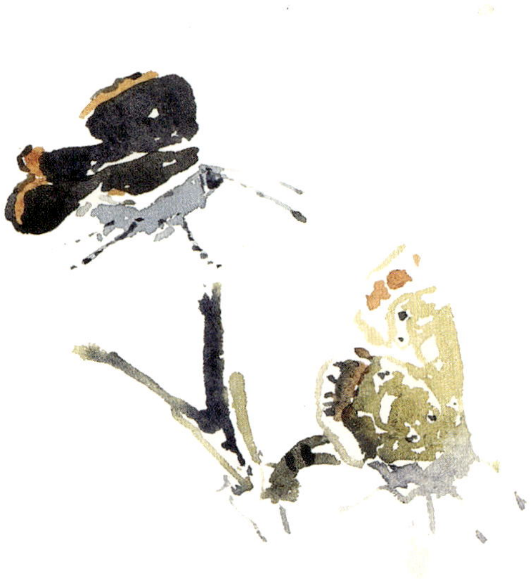

Northern Brown Argus
(watercolour, 440mm x 285mm)

11th July 2007.The Linn, Carlops, Borders. Lots of activity but very difficult to pin down. Breezy but warm.

From 13:00. Twenty degrees approx. in sun but feeling cooler in overcast spells and moderate south-westerly wind. Male constantly harassing female among section of Wild Thyme, 14:50. Constant tussling and bickering whilst hovering in the air as well as on ground. Male always trying to be in a position to present his abdomen, whilst female keeps her body still. Her much fresher wings consistently trembled. Whole sequence must have lasted twenty minutes or more, with male returning at least three times to same area of Thyme. At first attracted what appeared to be another male, but the joint participation did not last long. A t least four other Butterflies around at the same time. Sequence ended with female laying single egg on Rock Rose leaf – did final approach by male initiate egg-laying?

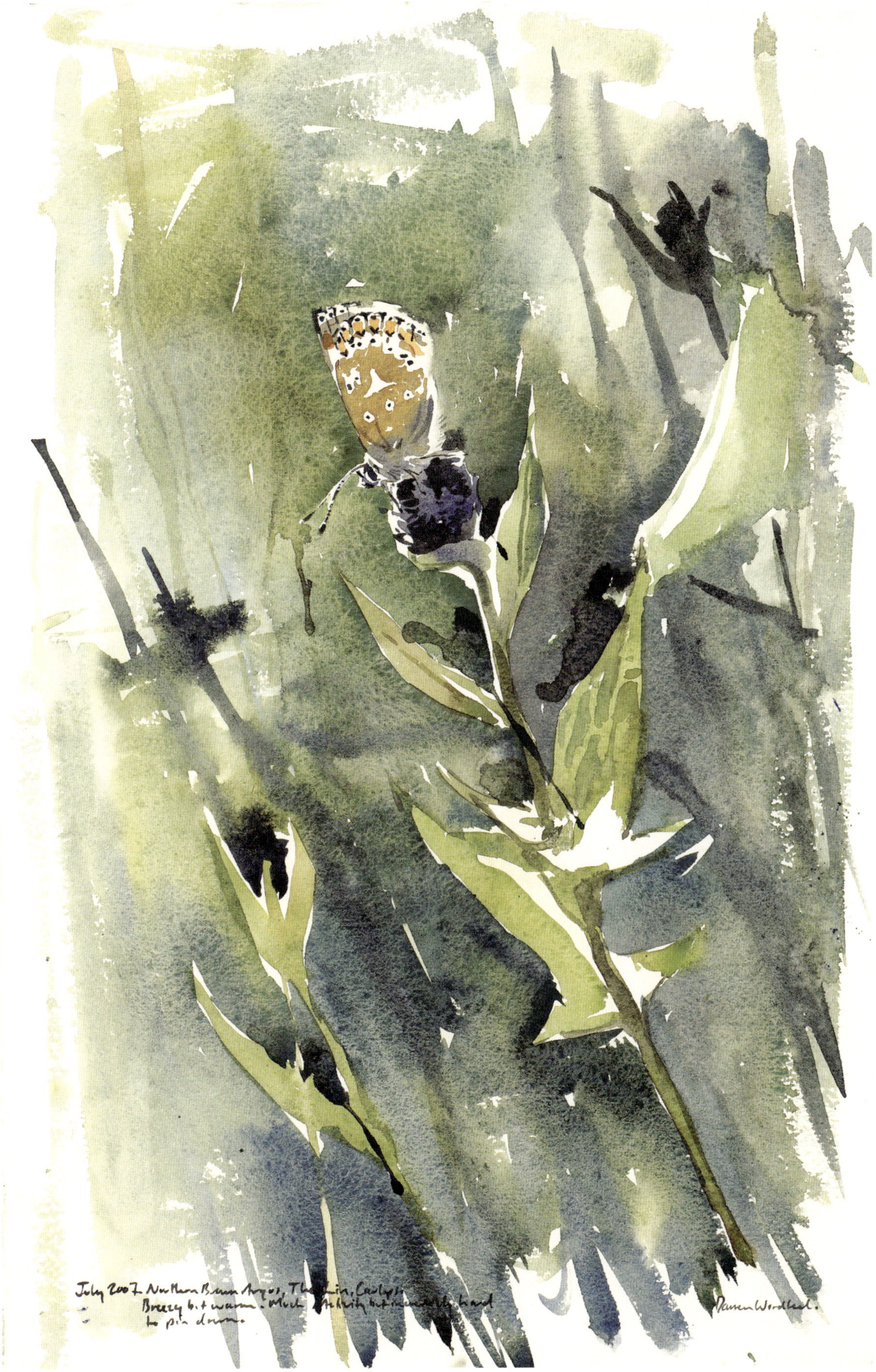

Northern Brown Argus
(watercolour, 440mm x 285mm)

11th July 2007, The Linn, Carlops. Breezy but warm. Much activity but incredibly hard to pin down.

Ringlet

(watercolour, 380mm x 280mm)

25th July 2007. (Probably male) Ringlet (*Aphantopus hyperantus*), Harbourcraig Heath. Overcast with periods of heavy showers. Early on looked good for Large Heath but nothing, not too much cotton on grass. So maybe too late this year. Only Butterfly, this Ringlet. Sheltering through showers, but as soon as temperature rose with brightness, off over heath.

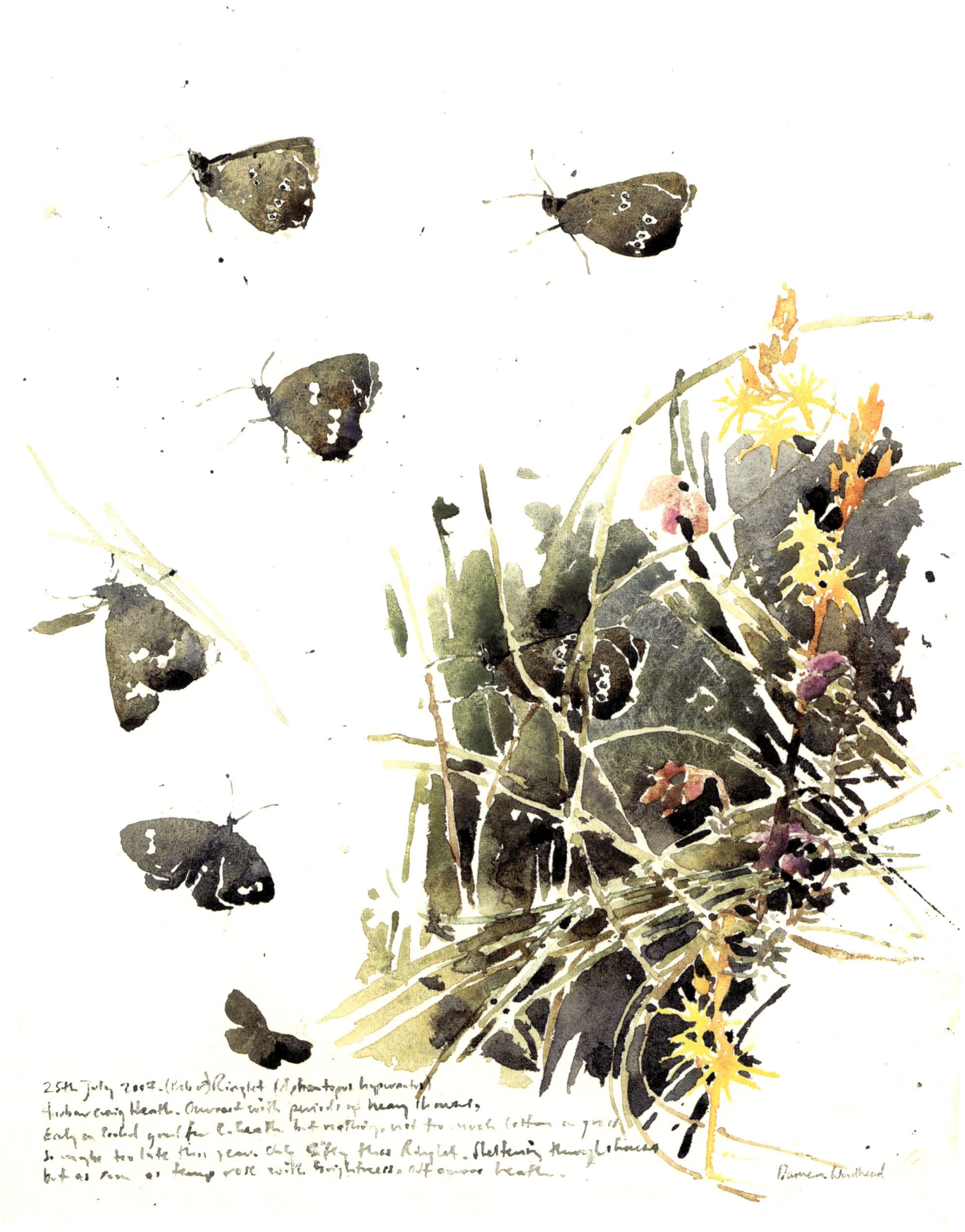

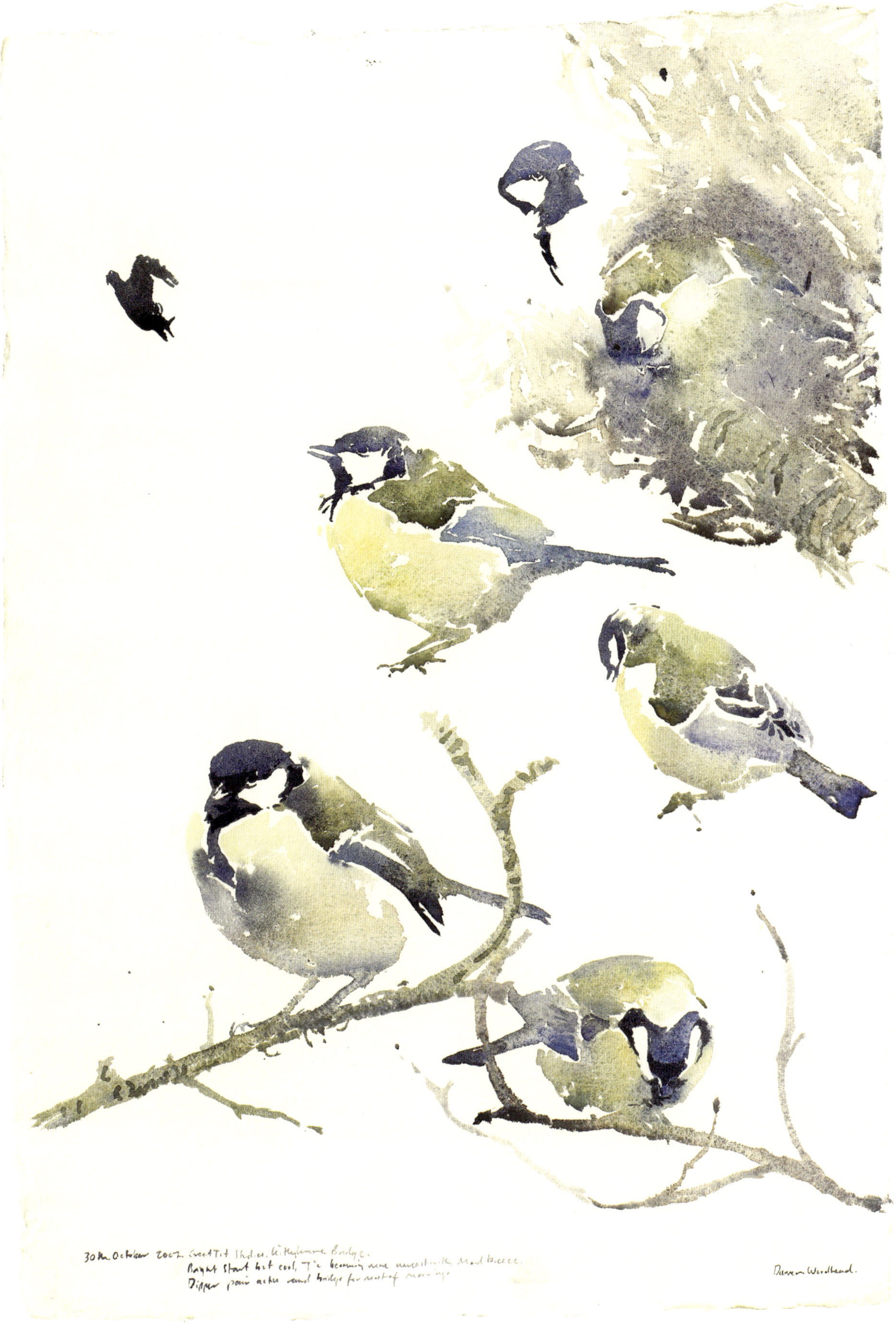

Great Tits feeding on Beech nuts
(watercolour, 560mm x 380mm)

30th October 2007, Great Tit studies, Kitleyknowe bridge. Bright start but cool, 7 degrees, becoming more overcast with moderate breeze. Dipper pair active round bridge for most of morning.

As I made my way towards the bridge my attention was drawn by a rustle and frenzied alarm calls from the bank of fallen Beech leaves. Looking down the side of the bridge I noticed many leaves being tossed aside as a pair of Great Tits voraciously fought within. Unperturbed by my presence, they tumbled down the slope until one bird held the other pinned on its back in the leaves. Both had their bills agape, napes widened as titmice do when showing aggression, with wings pressing into undergrowth to increase pressure. The tussle was short-lived, and all the birds headed back into the low-lying cover to begin feeding once again. The Beechnuts were always taken up from the ground onto low branches, where, held between both feet, they were subjected to energetic tapping until they split.

Amanita in among Scots Pine undergrowth *(watercolour and pen, 370mm x 275mm)*

8th November 2007. Clear and sunny after heavy early rain. Cool, with strong westerly wind.

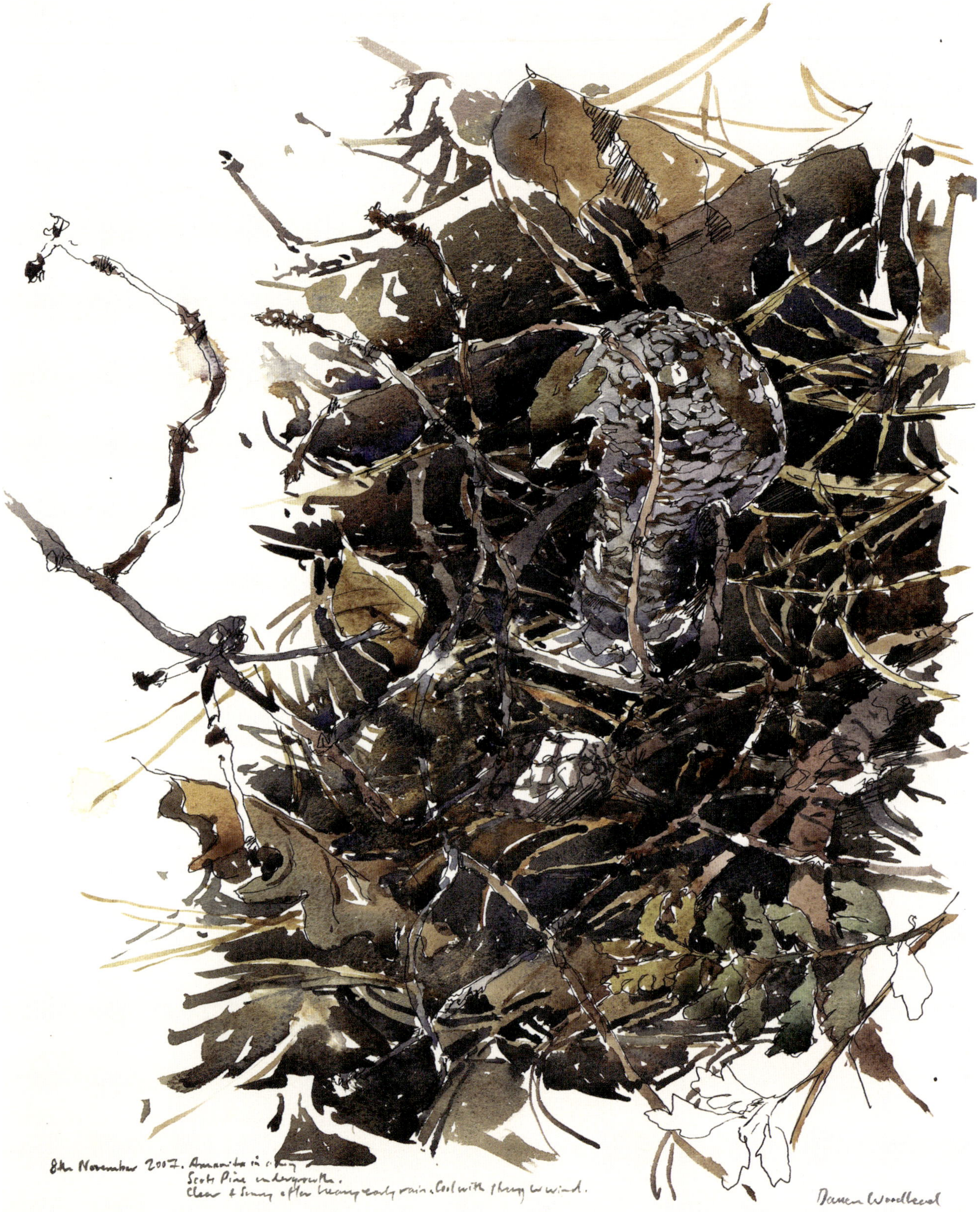

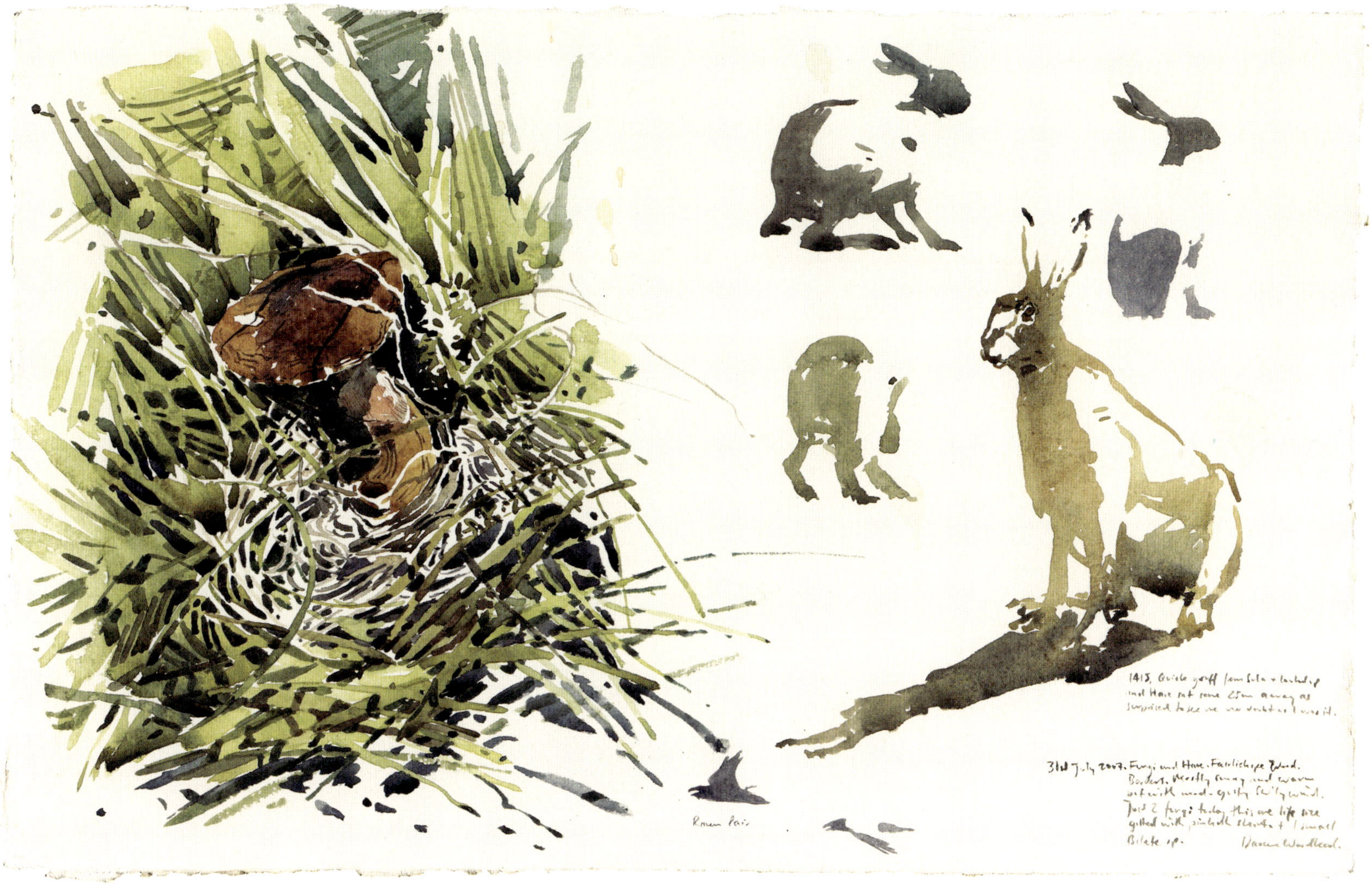

Fungi and Hare
(watercolour, 285mm x 440mm)

31st July 2007. Fairliehope wood, Borders. Mostly sunny and warm but with moderate to gusty south-westerly wind. Just two fungi today, this one life size gilled with pinkish skirt and one small Bolete species. 14:15. Quick gruff from Sula and looked up and Hare sat some 25 metres away as surprised to see me no doubt as I was to see it.

I had clear intentions for the coming autumn: I would try and concentrate solely on fungi, building on the foundations I had made the year before. However, conditions seemed to be against me. After a temperamental August, September started warm and very dry. With temperatures regularly reaching twenty degrees during the day, the ground appeared almost too dry to create the necessary conditions for fungi to flourish. It was not till the weekend of the 15th and 16th that a notable fall of rain occurred.

However, those warm, dry early September days still brought some magnificent rewards. Although they bleached my first Cep of the year almost beyond recognition, the dry weather possibly allowed it to stay unusually maggot-free. The woods were carpeted to a lesser extent with glowing yellow *Russulas* and beautiful small pockets of Primrose Brittlegills, intensely purple-hued on their flattened caps. Good numbers of Hedgehog Fungi could be seen in the moss. My first Chanterelles were earlier than last year, although my first large find was just a day before last year's, being on 30th October.

In addition, I found new species, including spectacular examples of *Boletus luridus*, which goes spectacularly inky blue instantly on cutting, a sure sign to leave it from the basket if ever there was one. I also saw many *Cortinarius purpurascens*, apparently a confusion species of Wood Blewitt, though I found it very different – a heavy dense fungus with deep brown gills and a purple-blue stem and certainly not even a tempting addition to the 'bag'. Being a *Cortinarius*, the younger ones show their characteristic web that encloses fresh gills. Differences from last year were striking, and I do think there were no Horn of Plenty at my usual spot. The amount of Ceps was well below that of last year, in fact numbers of *Boletes* in general were much lower. However, Wood Blewitts were

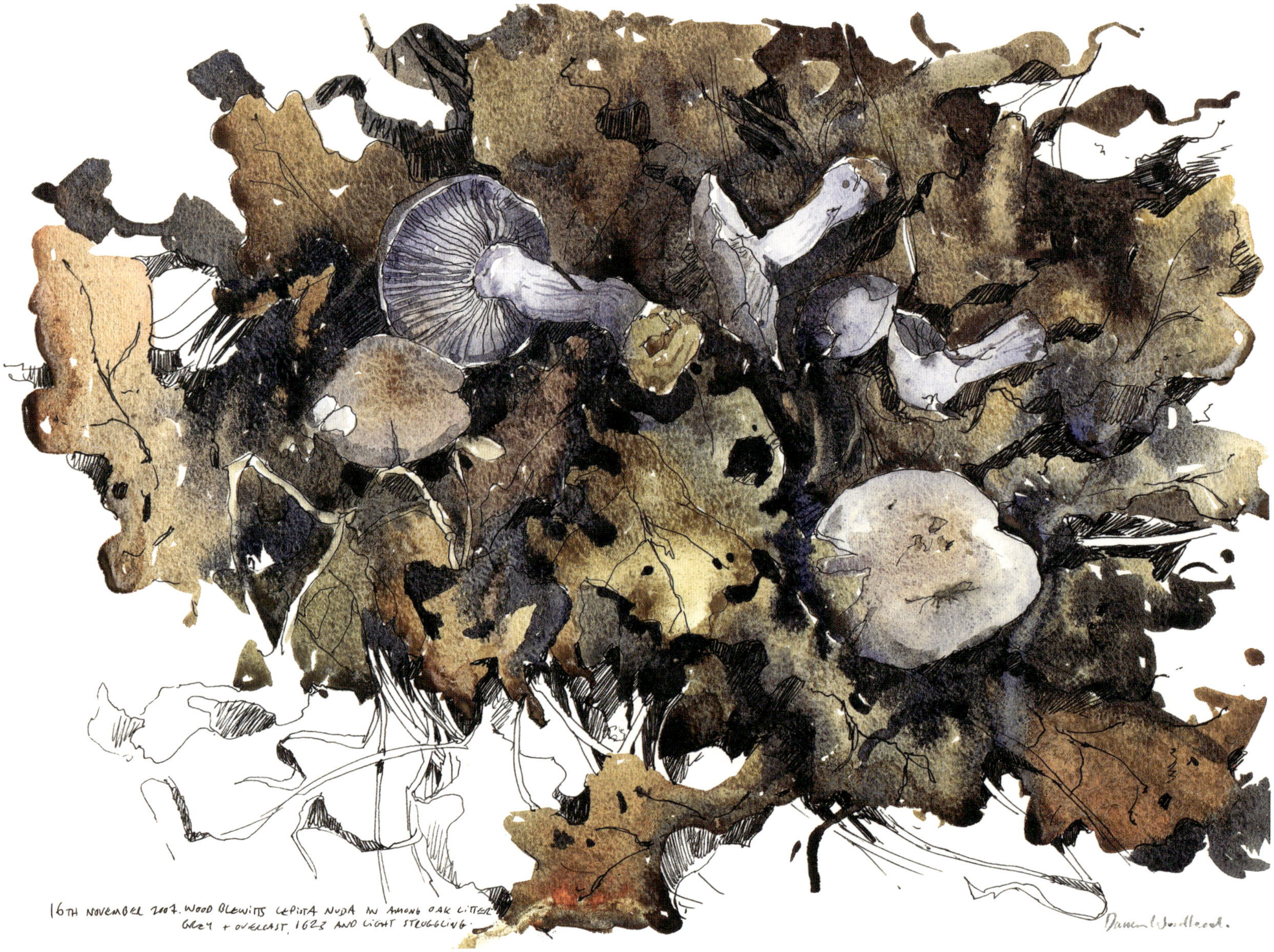

Wood Blewitts
(watercolour and pen, 275mm x 370mm)

16th November 2007. Wood Blewitts, *Lepista nuda* in among Oak litter. Grey and overcast, 16:23 and light struggling.

a different story. Just after I had noted in my diary the distinct lack of new fungi, a run of a week or so of cold but not frosty nights followed. Then, on 18th October, I found the first Blewitt of the season. Wonderfully fresh with domed deep brown cap and a neat pale rim, it was a gem. Following that, the floodgates opened. Maybe my eyes were sharper than the year before, or maybe it was just an exceptionally good year for them, but I was still finding Blewitts well into December!

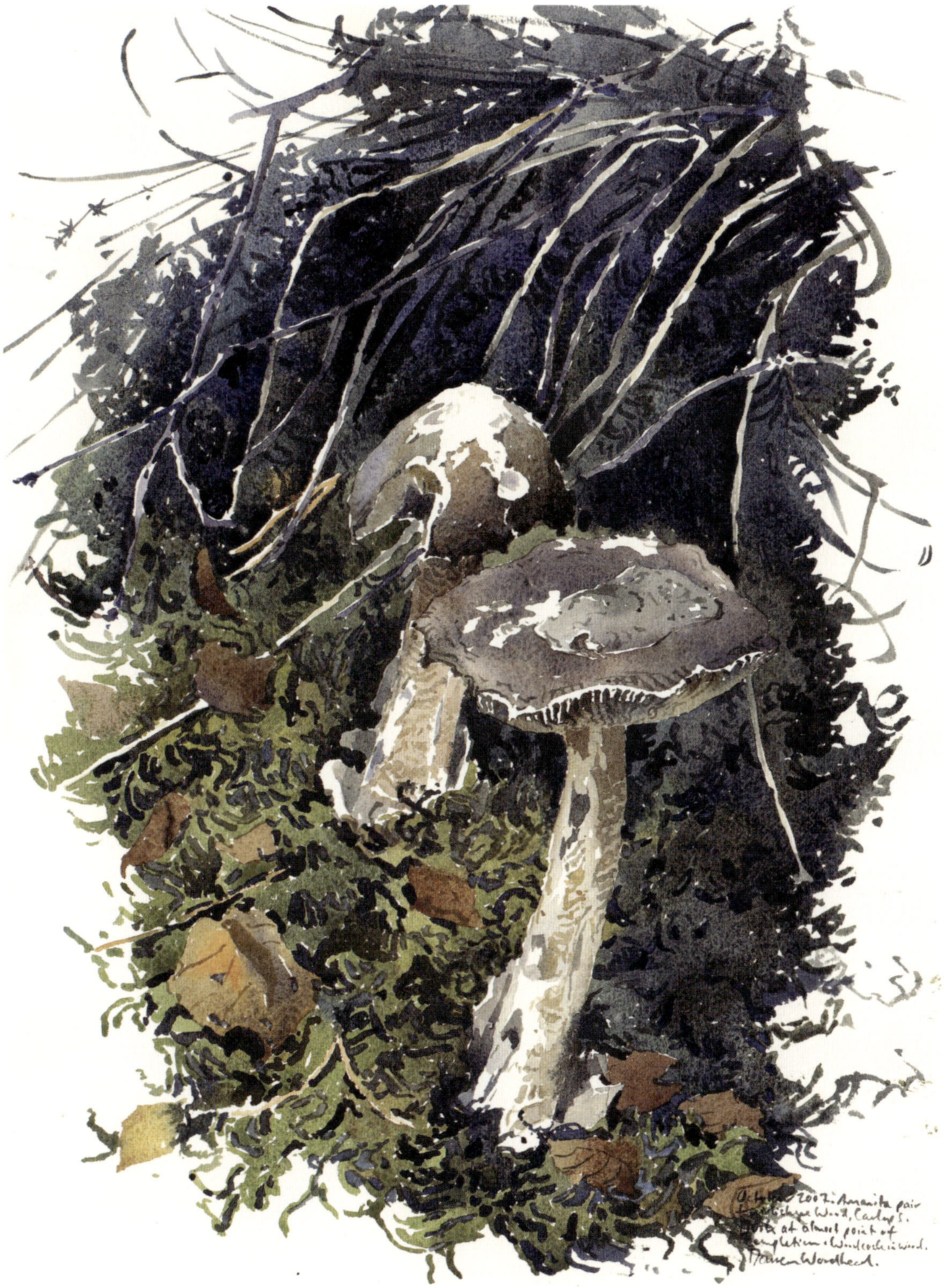

Amanita pair
(watercolour, 380mm x 280mm)

14th September 2007. Fairliehope wood, Carlops. Dusk at almost point of completion. One Woodcock in wood.

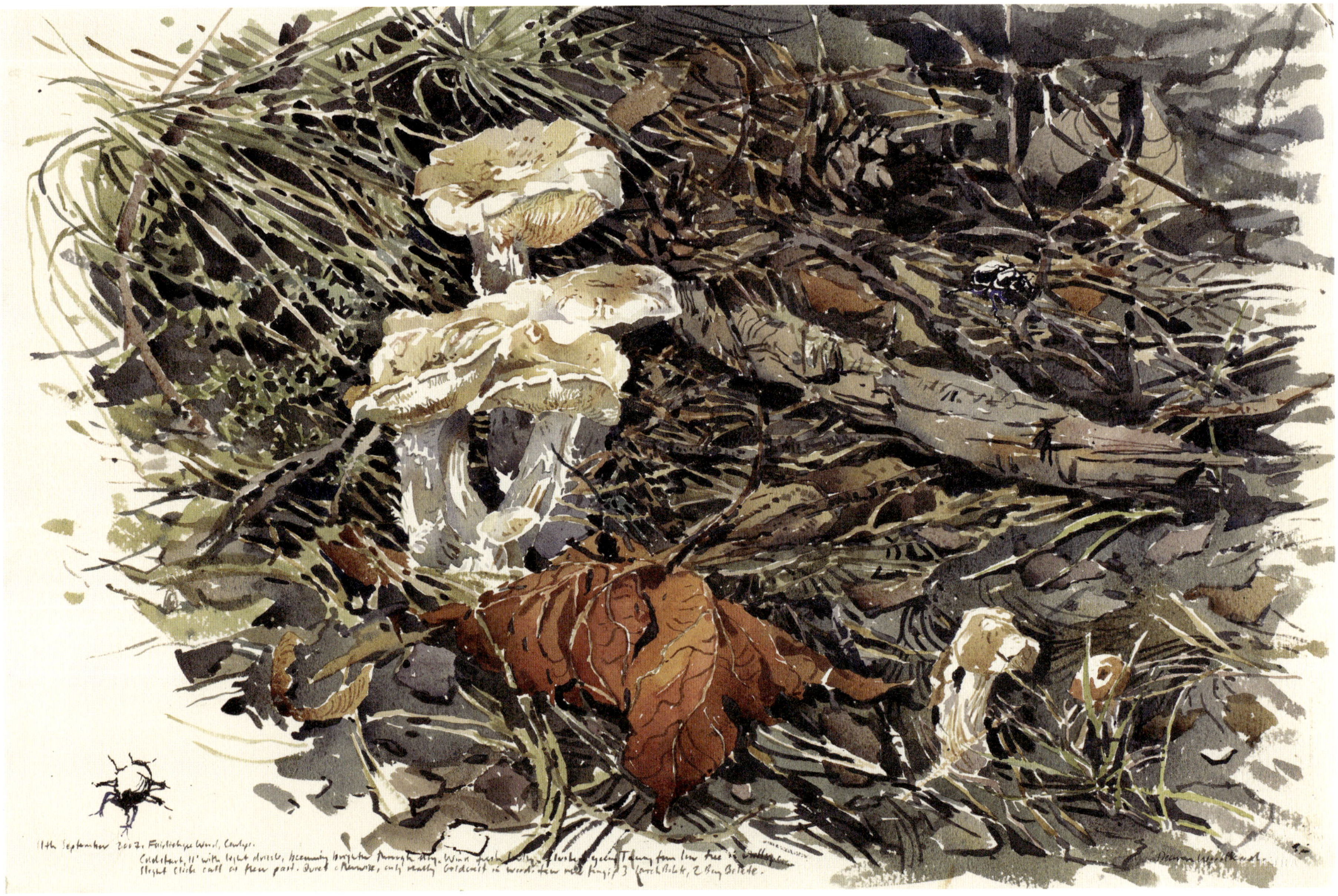

Spotted Toughshank and Passing Dung Beetle
(watercolour, 380mm x 560mm)

11th September 2007. Fairliehope wood, Carlops. Cold start, eleven degrees with light drizzle becoming brighter through day. Wind fresh south-westerly. Flushed young Tawny from low tree in valley. Slight click call as flew past. Quiet otherwise, only really Goldcrest in wood. Few new Fungi, three Larch Bolete, Two Bay Bolete.

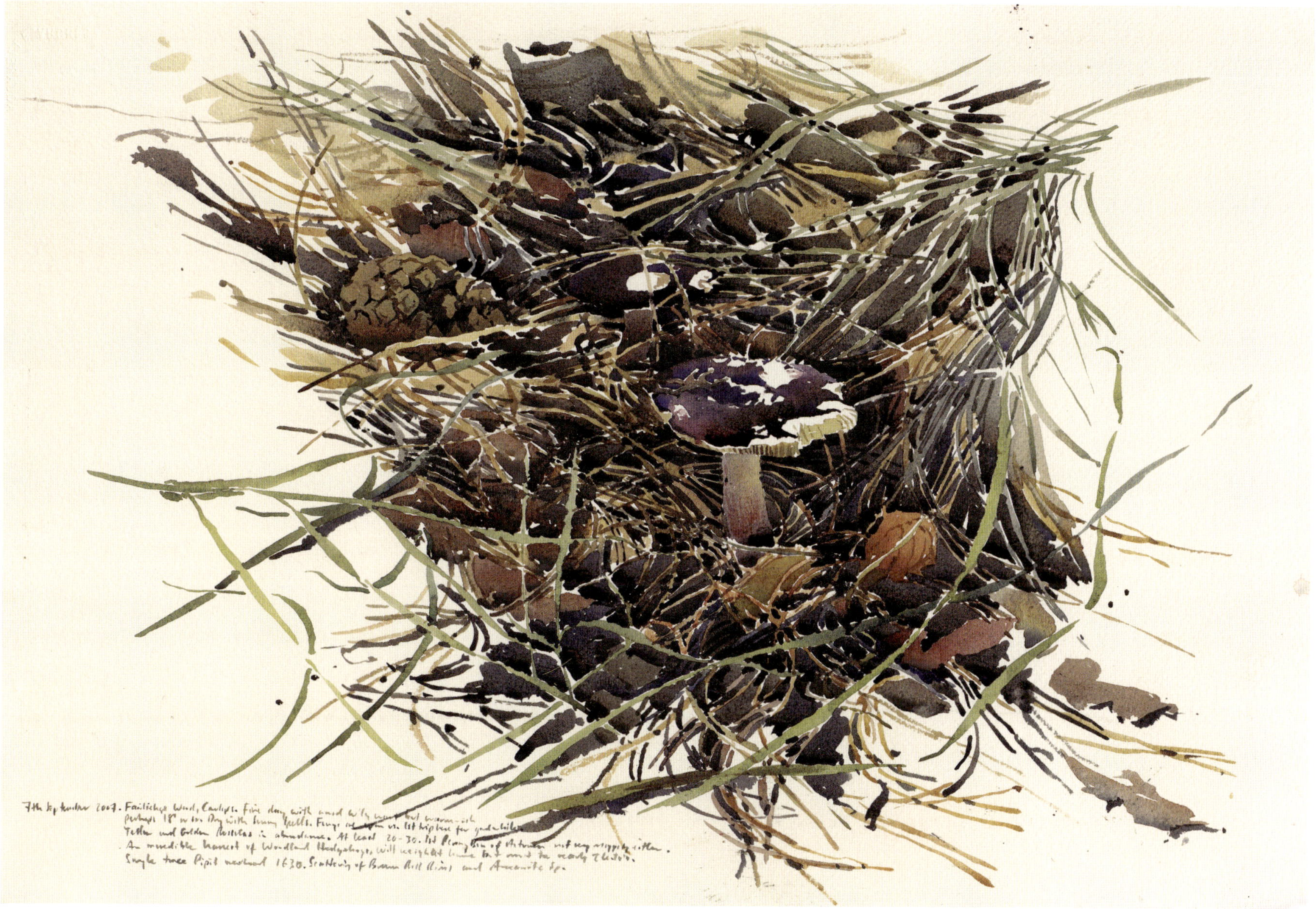

Primrose Brittlegill

(watercolour, 560mm x 380mm)

7th September 2007. Fine day with a moderate westerly wind but warmish, perhaps eighteen degrees or so. Dry with sunny spells. Fungi are upon us. First trip here for a good while. Yellow and Golden *Russulas* in abundance, at least twenty to thirty. First Penny Bun of autumn, not very maggoty either. An incredible harvest of Woodland Hedgehog, will weigh at home but must be nearly two kilos. Single Tree Pipit overhead 18:30. Scattering of Brown Roll-Rims and *Amanitas*.

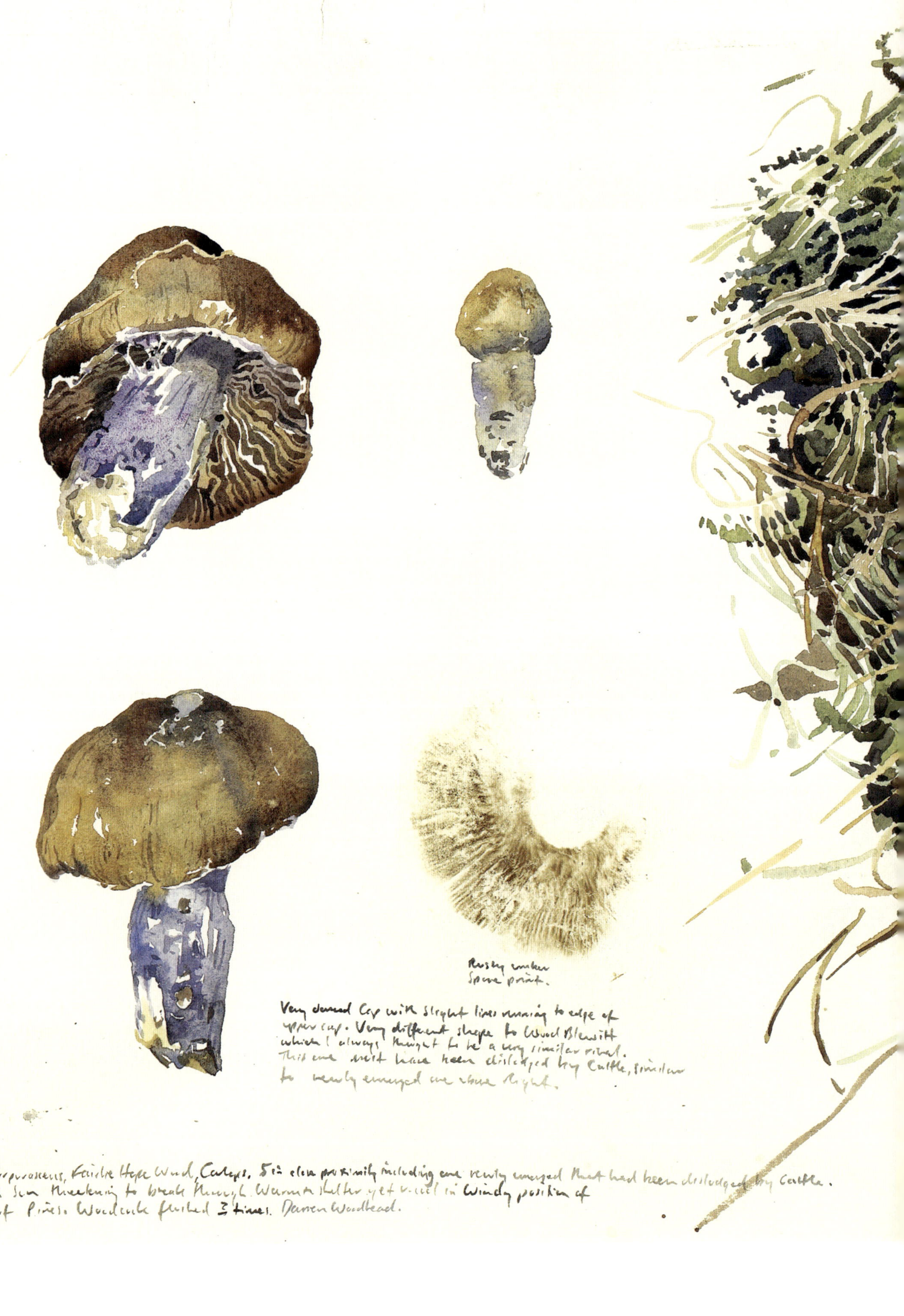
Rusty umber
Spore print.
Very domed Cap with slight lines running to edge of
upper cap. Very different shape to Wood Blewitt
which I always thought to be a very similar rival.
This one must have been dislodged by Cattle, similar
to newly emerged one above right.
19th October 2007. Cortinarius Purpurascens, Fairlie Hope Wood, Carlops. 5 in close proximity including one newly emerged that had been dislodged by Cattle.
Overcast with Sun threatening to break through. Warm in shelter yet cool in Windy position of
last Row of Pines. Woodcock flushed 3 times. Darren Woodhead.

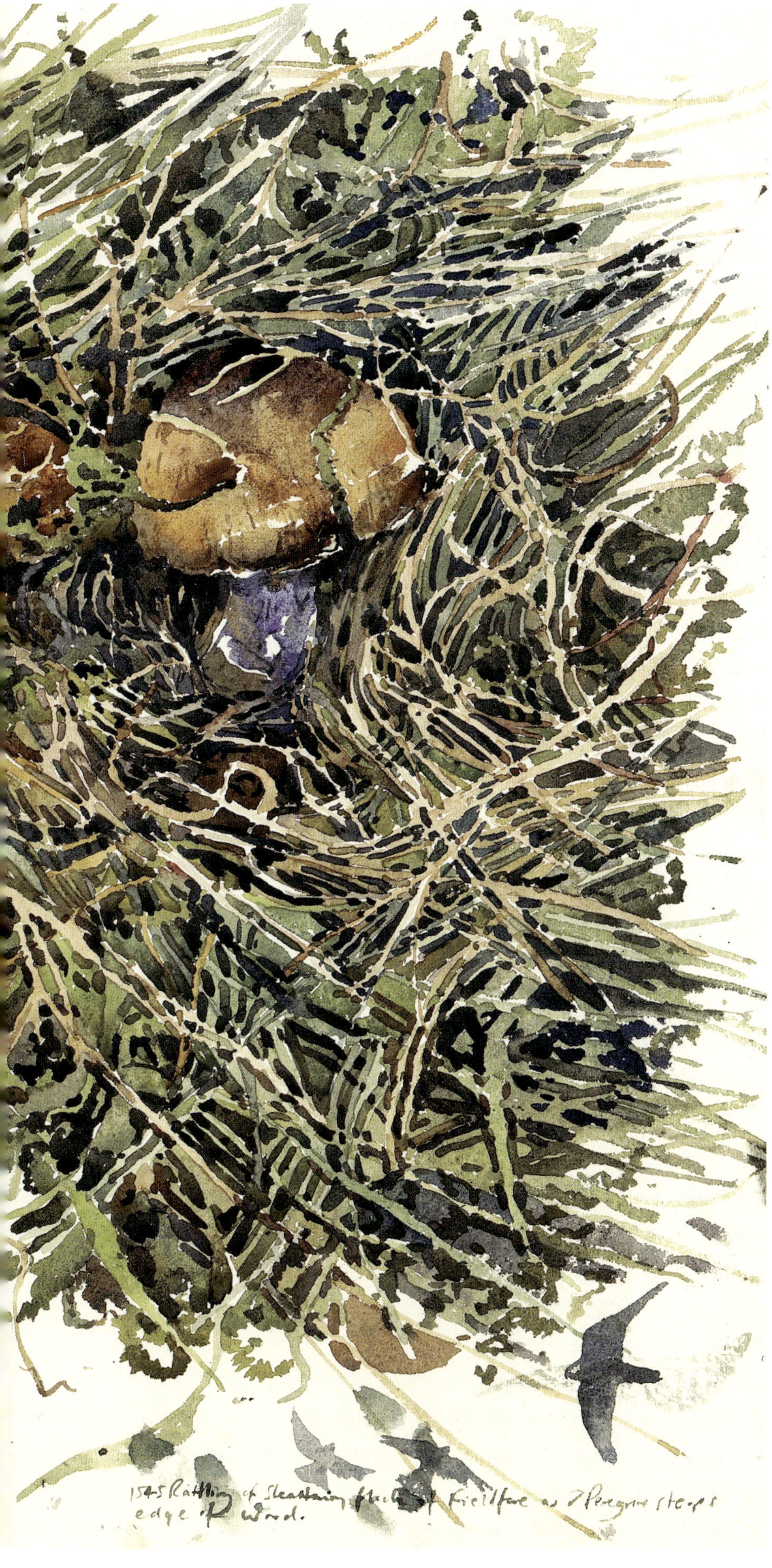

Cortinarius Purpurascens
(watercolour, 380mm x 560mm)

19th October 2007. Fairliehope wood, Carlops. Five in close proximity including one newly emerged that had been displaced by cattle. Overcast, with sun threatening to break through. Warm in shelter yet very cool in windy position of last row of Pines. Woodcock flushed three times. Rusty umber spore print. Very domed cap with slight lines running to edge of upper cap. Very different shape to Wood Blewitt which I always thought to be a very similar rival. This one must have been displaced by cattle, similar to newly emerged one above right. 15:45 Rattling flock of Fieldfare as male Peregrine stoops edge of wood.

Spectacular Rustgill at base of Beech
(watercolour, 560mm x 380mm)

26th October 2007. Spectacular Rustgill *Gymnopilus junonius*, on track between Kitleyknowe and road to Lamancha. Two caps tucked deep into base of Beech with three old Amethyst Deceivers. Many Deceivers days old, but three Red-cracked Bolete at least, one Matt Bolete collected as well as two Chanterelle. Wet from mid afternoon.

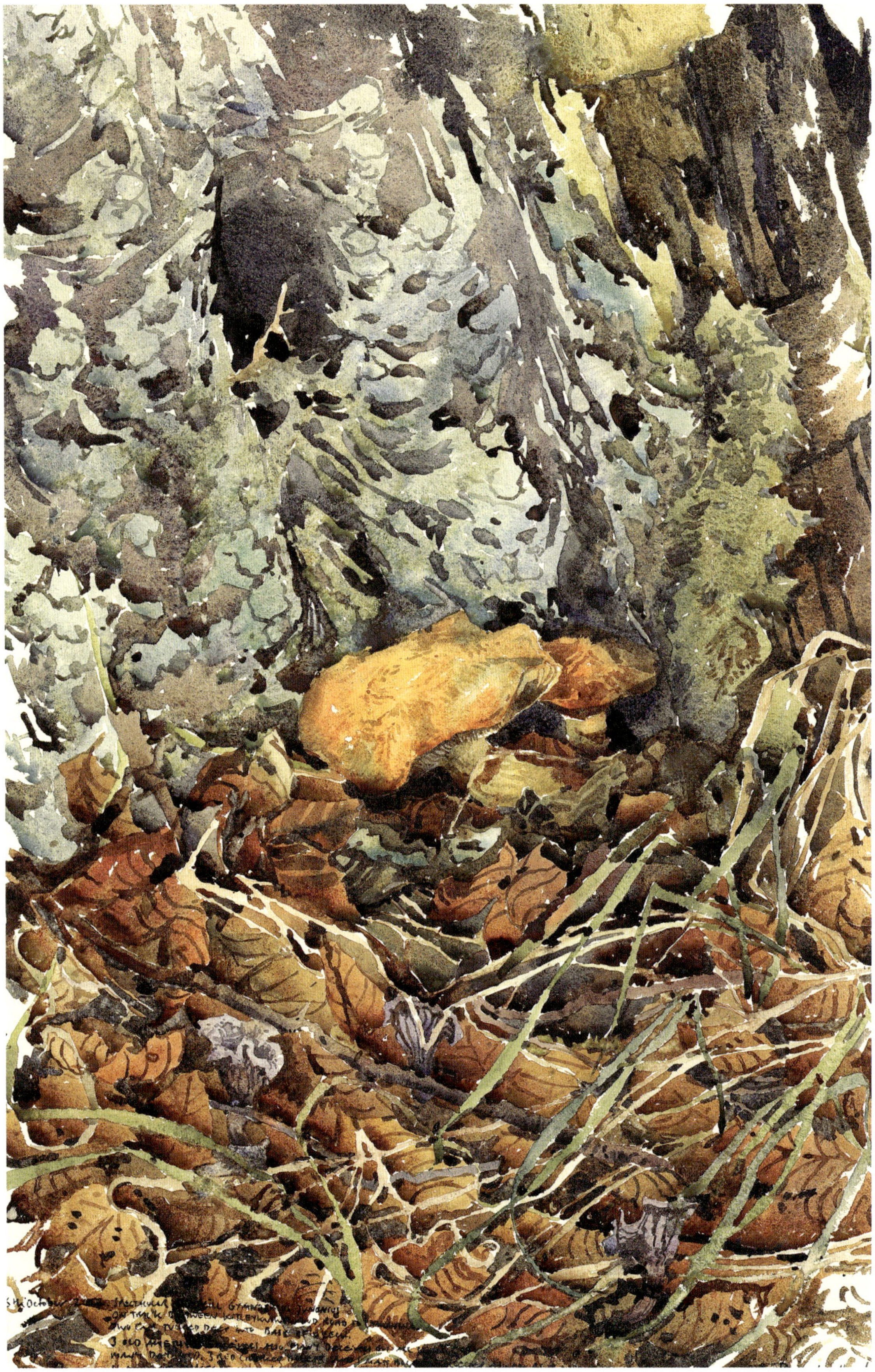

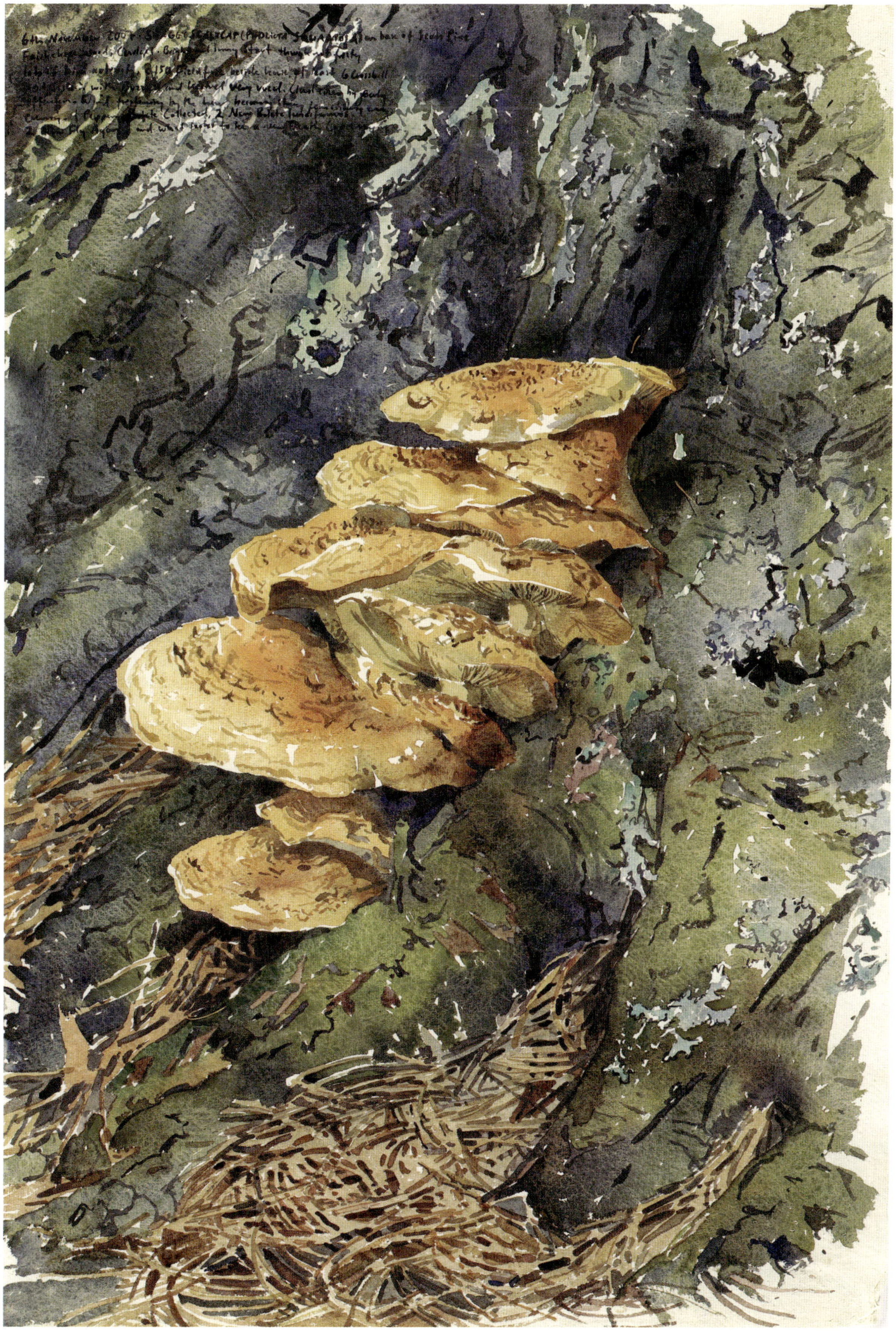

Shaggy Scalycap
(watercolour, 560mm x 380mm)

6th November 2007. Shaggy Scalycap *Pholiota squarrosa*, on base of Scots Pine, Fairliehope wood, Carlops. Bright and sunny start though not frosty. Lots of bird activity, approximately one hundred and fifty Fieldfare beside house, at least six Crossbill, thirty-plus Siskin with Buzzard and Kestrel very vocal. Cloud cover by early afternoon. Wind freshening by the hour becoming strong from still early evening. One Peppery Bolete collected, two new *Boletus luridus*. Two new Fly Agaric and what looked to be a new Deathcap emerging.

2008
Blizzards and Horizons

Black-faced Ewes
(watercolour, 760mm x 560mm)

22nd January 2008., Silverburn, Borders. Very cold first thing with snow after overnight fall. Bitter, with paint freezing instantly up to 10.30 a.m. From lunch warmed up to 5 degrees or so with a thaw beginning to set in.

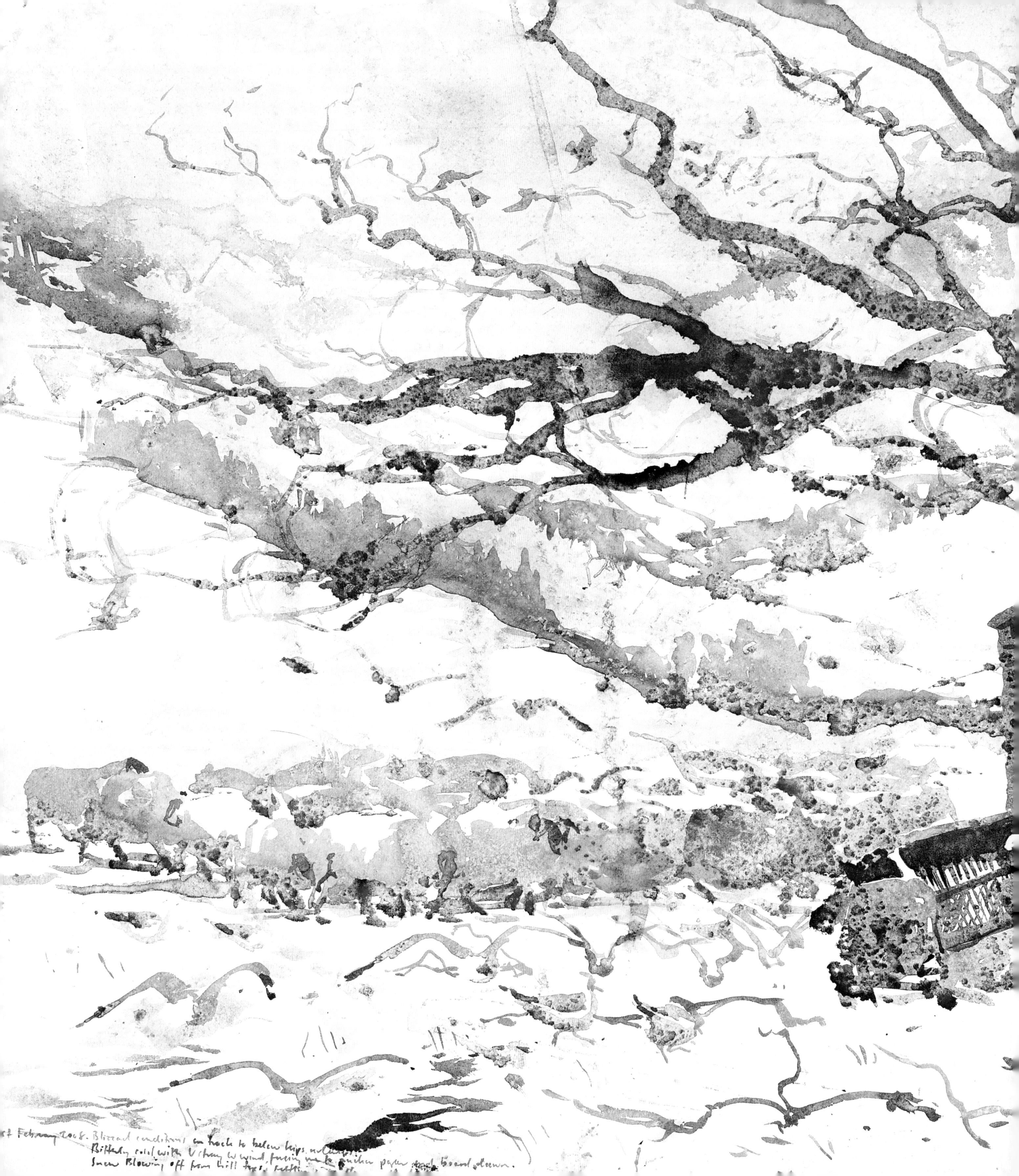
February 2008. Blizzard conditions

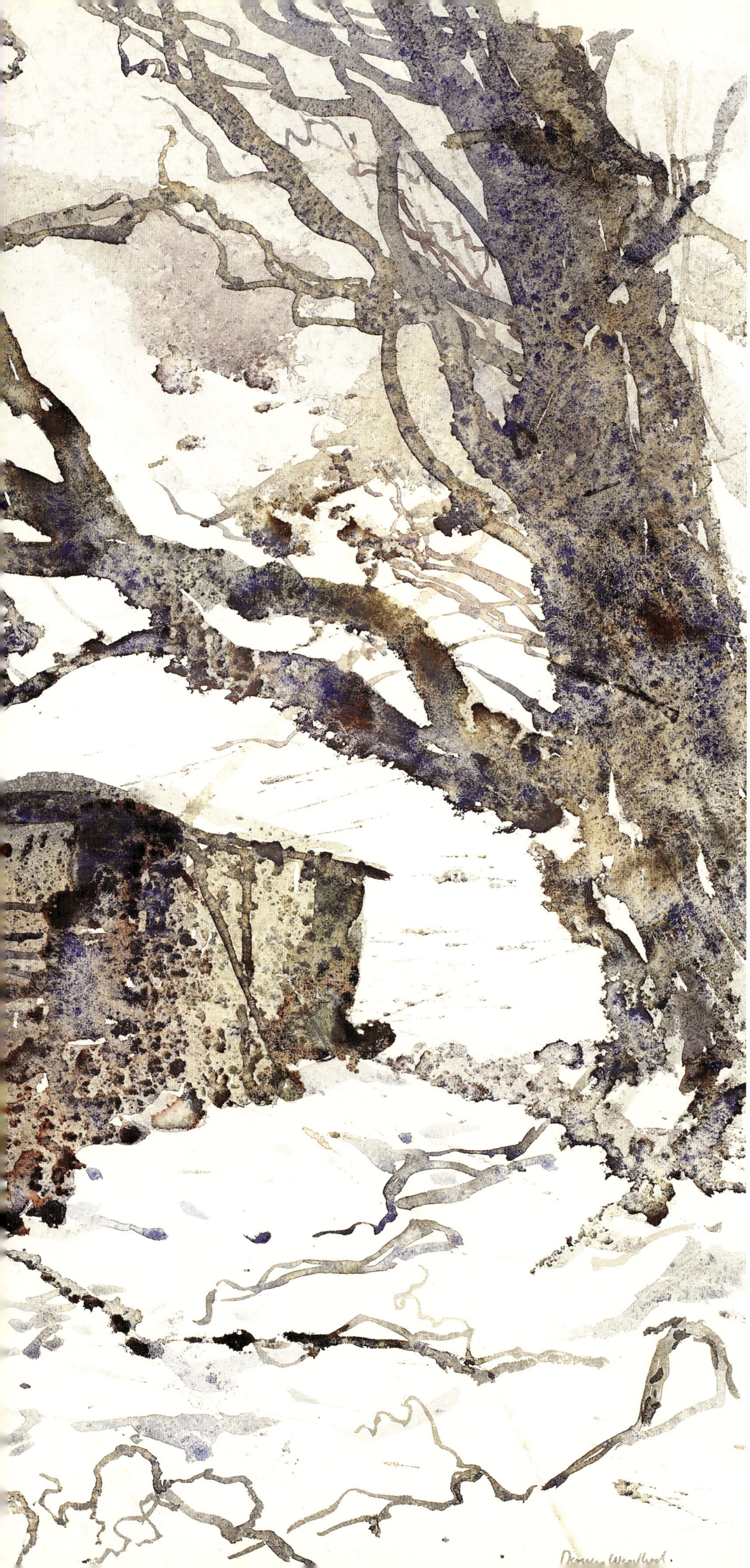

Winter track to Eastside
(watercolour, 560mm x 760mm)

1st February 2008. Blizzard conditions on track to Kips near Carlops. Bitterly cold with very strong westerly wind forcing me to wedge paper board down. Snow blowing off from hill tops and settling in gullies instead.

What a day. Blizzard conditions and total white out. Did not risk the hills but instead drove as far towards Eastside as I thought manageable. Weighed my drawing board down with rocks but even that wasn't enough. At one point both board and palette flying to the other side if the track, my metal palette coming off worst and snapping into two. Ice and snow gathering on the painting, with the occasional sounds of cracking branches and mewing of desperate Common Gulls, buffeted by the onslaught. The Sheep tight in a group and when the tops of the Kips visible, amazingly snow-less, violently blown drifts forming neat triangular shapes below.

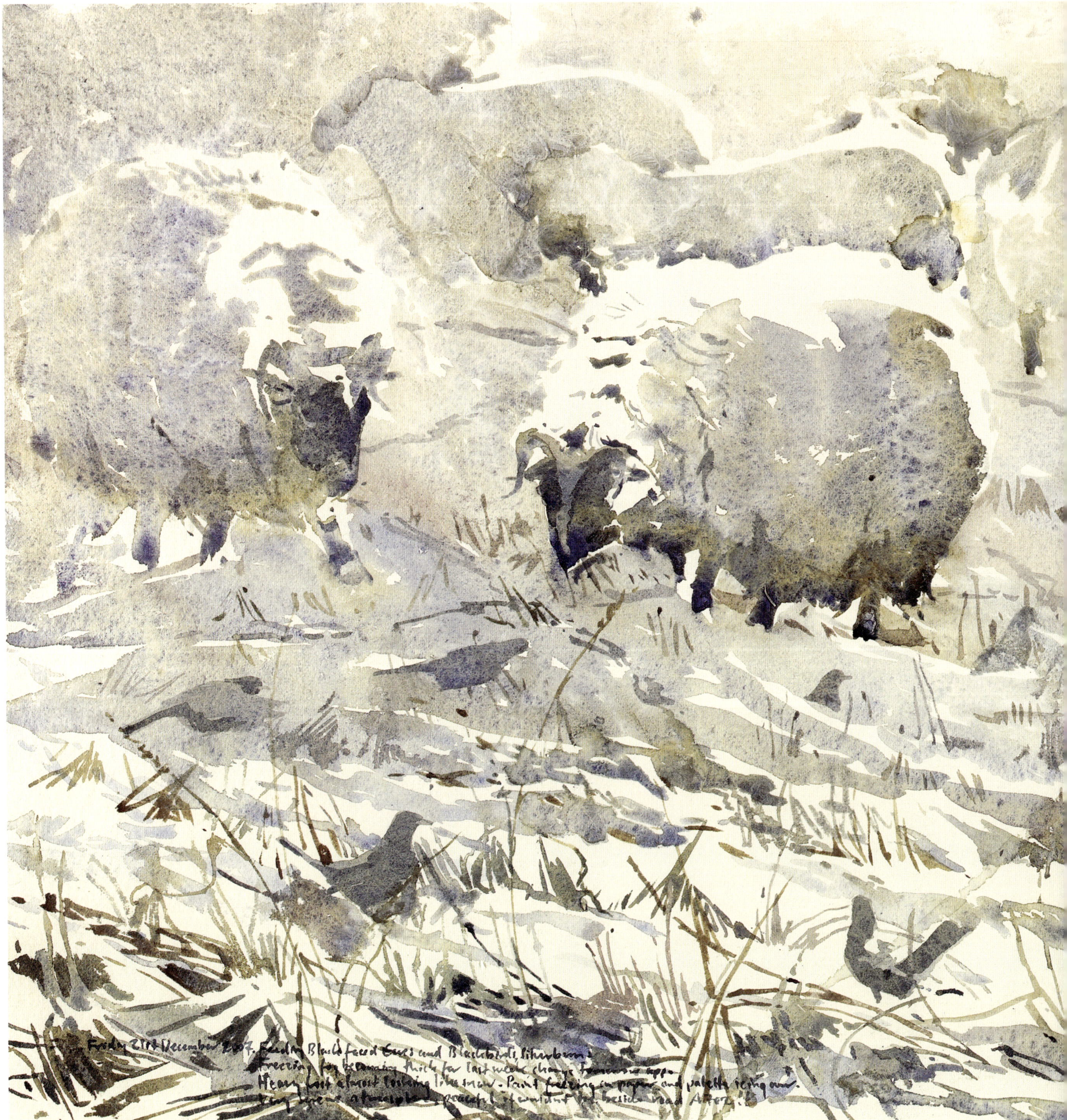

Friday 21st December 2007. Feeding Blackfaced Ewes and Blackbirds,
Heavy frost almost looking like snow. Paint freezing on paper and palette icing over.

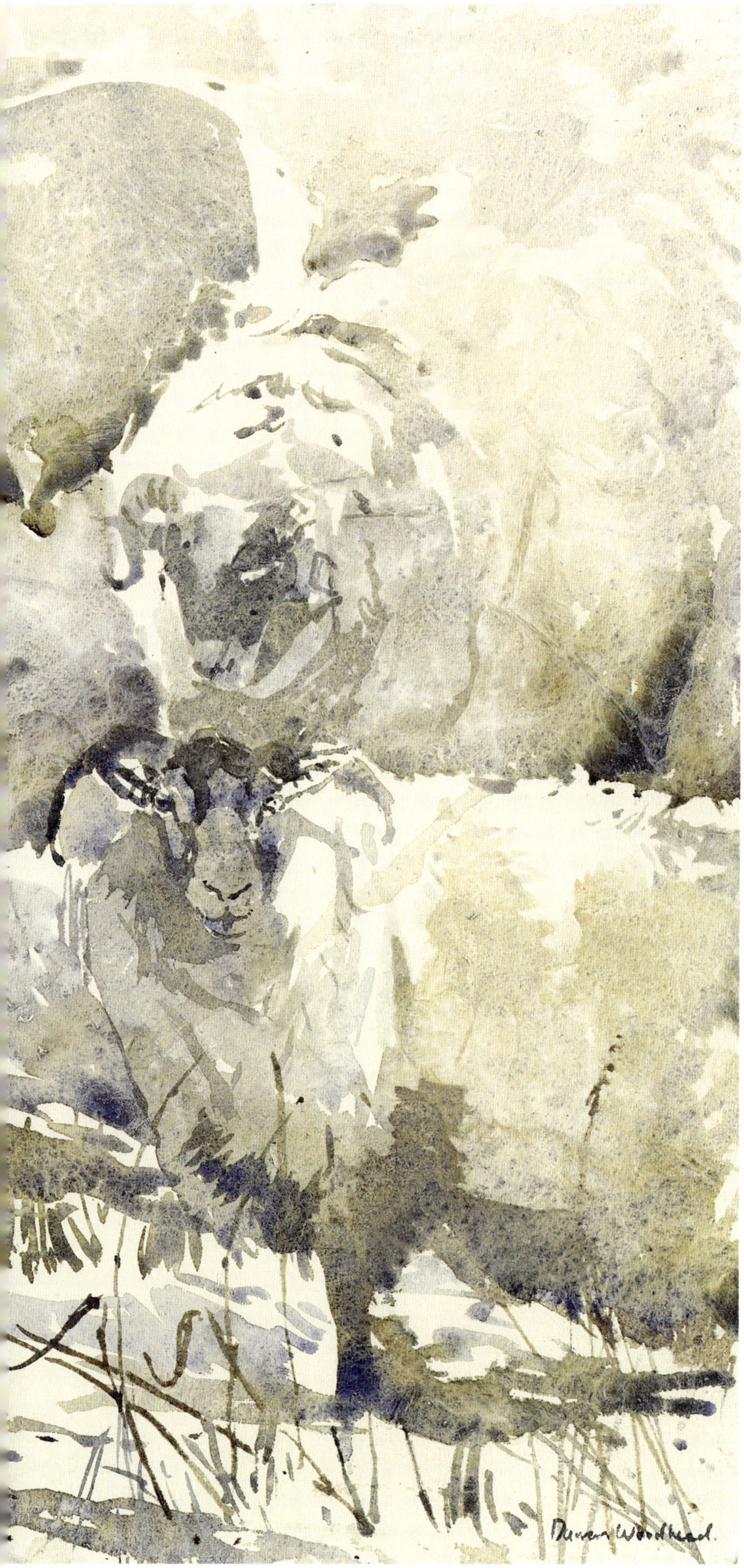

Ewes and fog
(watercolour, 380mm x 560mm)

Friday 21st December 2007. Feeding Black-faced Ewes and Blackbirds, Silverburn. Freezing fog becoming thick for last week, change tomorrow apparently. Heavy frost almost looking like snow. Paint freezing on paper and palette icing over. Very serene atmosphere, peaceful if it were not beside road A702.

A succession of below-freezing days accompanied by an ever-present dense fog created an unusually thick covering of frost on the ground and in the trees. The extremes of branches were coated so heavily that it seemed more like snow. Alongside the treacherous, iced tracks grasses were crisp and brittle, and sedges bowed with the weight of the days of frost. A group of Ewes at Silverburn drifted in and out of visibility as the fog thickened and thinned. I could not stop the paint freezing as it welled on the paper, and I struggled to keep it workable on my metal palette. Even my brushes began to stiffen when exposed to the cold air. At one point I lost everything in the thickening fog, even the Blackbirds that were actively hopping some twenty feet in front. As light faded and I made my way home from the hills, I looked back from the clearer outskirts of Edinburgh to the thick bank of fog that so decisively drew a border between the two worlds of city and country.

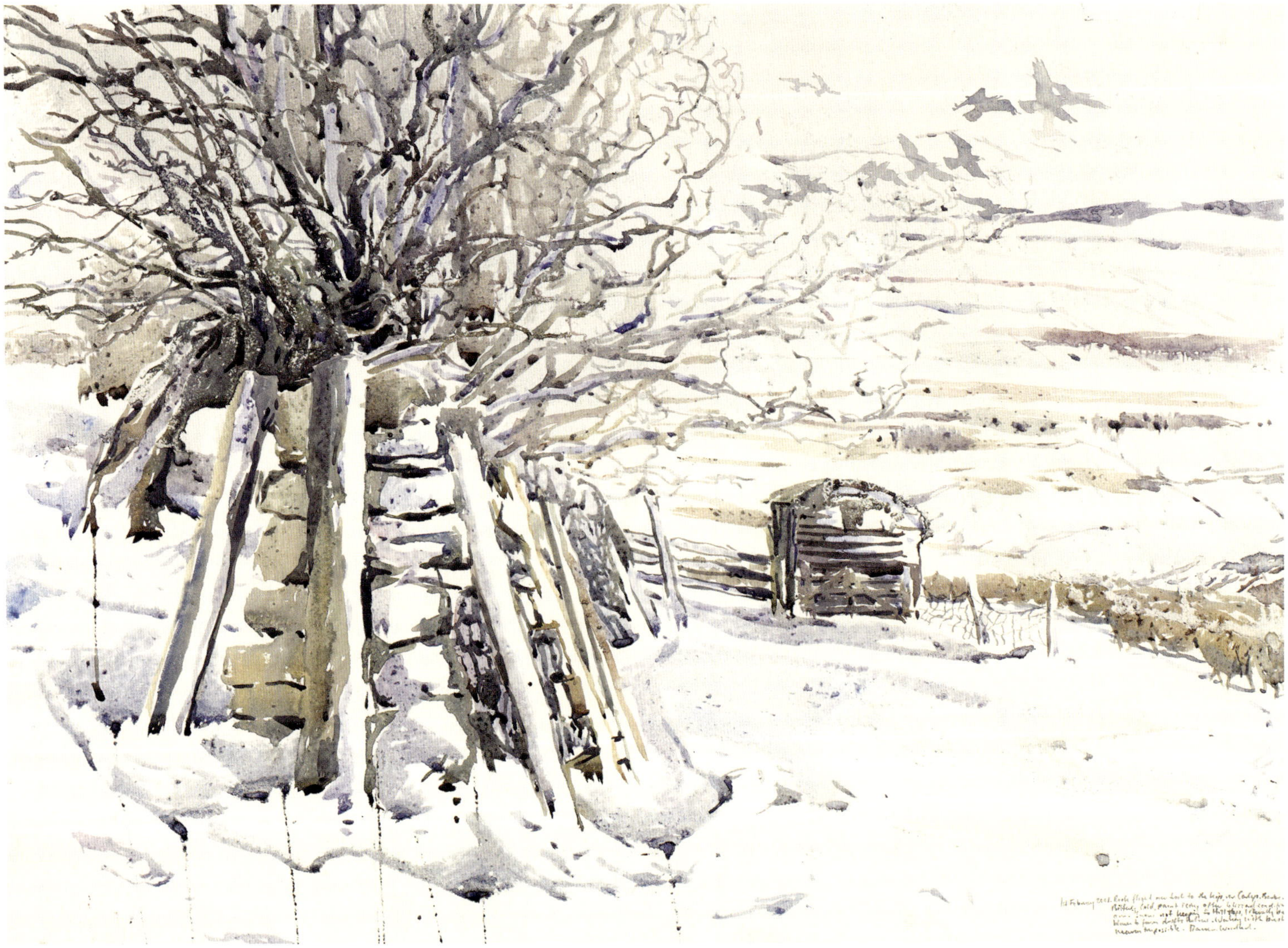

Looking south-east from the track to Eastside
(watercolour, 560mm x 760mm)

1st February 2008. Rook flight over track to the Kips near Carlops, Borders. Bitterly cold, icing over after blizzard conditions a.m. Snow not keeping to hill tops, literally been blown down to form drifts below. Working with brushes near on impossible.

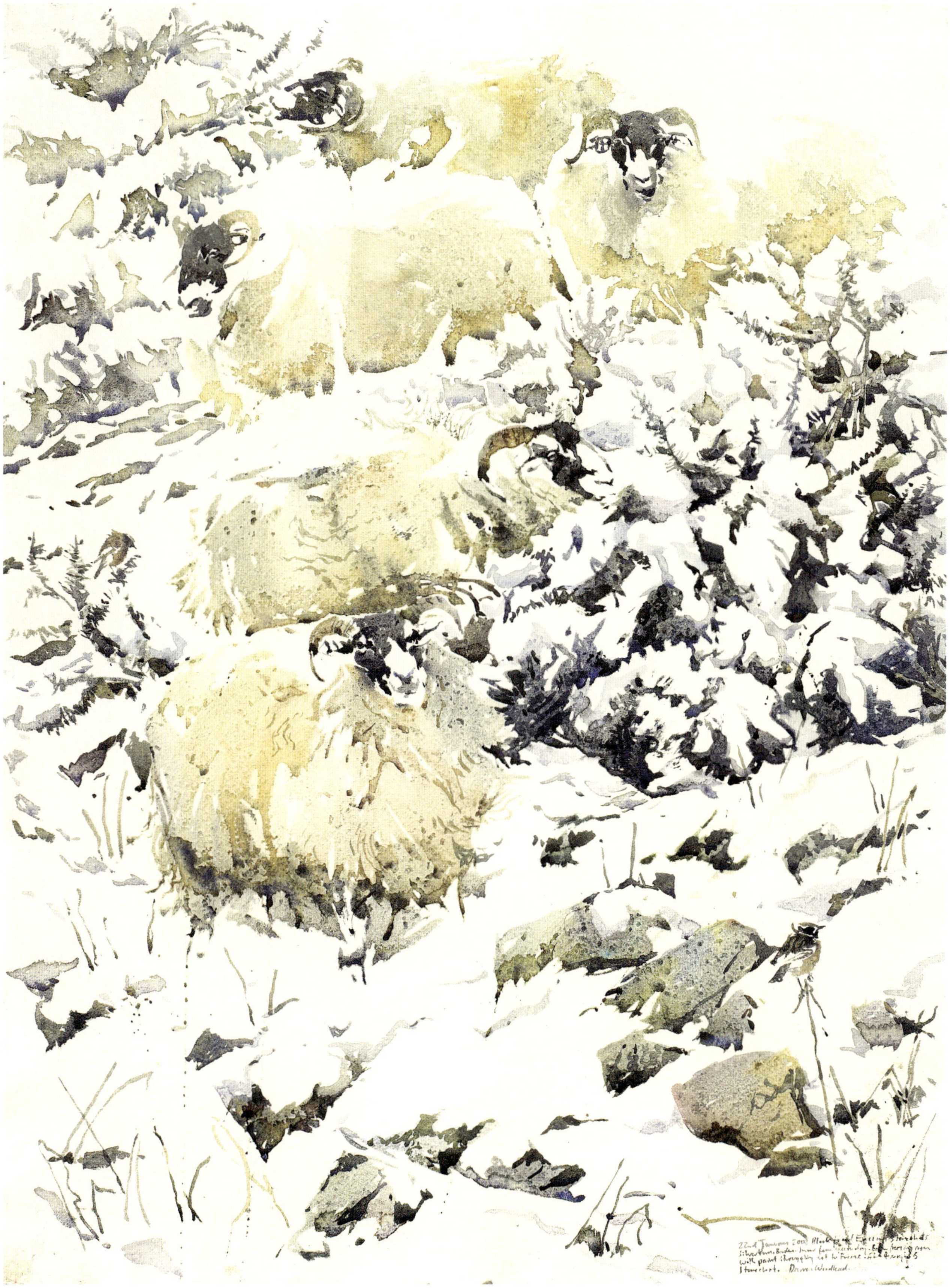

Ewes and Stonechats
(watercolour, 760mm x 560mm)

22nd January 2008. Black-faced Ewes and Stonechats, Silverburn, Borders. Snow from yesterday, below freezing a.m. with paint struggling not to freeze. Afternoon 4 maybe 5 degrees.

The textures on the coats of the ewes come from the instantly freezing washes of paint, at times making the laying down of any colour impossible. When paint freezes like this it tends to stain the paper surface, leaving a subtly distinctive mark. Although where there are frozen wells these will rapidly thaw and at that point it can be hard transporting the work without causing drips, even the slightest hole in the road can initiate a drip and ruin a painting.

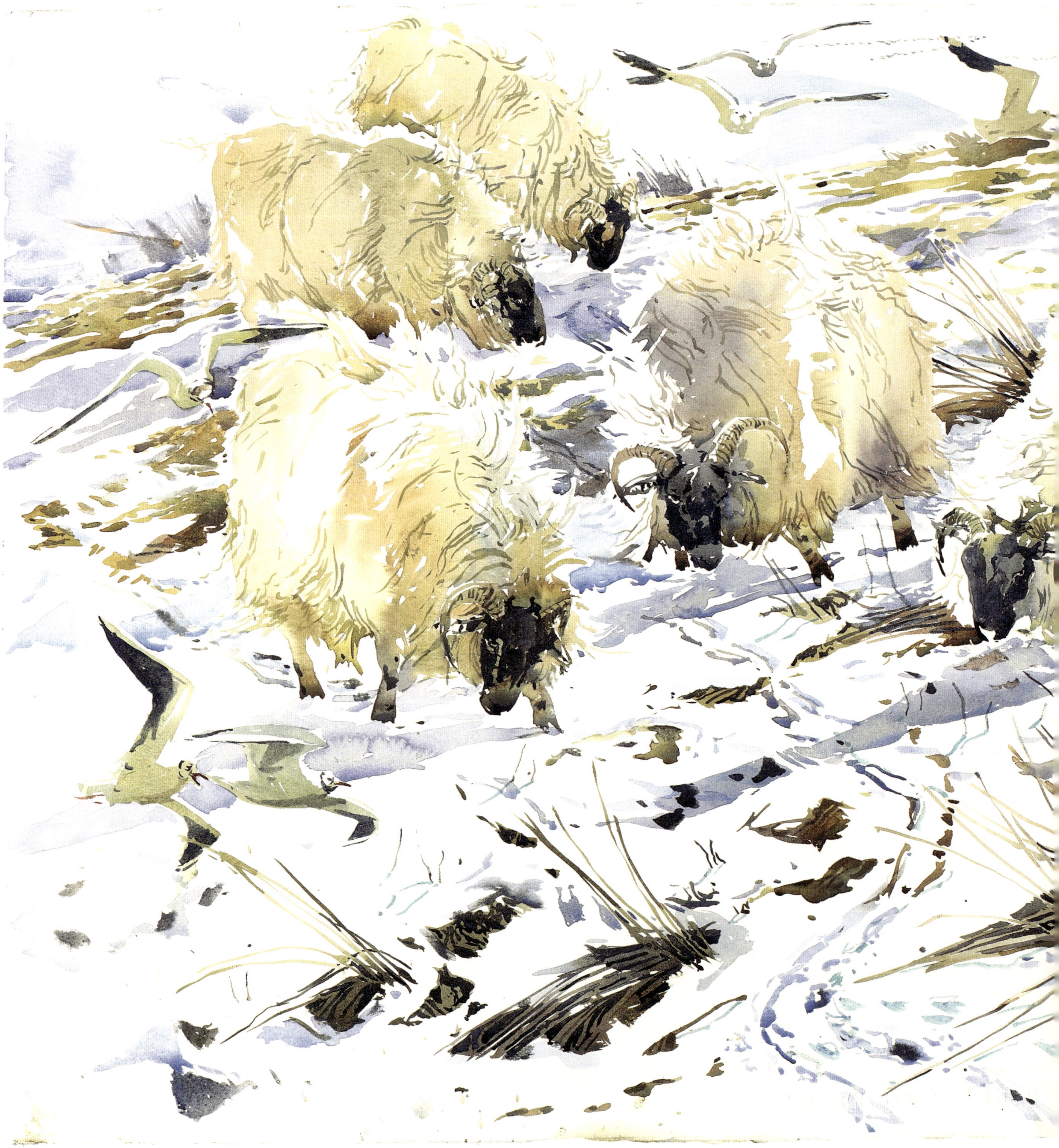

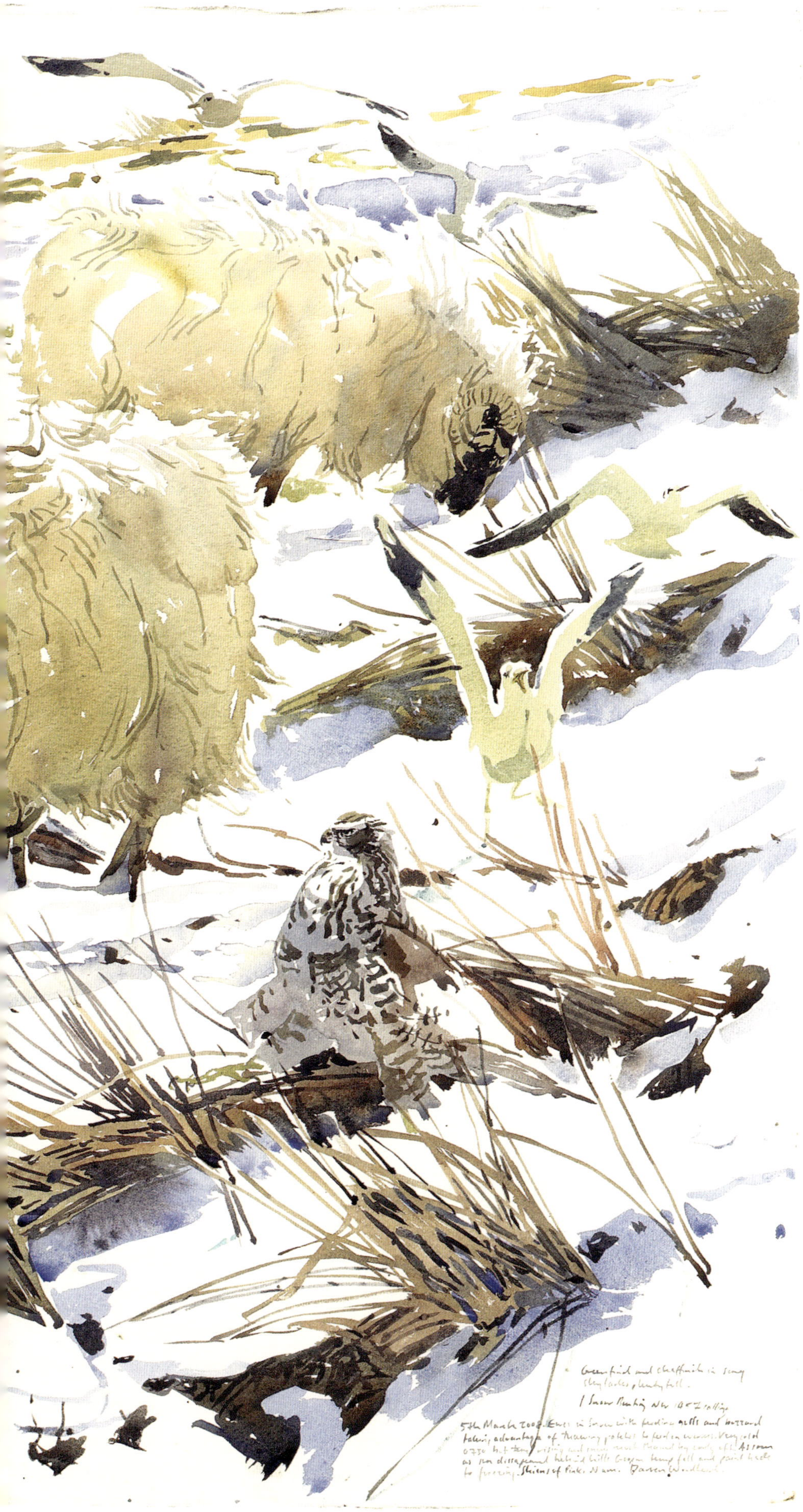

Ewes, Gulls and Buzzard

(watercolour, 660mm x 1016mm)

5th March 2008. Ewes in snow with feeding Gulls and Buzzard taking advantage of thawing patches to feed on worms. Very cold 07:30 but temperature rising and snow much thawed by early afternoon. As soon as sun disappeared behind hills 18:00, temperature fell and paint back to freezing. Skeins of Pink-footed Geese north a.m. Greenfinch and Chaffinch in song, Skylarks plentyfull. One Snow Bunting north-west 14:57, calling.

Whooper Family

(watercolour, 560mm x 380mm)

12th February 2008. Whooper Swan family on the North Esk reservoir, Carlops. Beautiful morning with barely a breeze, the mirrored surface only broken by wake of Swans, occasional whiff of wind or termination of a Mallard chase.

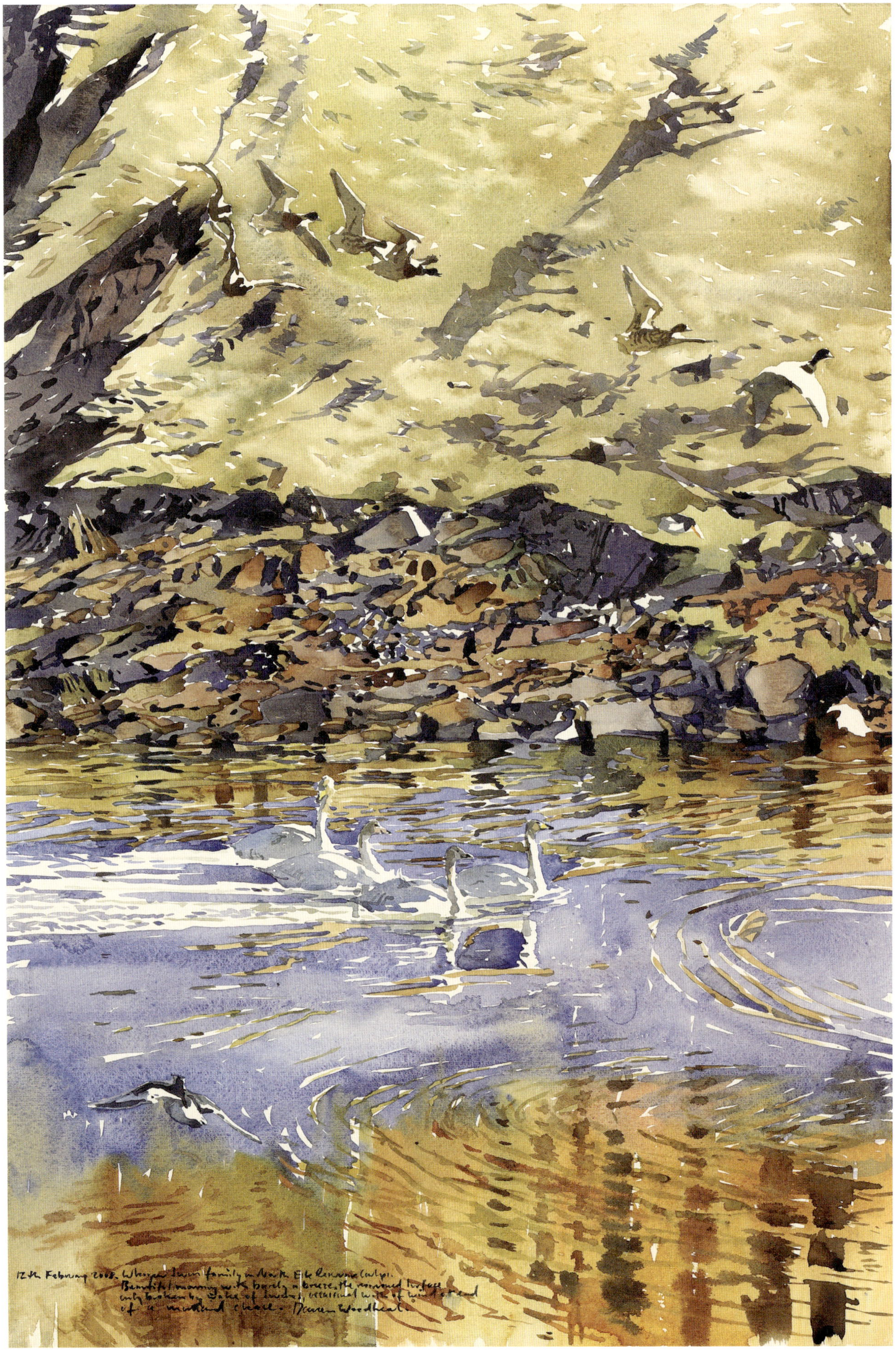

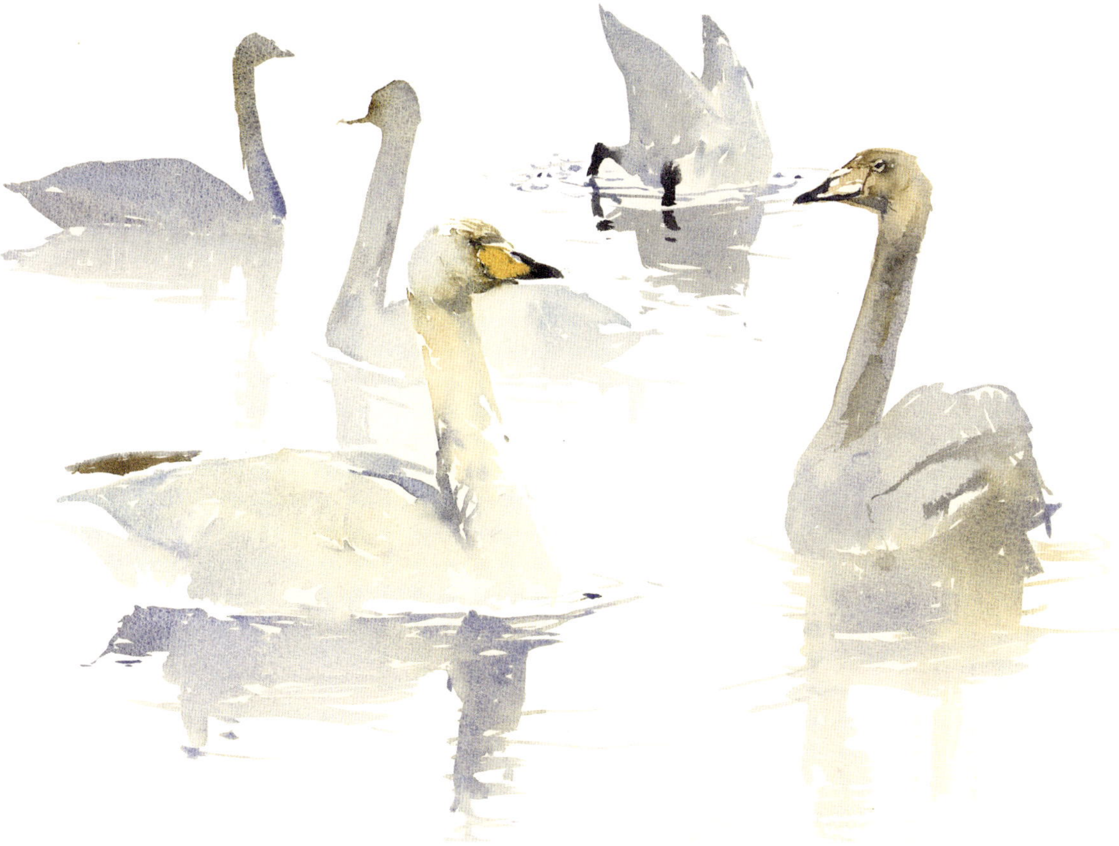

Whooper Swan Studies
(watercolour, 380mm x 560mm)

12th February 2008. Whooper studies, North Esk reservoir. Adult with yellow ring on left leg 9UZ and seemingly written 3–4 times repeatedly around ring. Mate with silver ring on left leg.

My reading of the yellow ring on 12th February 2008 was the first positive record of 9UZ at the reservoir. Details show that she was ringed as a cygnet at Caerlaverock, Dumfries and Galloway on 10th December 1997 (metal ring number Z88257). This particular season, her family group of four had arrived at the reservoir by the 15th December, and stayed until ice forced them elsewhere by the 27th They had returned by the 8th January and were last seen that season on 14th March 2008.

In the winter of 2008/2009, she returned with her partner and, this time, four cygnets by 29th October 2008 and stayed fairly consistently until 12th January 2009, when once again the reservoir became heavily iced over.

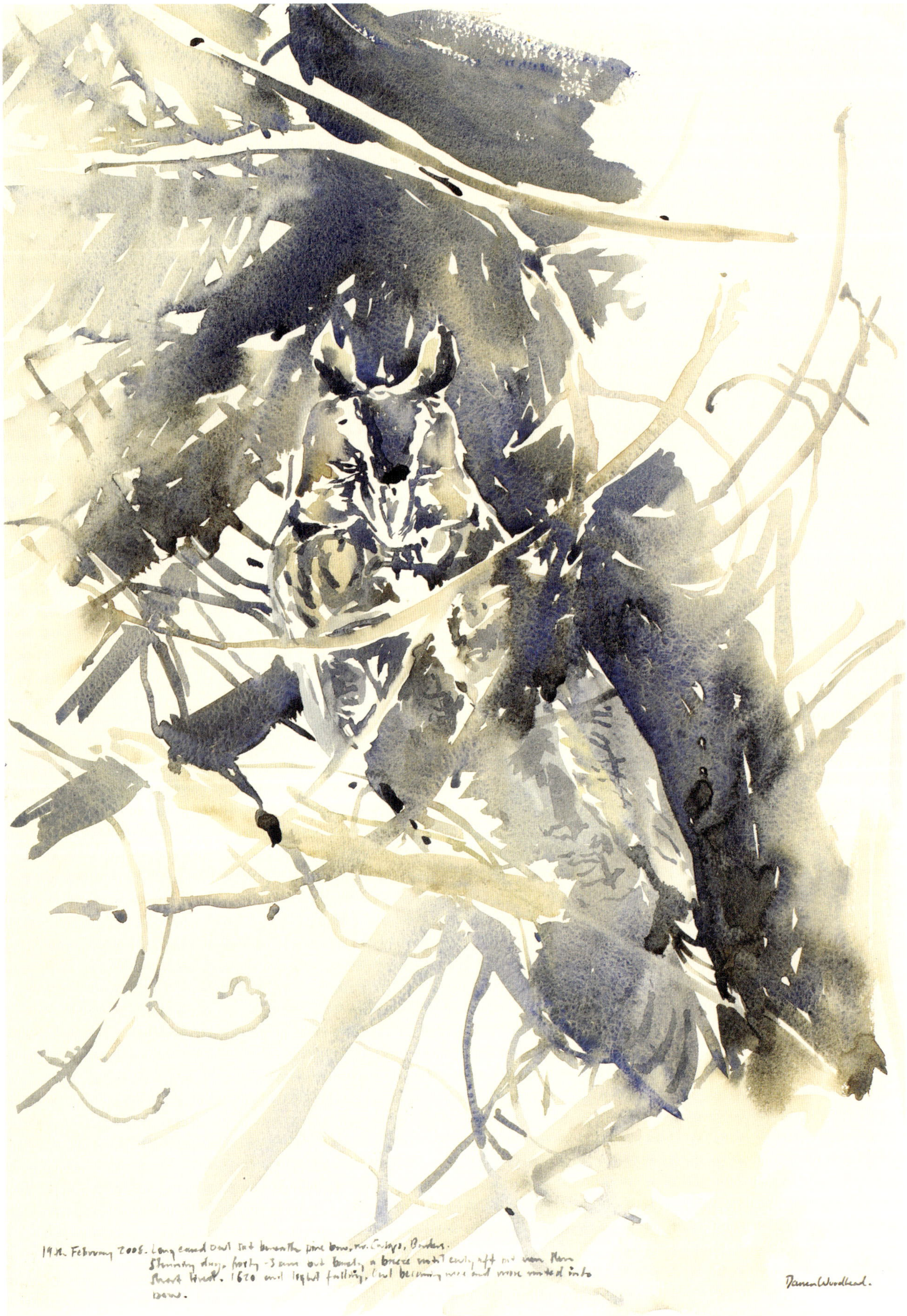

Long-eared Owl
(watercolour, 560 x 380 mm)

19th February 2008. Long-eared Owl sat beneath Pine bow, near Carlops, Borders. Stunning day, minus 3, a.m., but barely a breeze until early afternoon but even then short-lived. 16:20 and light falling. Owl becoming more and more muted into bow.

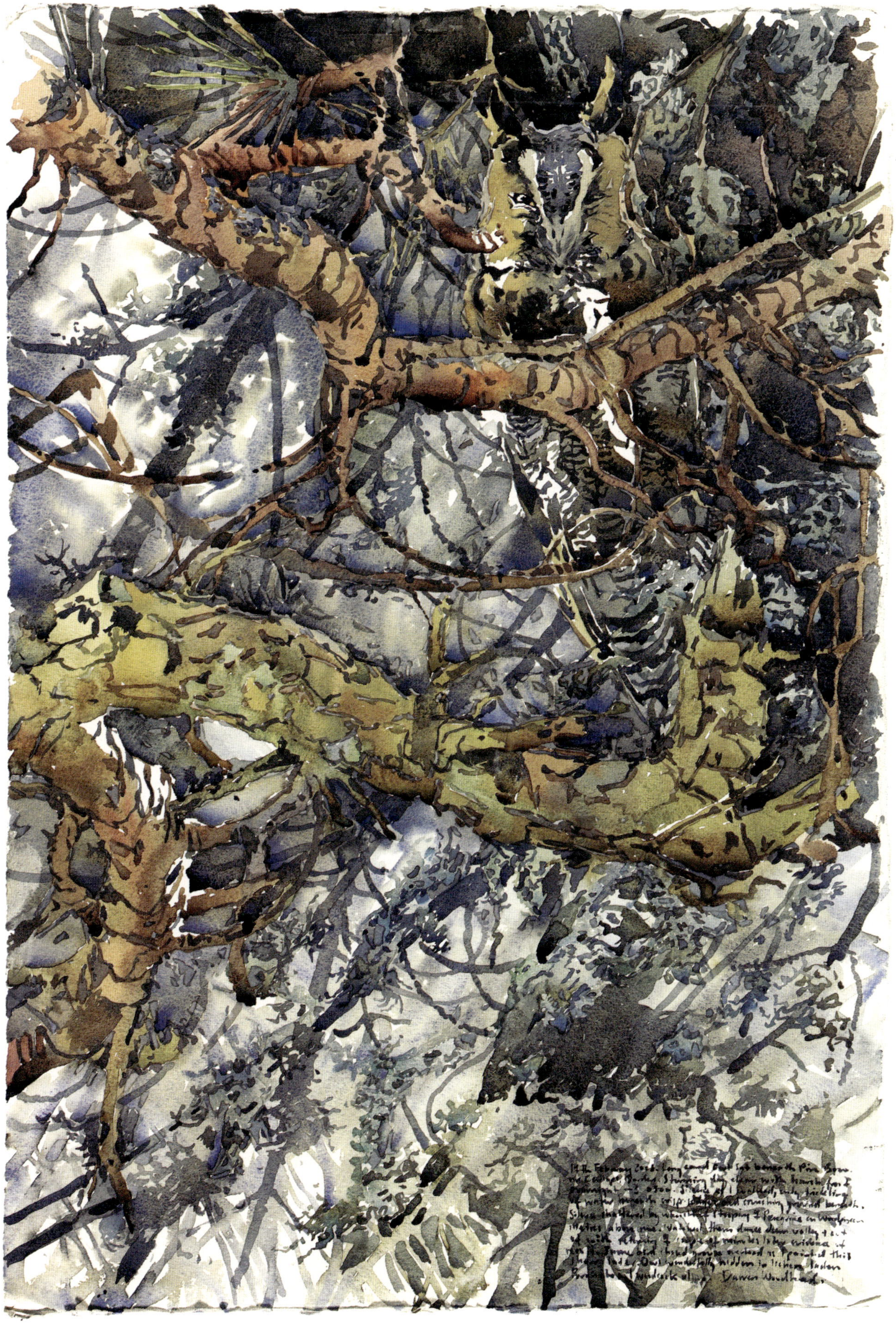

Long-eared Owl in shadow of Pine
(watercolour, 560mm x 380mm)

19th February 2008. Long-eared Owl sat beneath Pine bow, near Carlops, Borders. Stunning day, clear with harsh frost overnight, minus 3, 08:00. Silence as I walked, only tricking of water beneath crisp sedges and crunching ground. Silence shattered by whoosh of stooping female Peregrine on Woodpigeon, metres above me. Watched them dance down valley and out, with returning female couple of minutes later evidence of miss. Same bird chased Grouse overhead as I painted this sheet later. Owl wonderfully hidden in Lichen-laden branches. One Woodcock also.

Blackbird in Winter Hawthorn

(watercolour, 1016mm x 660mm)

Tuesday 5th February 2008. Lone male Blackbird in Hawthorn. Overcast, with rain becoming heavy and persistent. Mild though, 8 degrees or so after period of cold and frosty weather. Thirty or so Redwing in fields nearby. Goldcrests and Coal Tits vocal. A good fifteen or so Blackbirds in Hawthorns. Quiet for Bullfinch. Hare fending off Buzzard stoop at 08:20 this morning!

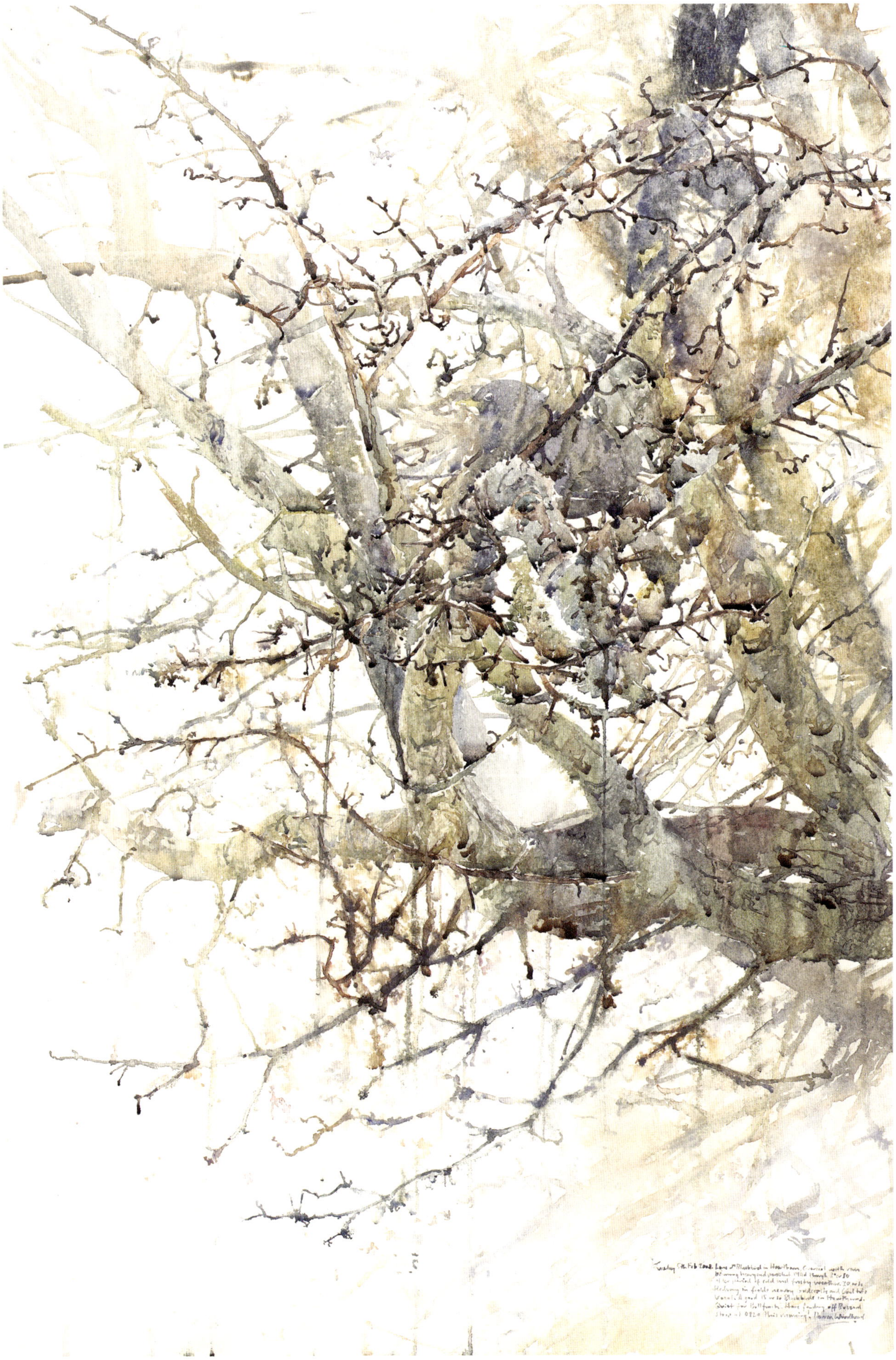

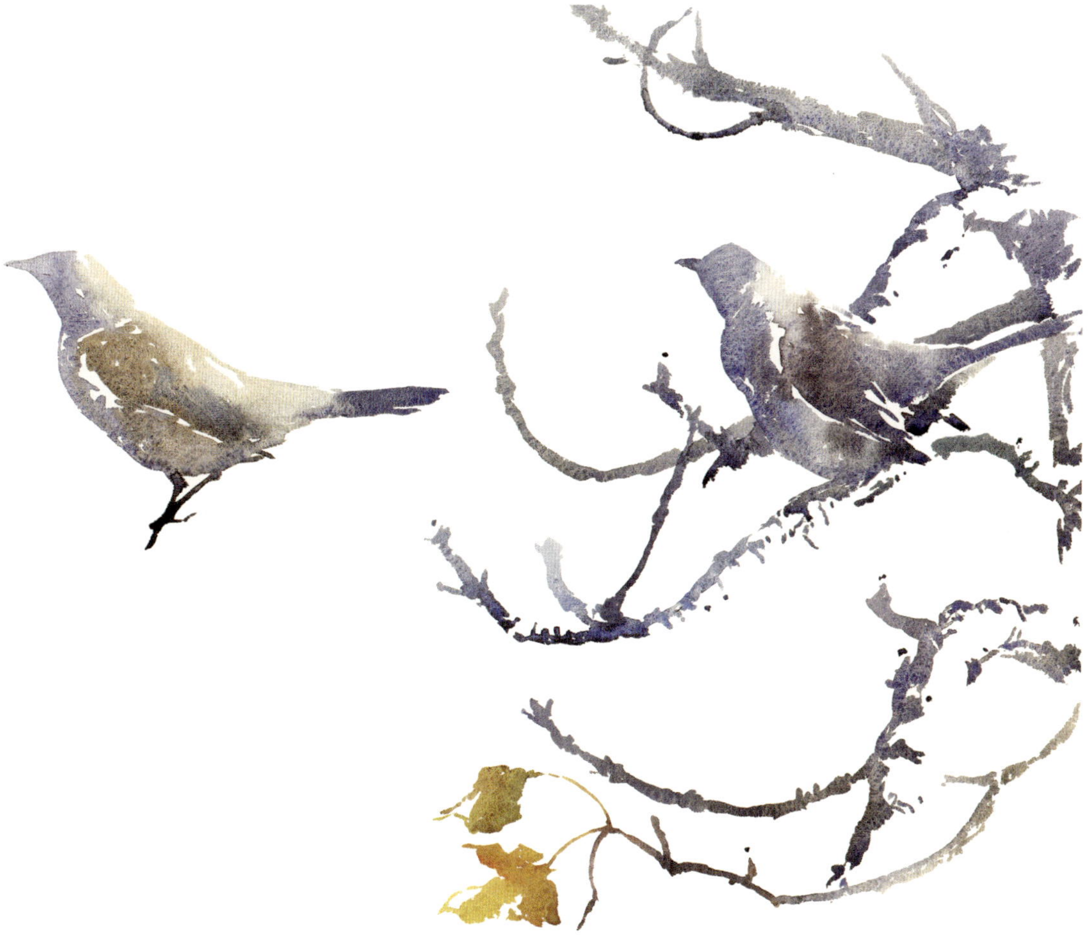

Fieldfare studies , 6th November 2007.
(watercolour, 380mm x 560mm)

Tuesday, 5th February 2008. Early heavy mist finally succumbed to the onset of rain that had loomed to the west. I begin to paint a winter Hawthorn alive with colour – ochres, browns and greens alongside velvet purples and slate greys. In among this and the bank below is the constant chatter of feeding winter Thrushes, Blackbirds, Redwing and the odd boisterous Fieldfare. My brushmarks almost float above the paper surface. I feel the paper's fibres have absorbed so much of the surrounding dampness that it is saturated, not allowing the usual immediate absorption of colour. Still, the colour is keeping vibrant and fresh. The greens and greys that well in pockets on the paper result in a separation of pigments and an array of texture. The first occasional drip trespasses through my umbrella above and down the page, summing up the day. I become absorbed in drawing the patterns of Hawthorn twigs and complex structures of thorns and buds, knowing that if the last wet area touches the one I am working on now the colours will run together becoming one dull uniform tone.

The painting took until the following evening to dry, such had been the conditions that day. I had to leave it in the car until it was safe to move it late that second evening. Sometimes when colour takes so long to dry, the pigments retain a certain vibrancy. One of the many joys of winter painting.

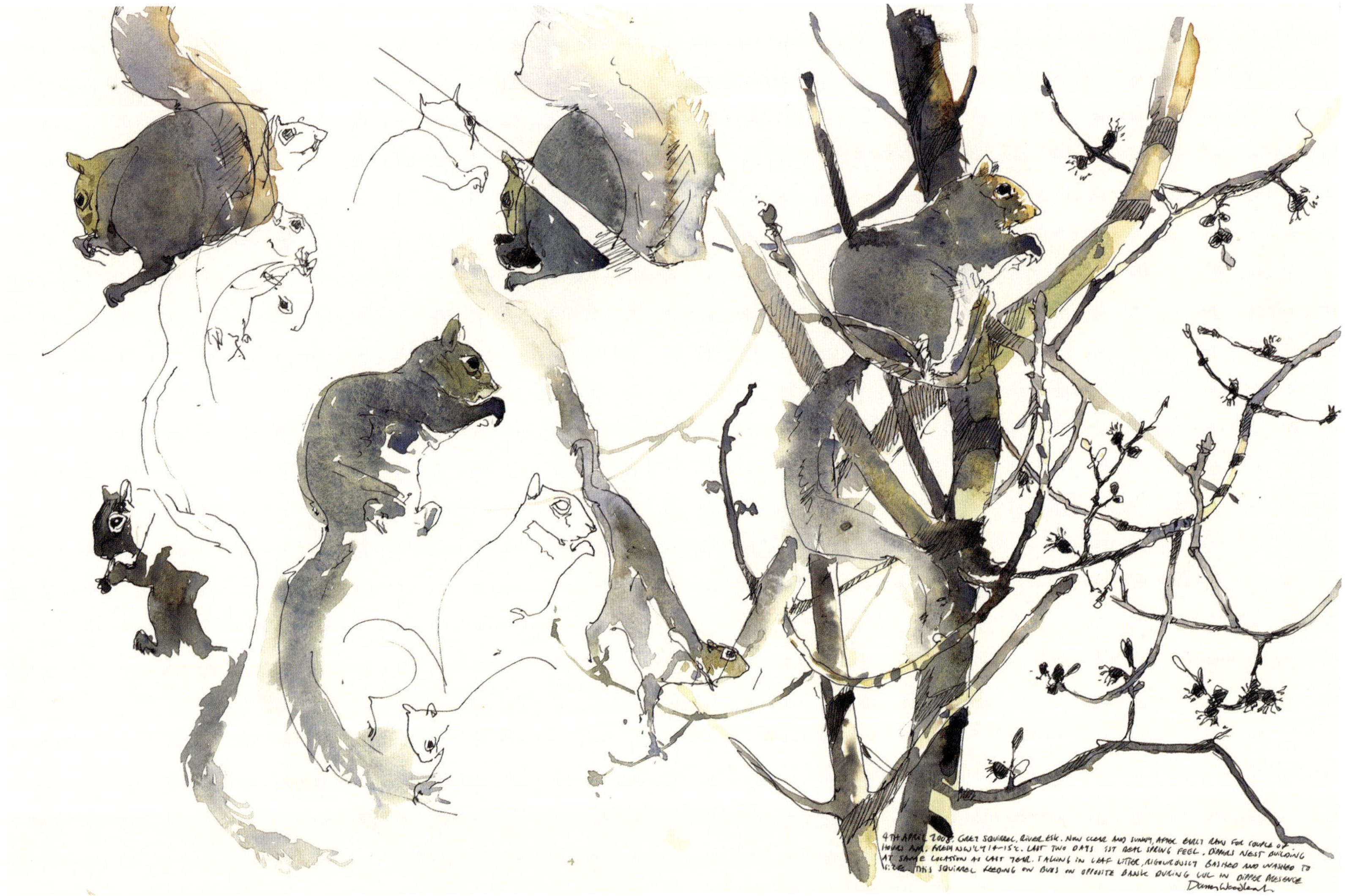

Grey Squirrel feeding on buds
(watercolour and pen, 380mm x 560mm)

4th April 2008. Grey Squirrel, River Esk. Now clear and sunny after rain for couple of hours a.m. Fresh north-westerly 14–15 degrees. Last two days real spring feel. Dippers nesting at same location as last year. Taking leaf litter, rigorously bashed and washed to size. This Squirrel feeding on buds on opposite bank during lull in Dipper activity.

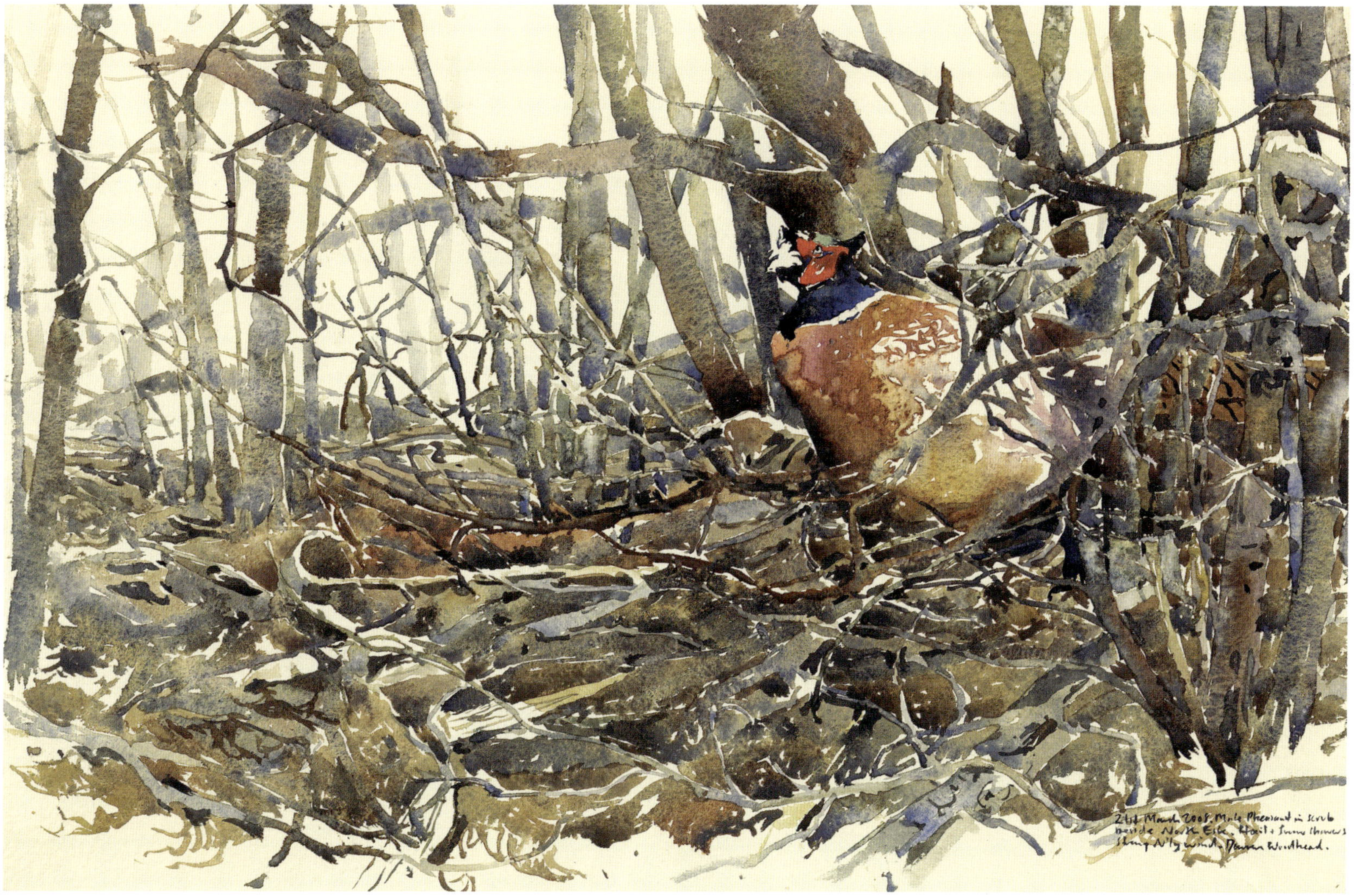

Male Pheasant
(watercolour, 380mm x 560mm)

21st March 2008. Male Pheasant in scrub beside North Esk. Hail and snow showers, strong northerly wind, cold.

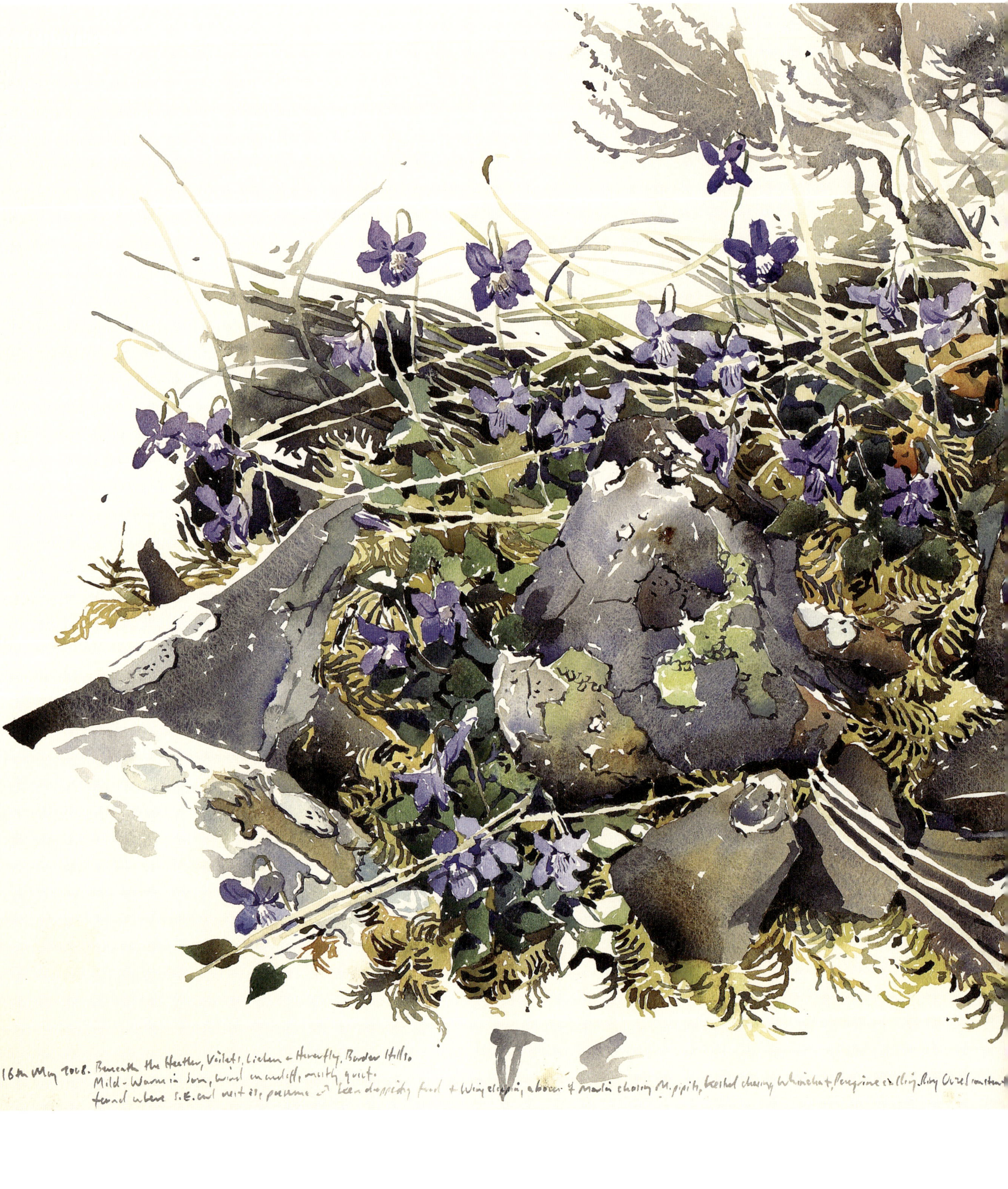
16th May 2008. Beneath the Heather, Violets, Lichen & Hoverfly, Border Hills.
Mild - Warm in sun,

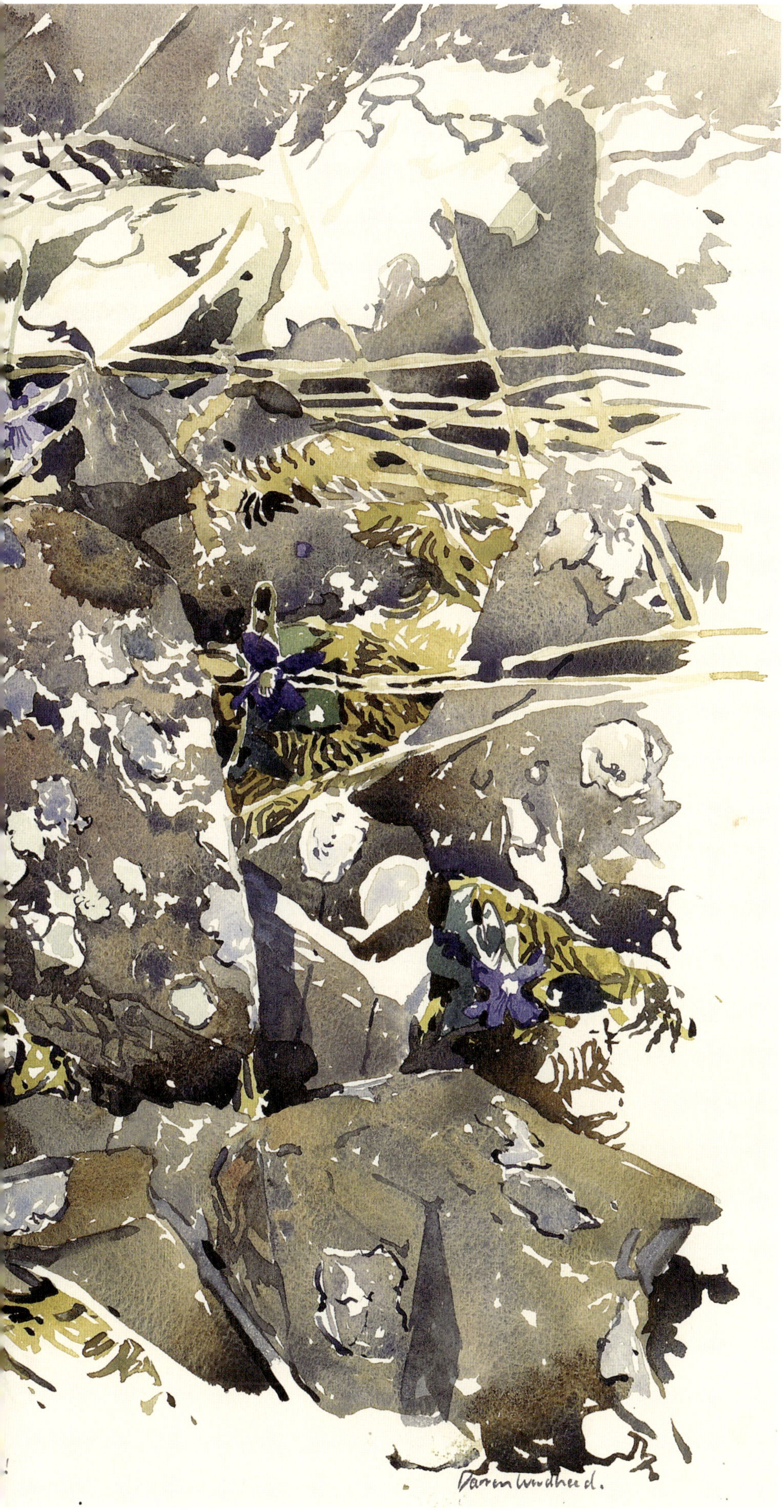

Violets and Hoverflies among lichened rocks
(watercolour, 380mm x 560mm)

16thMay 2008. Beneath the Heather, Violets, Lichen and Hoverfly, Border hills. Mild to warm in sun, wind on and off, mostly quiet. Found where Short-eared Owl nest is; (presume) male seen dropping food and wing-clapping above. Female Merlin chasing Meadow Pipits, Kestrel chasing Whinchat, Peregrine calling. Ring Ouzel constant but so mobile!

Walked over a brow of heather for Sula to launch into a motionless and purposeful point. There was a determination in the way that she held her transfixed pose. I looked in front, could not see anything. As I crept forth Sula occasionally glanced at me but was soon again fixated, her brow occasionally raised, head low to the heather, tail solid and still. I moved further on, and there it was, within two metres of me, deep within the base of the heather – the wings and tail of an owl. Almost invisible, the complex patterns perfectly colliding with fragmented heather textures. Presuming Short-eared, as I had seen one earlier, I suddenly caught glimpse of two orange eyes and extended ear tufts: not Short-eared but Long-eared and on the ground in heather! I was not aware that Long-eared nested on the ground, as they usually favour old crow nests, but reading up about it I discovered it is not unknown. I moved away to try and see it from a distance, but it was impossible. Within the same day and same few hundred feet, nests of two very similar and spectacular Owls.

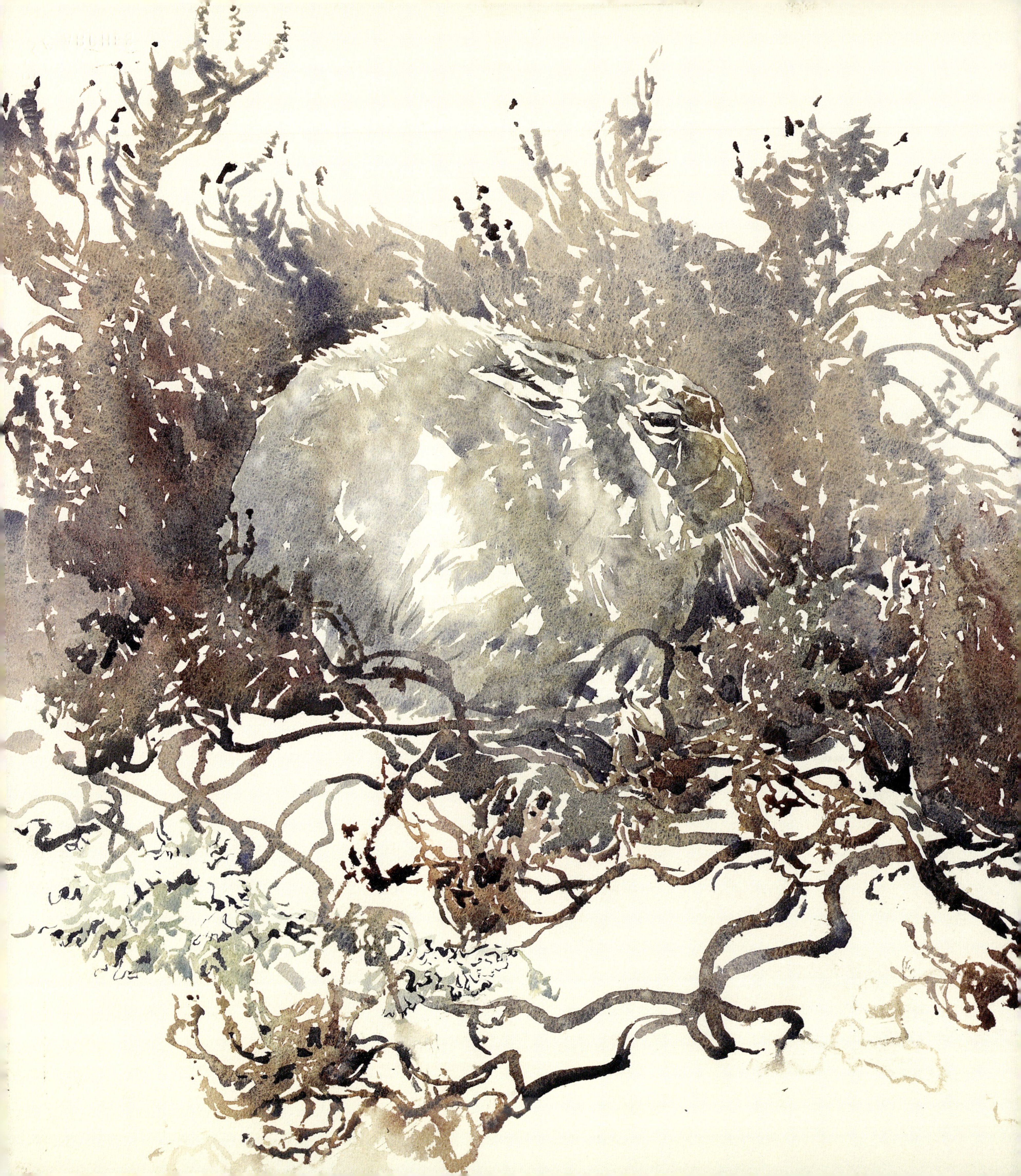

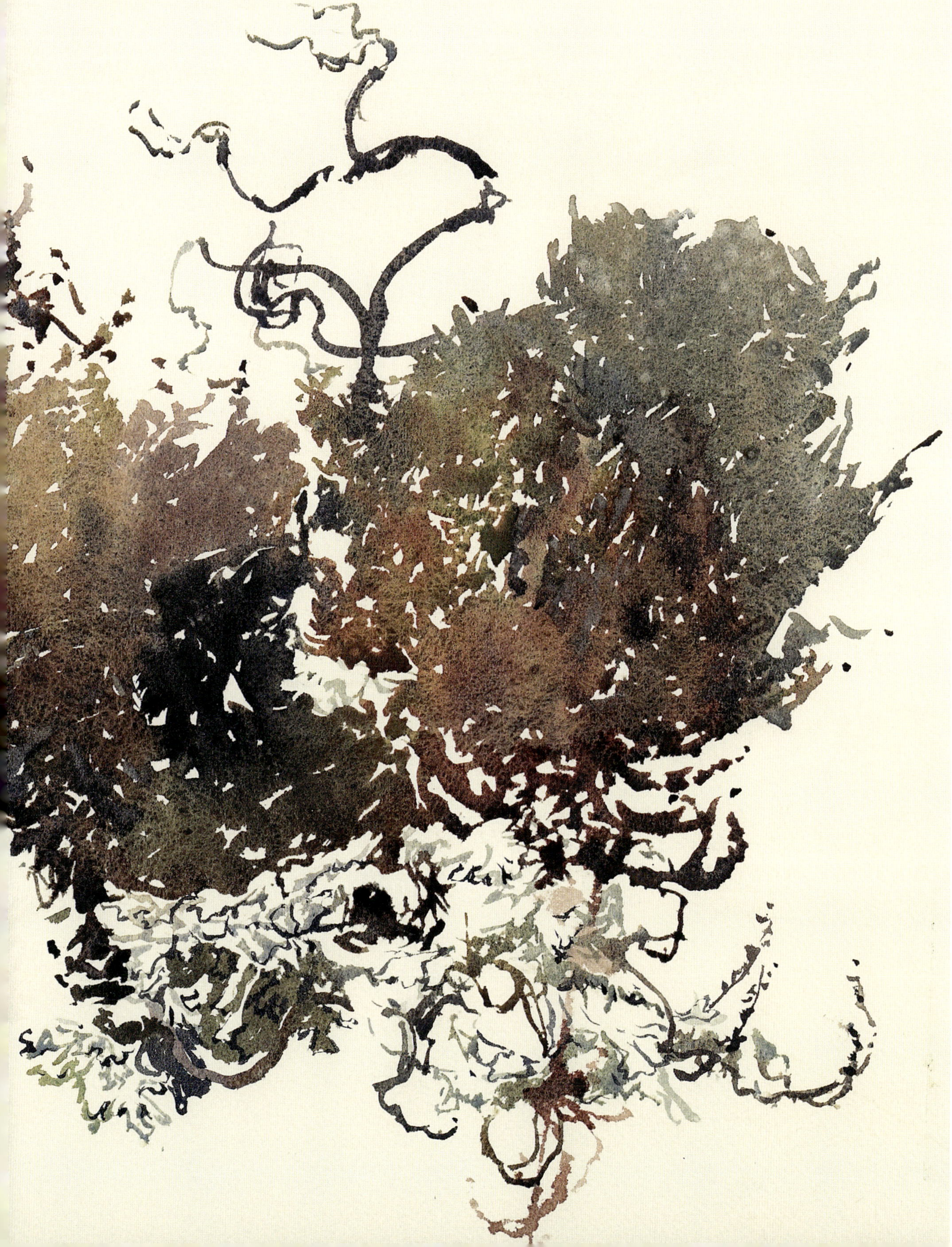

Mountain Hare among
Heather twists
(watercolour, 380mm x 560mm)

18th April 2008. Overcast and freezing cold, strong easterly wind, rain constant from 08:30 to 15:30, patchy thereafter. Occasional sunny spells though cloud descended 14:00 to 40/50 metres, visibility. At least one singing Ring Ouzel, pair Common Sandpiper and female Peregrine west as soon as I arrived.

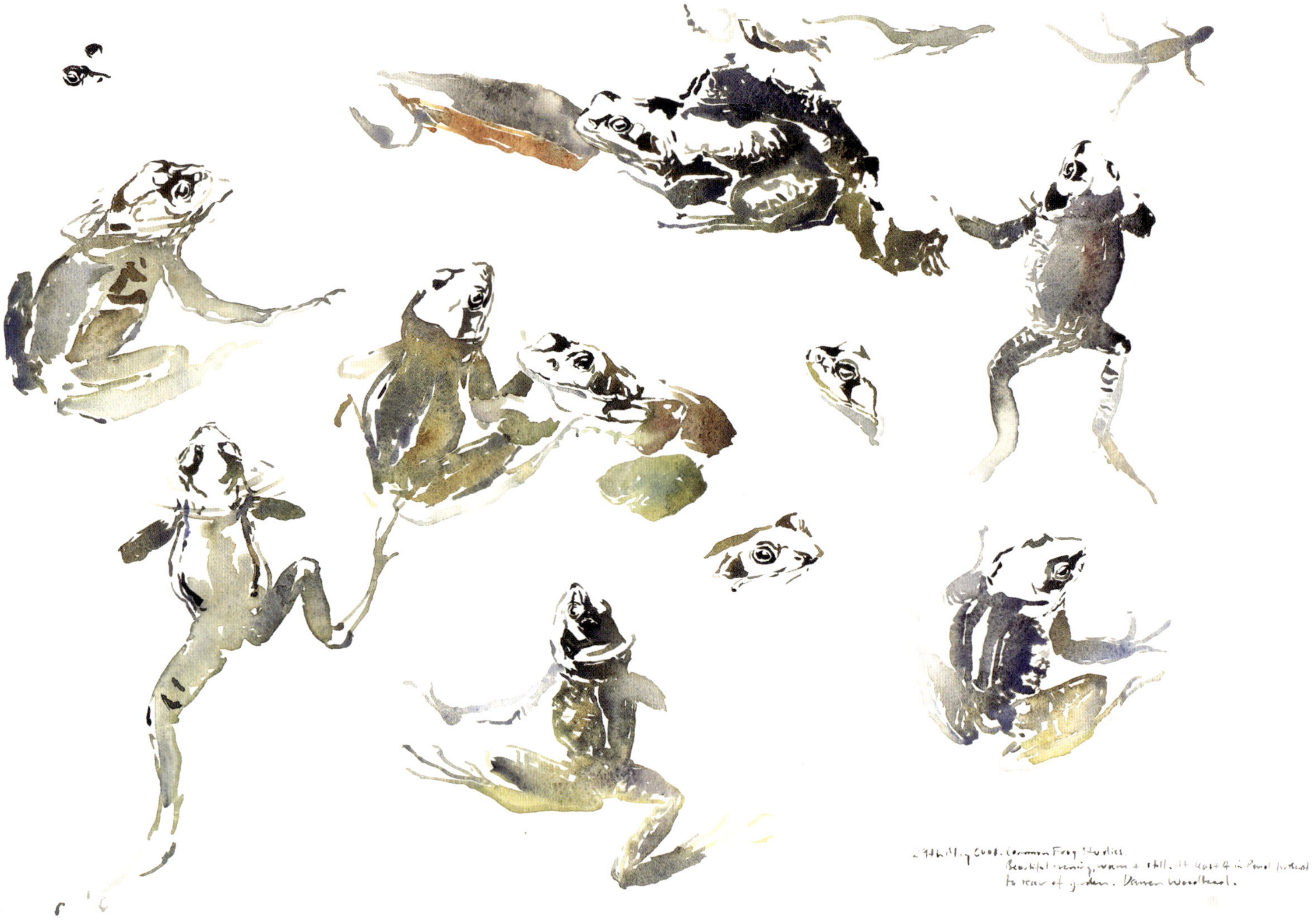

Common Frog Studies
(watercolour, 380mm x 560mm)

29th May 2008. Beautiful evening, warm and still.

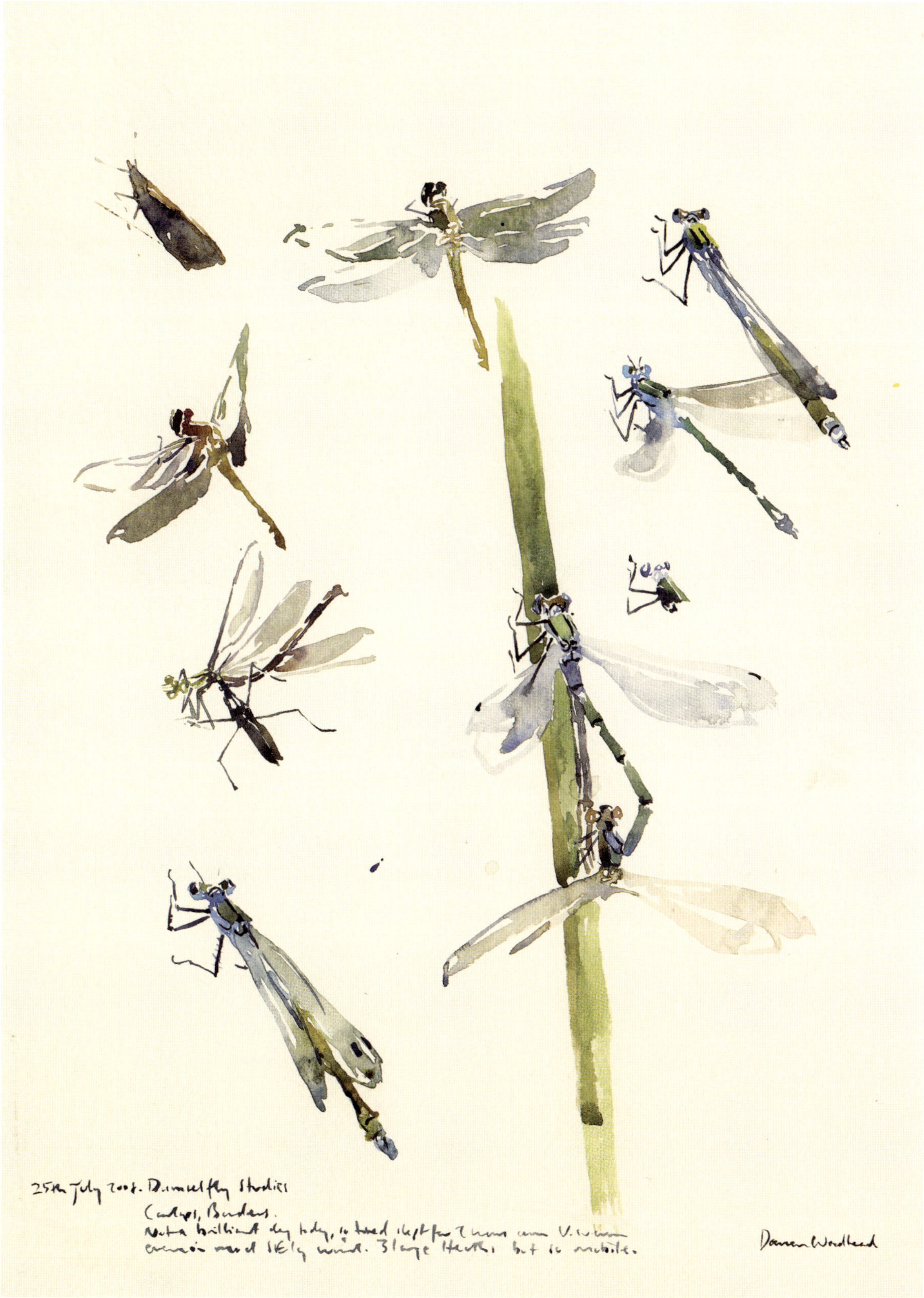

Emerald Damselfly
(watercolour, 380mm x 280mm)

25th July 2008. Damselfly studies, Carlops, Borders. Not a brilliant day today, so tired, slept for two hours a.m. Very warm. Overcast in moderate south-easterly wind. Three large Heaths but so mobile.

I watched a struggling Damselfly that had somehow become waterlogged come under attack from a Pond Skater. Defenceless, the Damselfly struggled to lever itself out as the Pond Skater made its move, and sharply manoeuvred its prey into position before easily piercing its body with ease with its mouth parts.

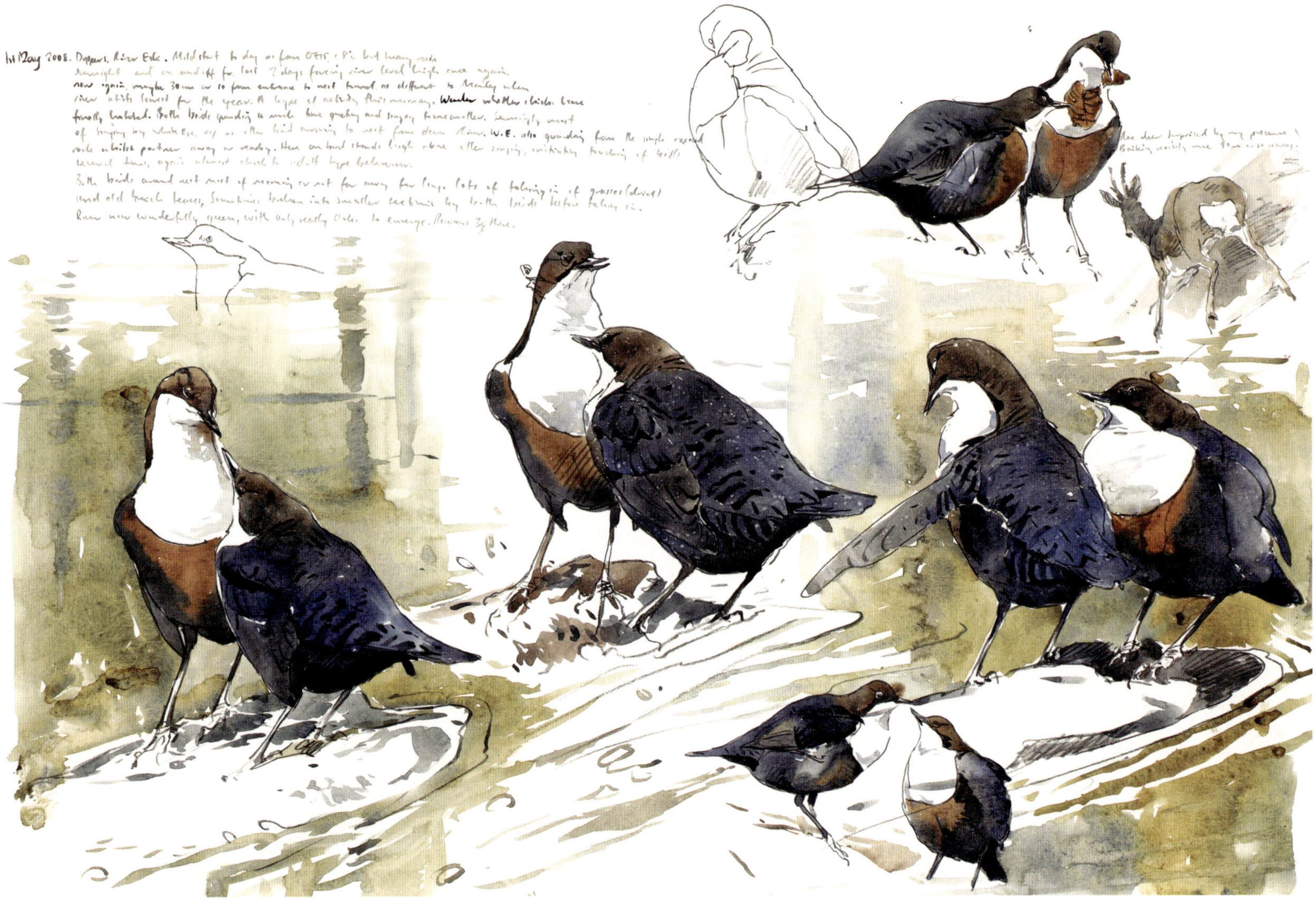

Dipper studies
(watercolour and pencil, 420mm x 594mm)

1st May 2008. Dippers, River Esk. Mild start to the day as from 07:45. Circa 8 degrees but heavy rain overnight and on and off for last two days forcing river level high once again. Now again maybe thirty centimetres or so from entrance to nest tunnel, as different from Monday when river at its lowest for the year. A hive of activity this morning; wonder whether chicks have finally hatched. Both birds spending so much time greeting and singing to one another. Seemingly most of singing by white eye, especially as other bird arriving to nest from down river. White eye also guarding from the single exposed rock whilst partner away or nearby. Here one bird stands high above the other singing, initiating touching of bills several times, again almost chick- to-adult type behaviour.

Both birds around nest most of morning or not away for long. Lots of taking in of grasses (dried) and old beech leaves, sometimes broken into smaller sections by both birds before taking in. River now wonderfully green, with really only Oak to emerge. Rowans two thirds there.

Roe deer surprised by my presence, barking noisily once 40 metres or so away.

I observed the same pair of Dippers that I had seen in both 2006 and 2007 again in 2008. This year I spent more time watching courtship and nest-building. Having a good idea when incubation had occurred I was able to calculate when I could expect the river to come alive with the sounds of a young Dipper family. Despite a bad spell at the beginning of May, the weather became more settled and all seemed well. Activity was normal, but then I felt strangely concerned by a sudden change in the Dippers' behaviour. On one visit I saw both birds actually taking nesting material out with purpose. My suspicions were now fully aroused – by this point activity at the nest should have been reaching a crescendo, but all was quiet – a stark contrast with the rest of the riverside, which was

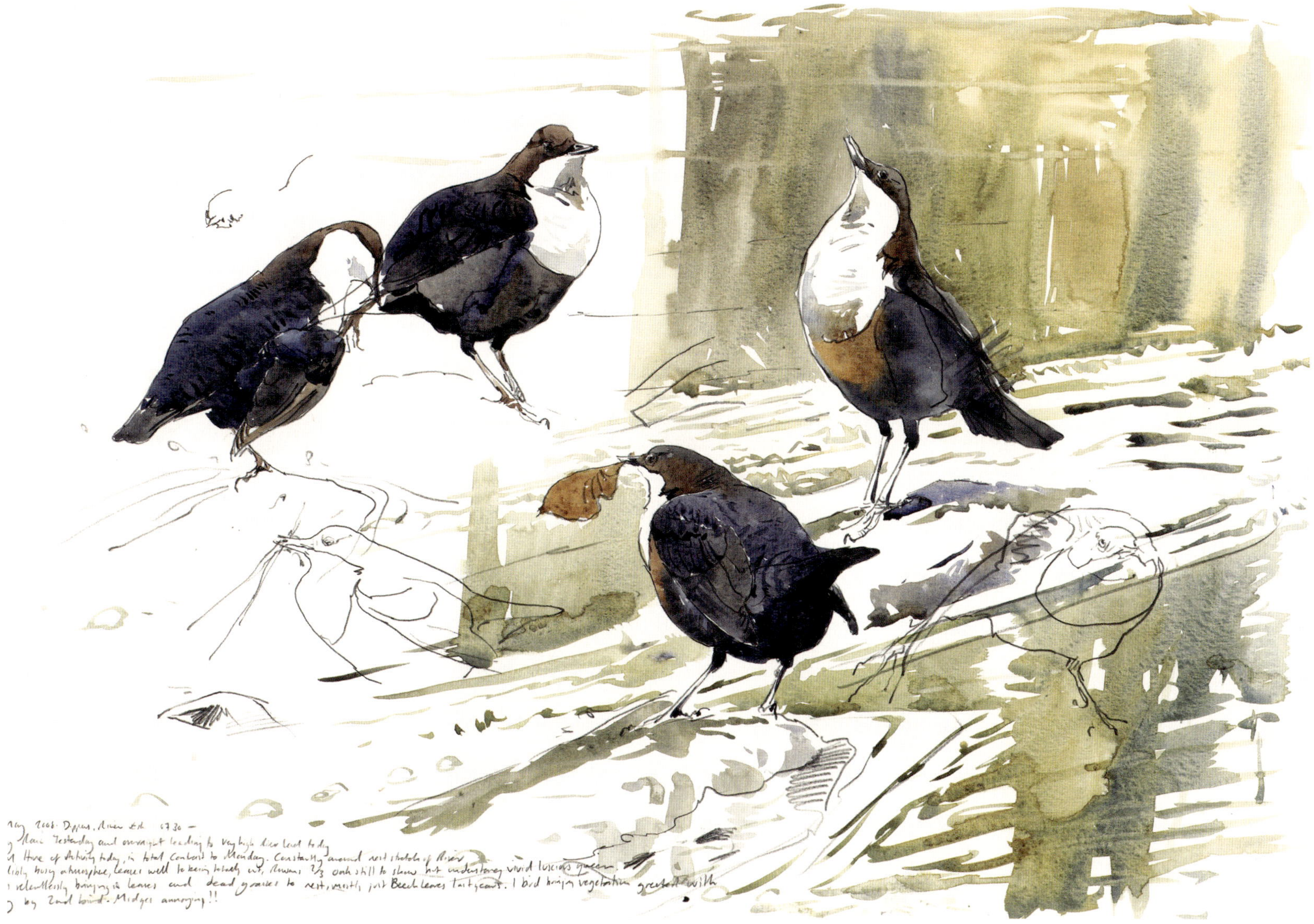

now full of greenery and life. Looking into the nest entrance from a distance everything seemed in order. I gave it a good week until I was sure there was no activity before going and looking into the nest itself. Everything looked in order, yet for some reason they had failed. Two possibilities came to mind. Either the nest had been raided by a small mammal, perhaps Rat or Mink, which had left little trace, or the eggs had been infertile. In early March 2009 I again began to watch the same pair. Interestingly, they chose a new site a hundred metres or so further downstream, higher up the bank and with the fortified protection of an outcrop of rocks below, a good metre and a half above river level. They built the nest in good time and all seemed well. But, as I finalise the text for this book in May, a similar occurrence has just happened again, so for another year the river is quiet to the sound of Dippers.

Dipper studies
(watercolour and pencil, 420mm x 594mm)

1st May 2008. Dippers, River Esk 07:30 onwards. Heavy rain yesterday and overnight leading to very high river level today. A total hive of activity today in total contrast to Monday. Constantly around nest stretch of river. Incredibly busy atmosphere, leaves well on the way to being totally out; Rowans two-thirds, Oak still to show but under-storey vivid luscious green. Dippers relentlessly bringing in leaves and dead grasses to nest, mostly just Beech leaves – last year's. One bird bringing vegetation greeted with song by second bird. Midges annoying!

Peregrine catching Teal
(watercolour, 560mm x 380mm)

8th October 2008. Brighter day than yesterday, with fresh south-westerly breeze. Mild, though – 14–16 degrees. When Peregrine struck seemed to catch everything by surprise, it was only on impact that the usual fear and chaos ensued.

13:35 Peregrine came low from north-west and immediately grabbed female Teal. Upon impact struggled to keep in flight, carrying prey to ground, and only 20 metres from me! Sat on flaying Teal, duck's legs still kicking. Peregrine gape slightly open. Heard feathery impact and vocal call from Peregrine on landing.

After escaping Teal, swam sharply across pool and into reed edge, holding neck and bill low to water, before ten seconds later swimming out and moving normally, if not slightly edgy.

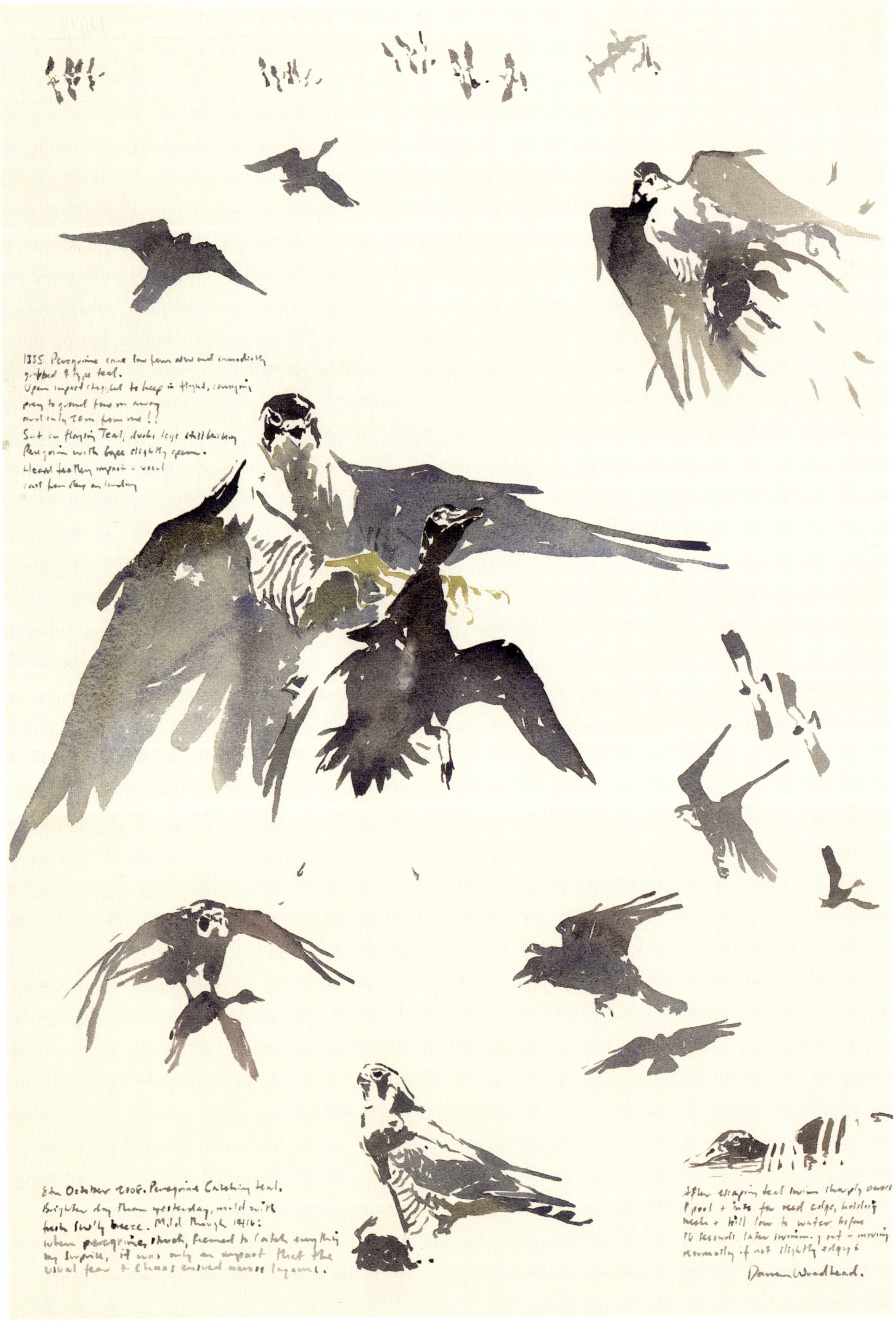

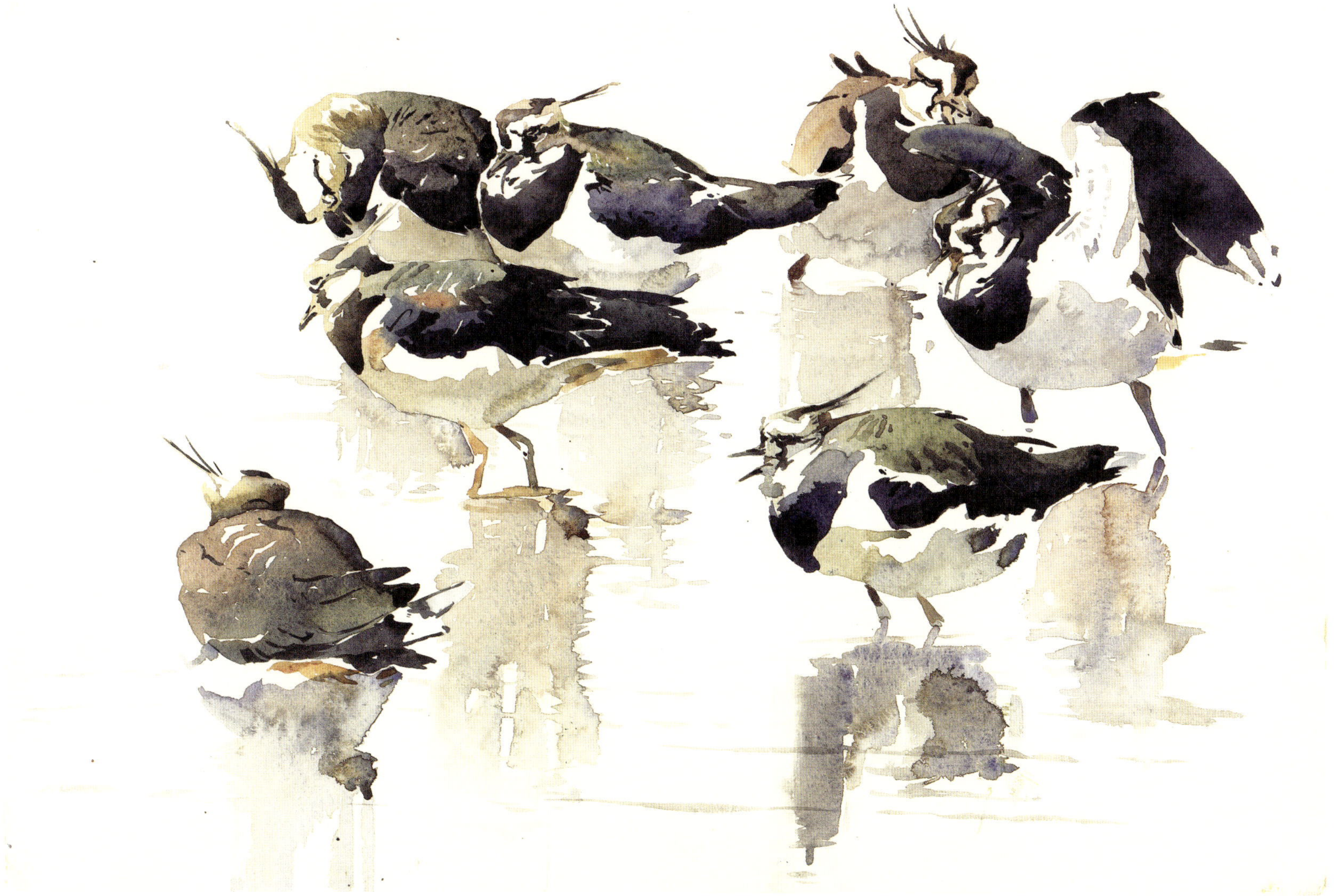

Lapwings
(watercolour, 380mm x 560mm)

27th July 2007. Lapwing late afternoon. At last a day and afternoon without showers. At least 260 Little Gulls.

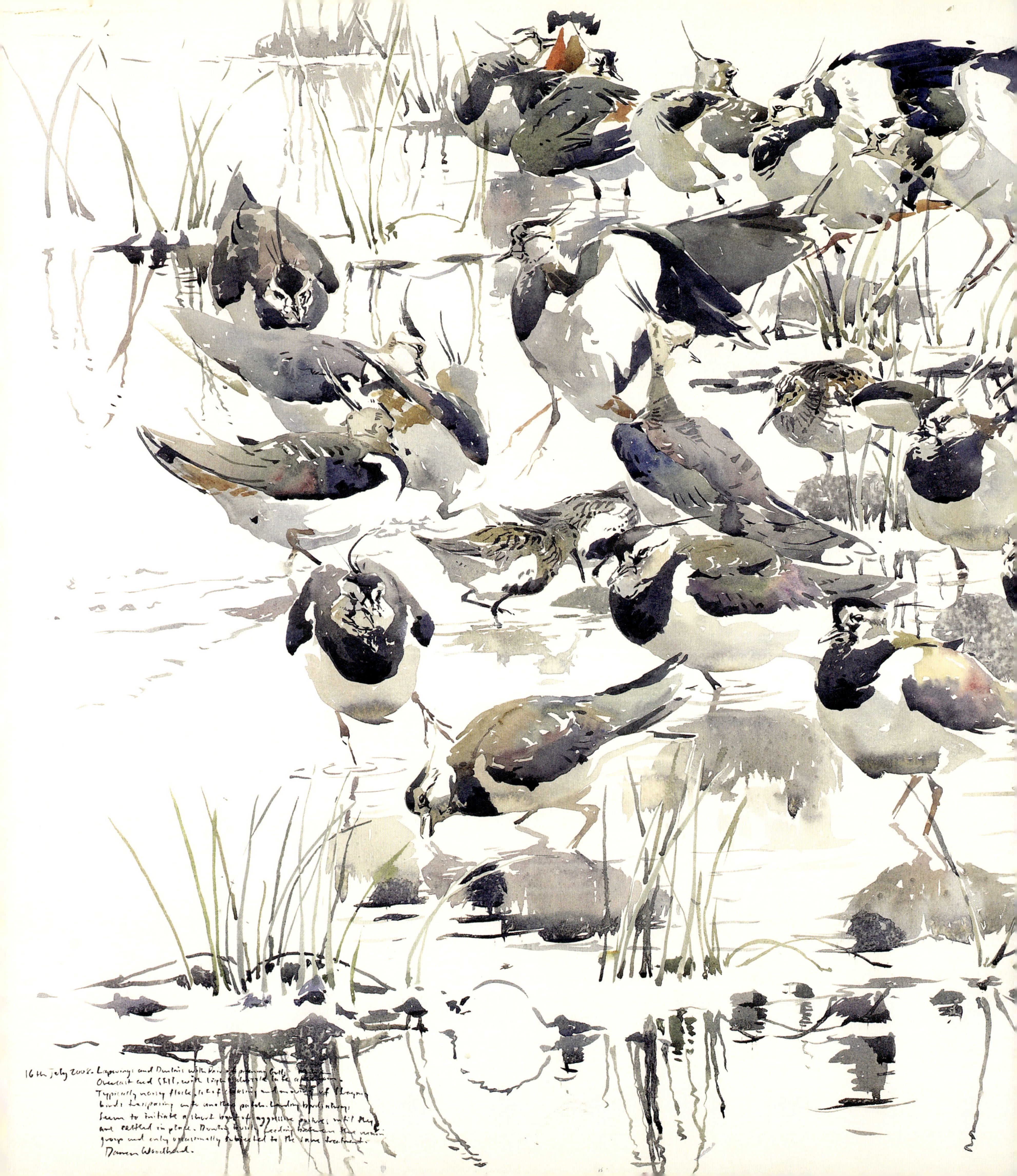
16th July 2008. Lapwings and Dunlins with pair of preening Gulls
Overcast and still, with light
Typically noisy flock, lots of chasing and moving of
birds onto another patch. Landing birds always
seem to initiate a short bout of aggressive posturing until they
are settled in place. Dunlins busily feeding between the main
group and only occasionally subjected to the same treatment.
Darren Woodhead.

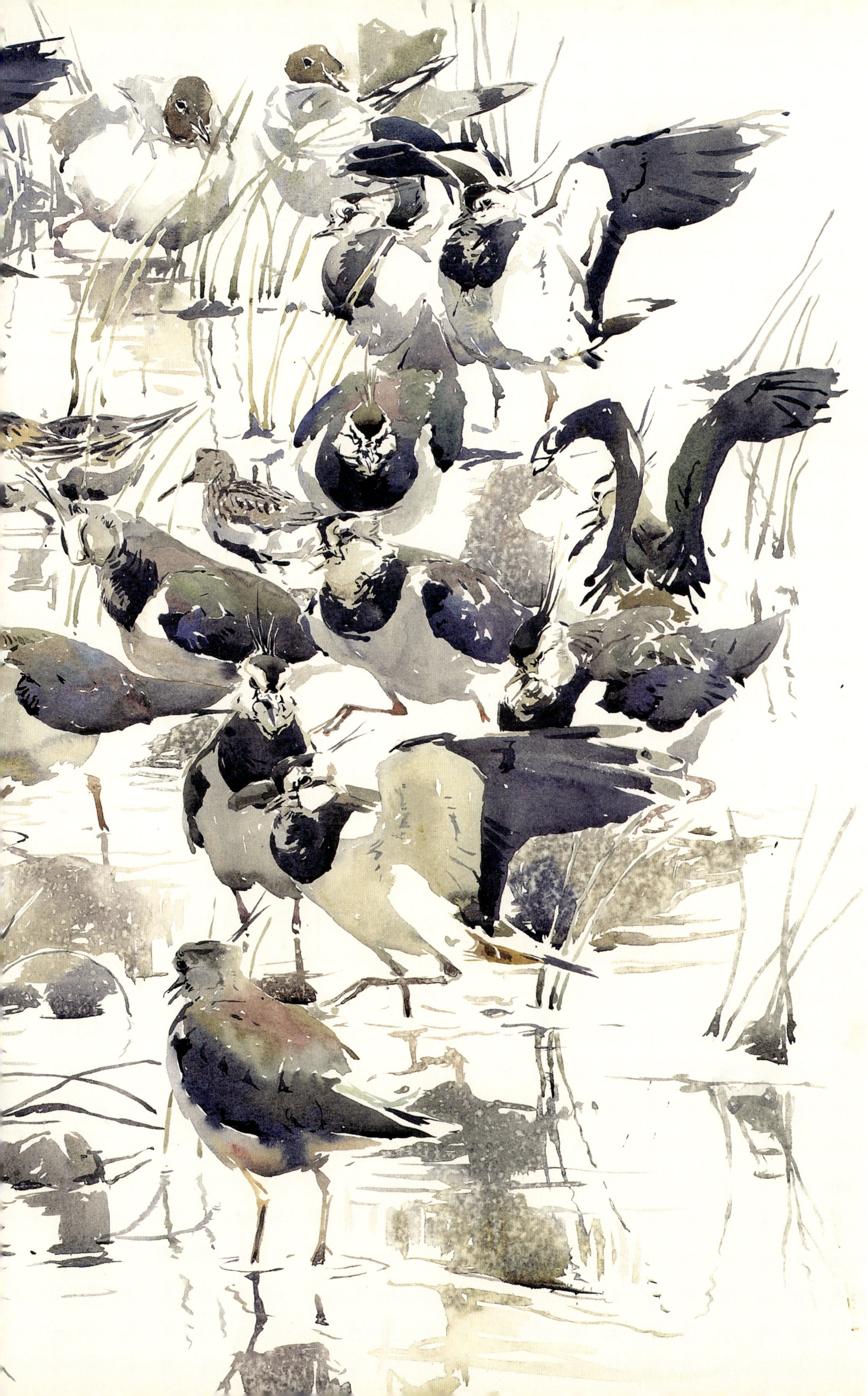

Lapwing Flock
(watercolour, 660mm x 1016mm)

16th July 2008. Lapwings and Dunlins with pair of preening Gulls. Overcast and still, with light drizzle late afternoon. Typically noisy flock, lots of chasing and moving of straying birds trespassing onto each others' patch. Landing birds always seem to initiate a short bout of aggressive postures until they are settled in place. Dunlin busily feeding between the main group and only occasionally subjected to the same treatment.

Singing Redstart

(watercolour, 560mm x 380mm)

22nd May 2008. Singing male Redstart among freshly emerging Oaks. Cool and overcast, becoming brighter, fresh westerly. Singing constantly from mid morning till at least 13:30, not so much when cold first thing.

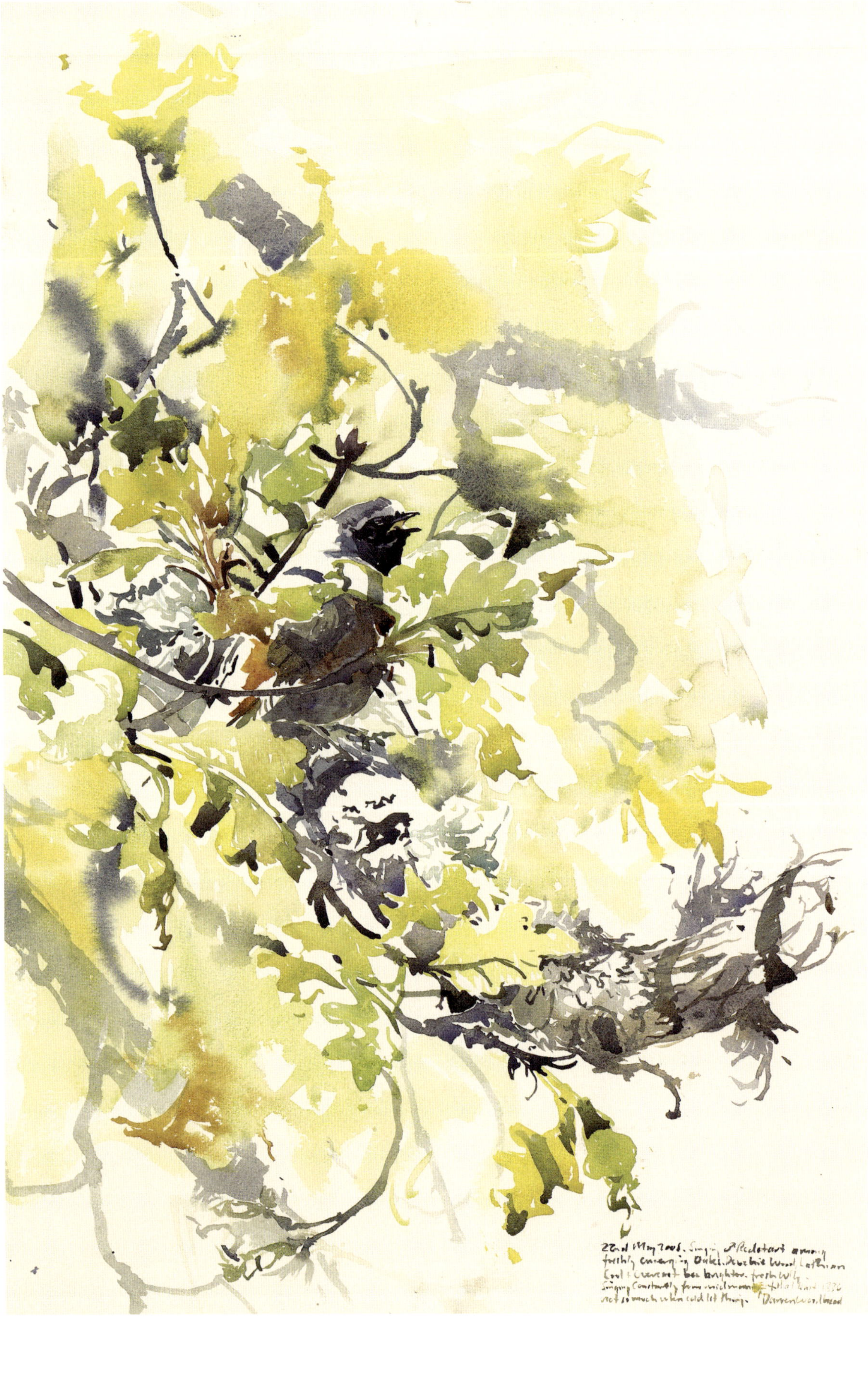

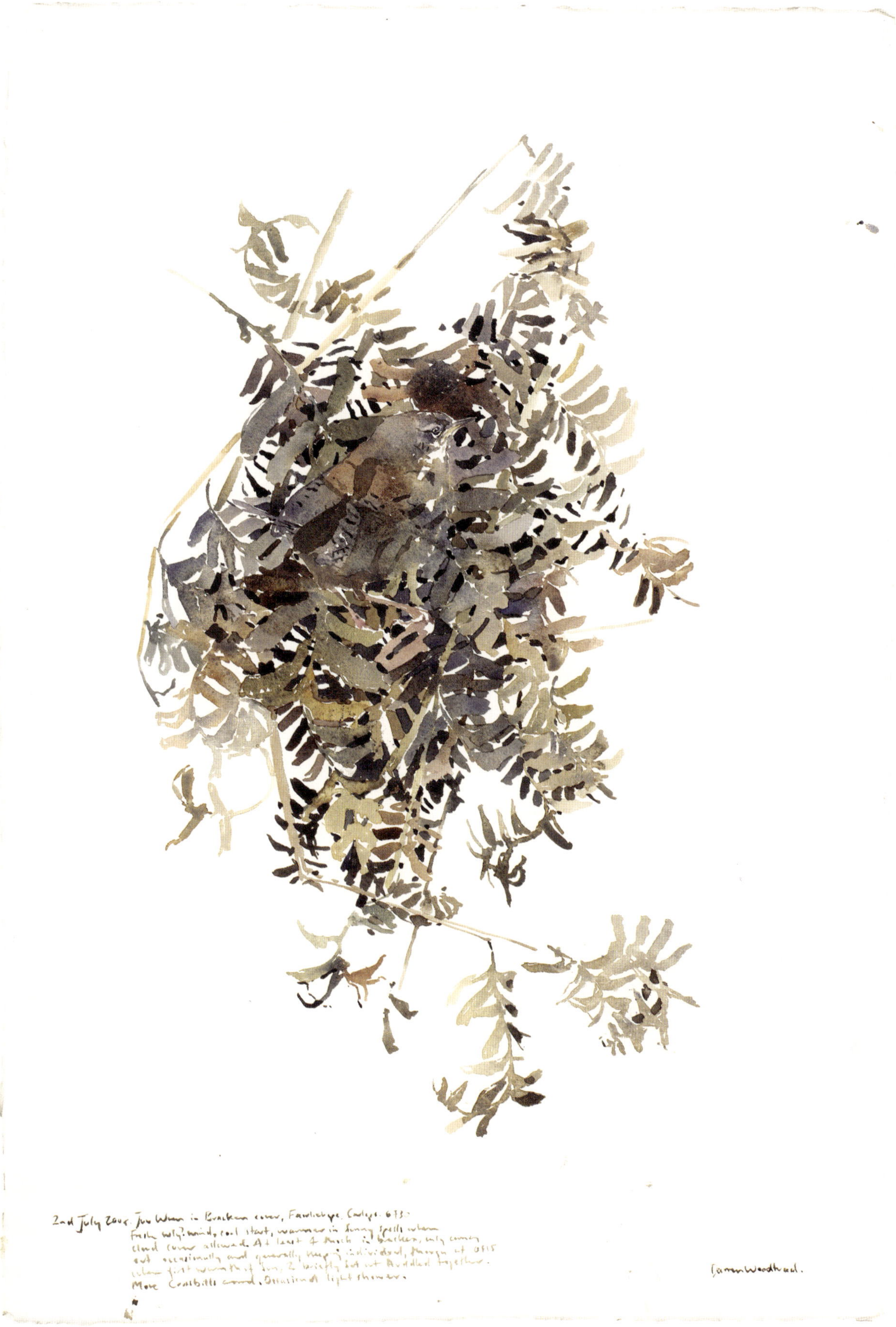

Wren fledgling
(watercolour, 560mm x 380mm)

2nd July 2008. Juvenile Wren in Bracken cover, Fairliehope, Carlops, 07:30. Fresh westerly wind, cool start, warmer in sunny spells when cloud cover allowed. At least four chicks in bracken, only coming out occasionally and generally individually, though at 08:15 when first warmth of sun, two briefly sat out huddled together. More Crossbills around. Occasional light shower.

Buzzard chick in Scots Pine
(watercolour, 560mm x 380mm)

30th June 2008. Buzzard chick on nest 17:00. Overcast with fresh south-westerly. Feeling cool, though – probably 16–17 degrees. Occasional sunny break. Just looks like the one chick, though difficult to really see; certainly only one moving.

The same nest as last year and but with only the single young reaching near fledging stage this year.

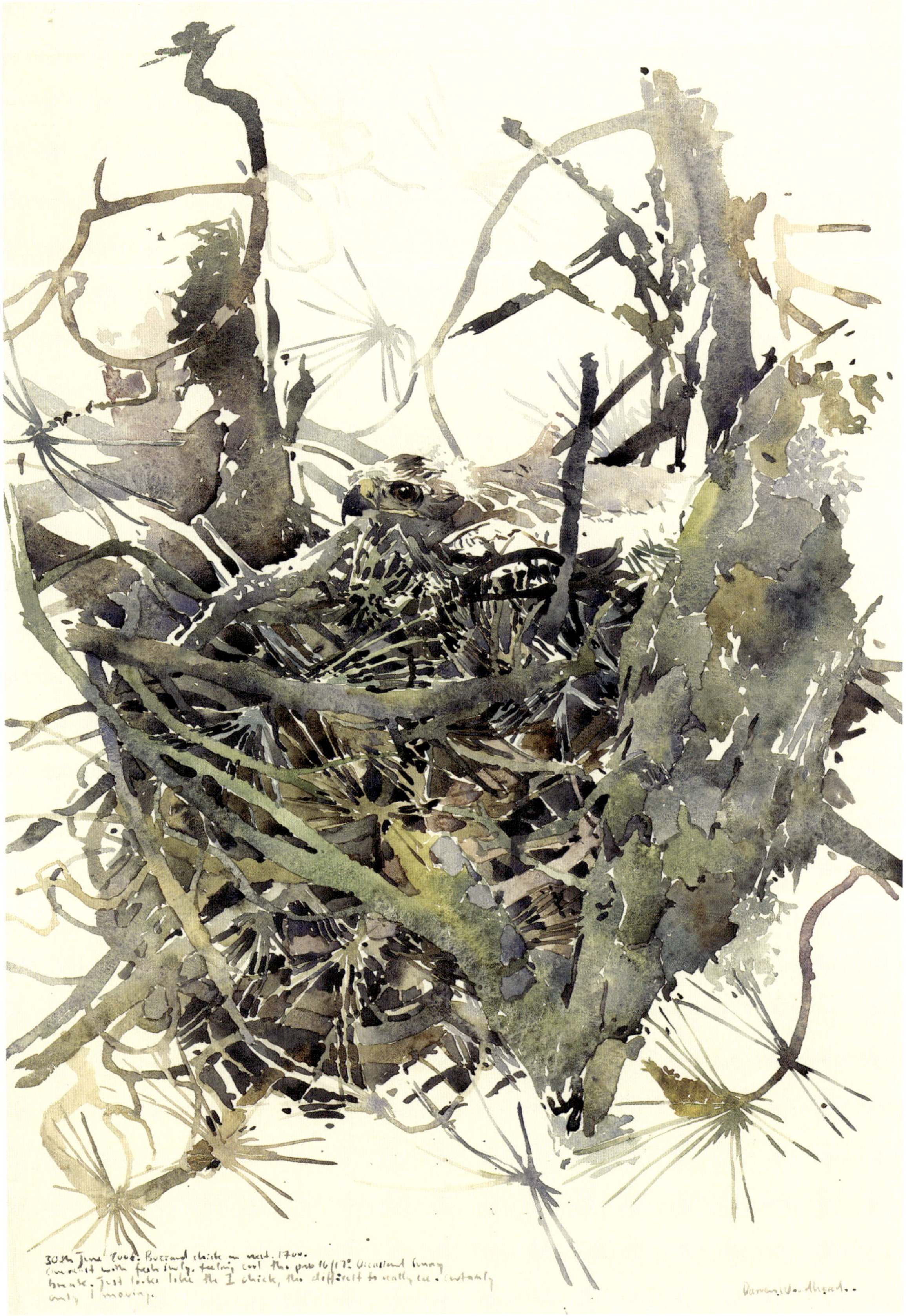

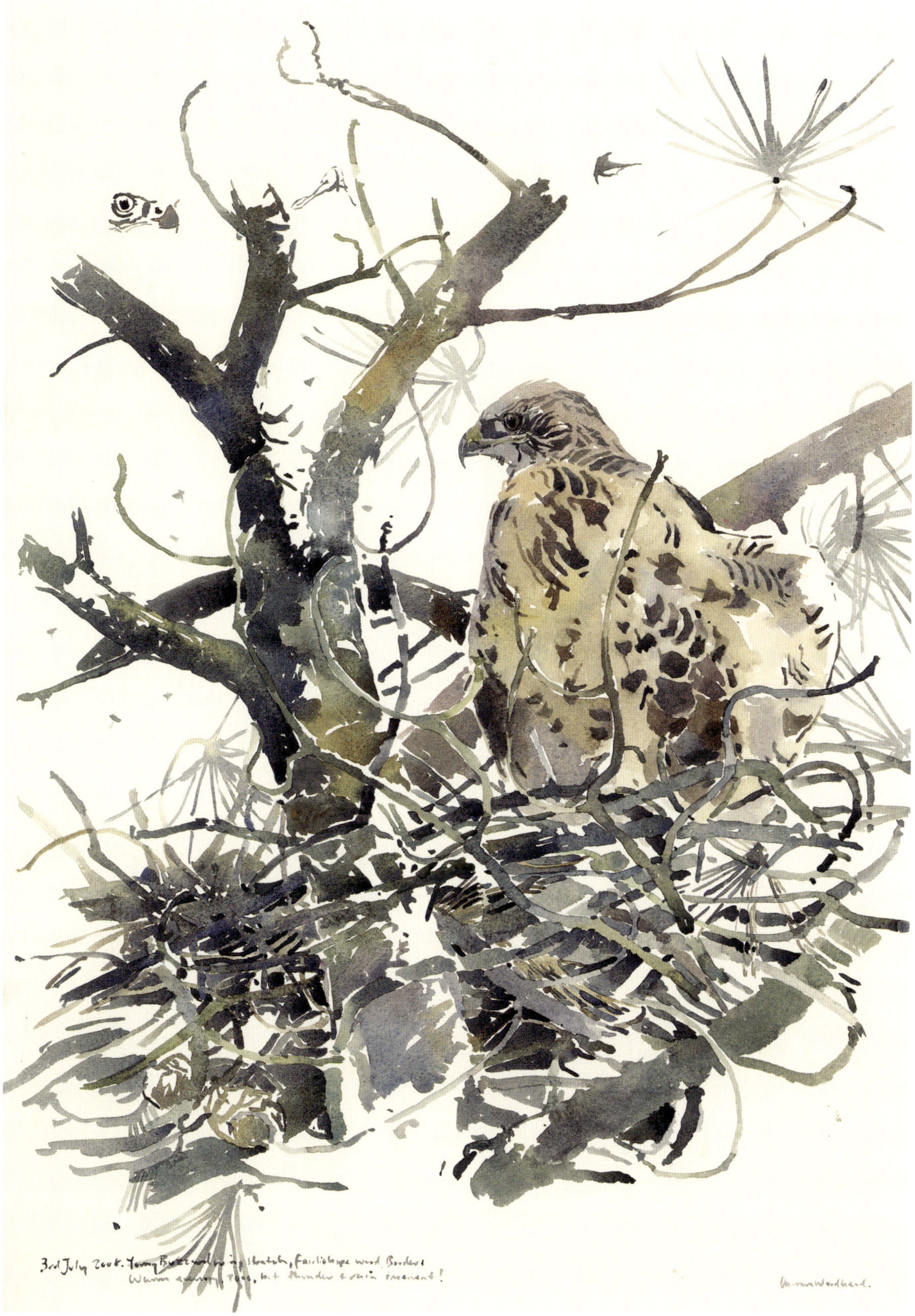

Young Buzzard on nest
(watercolour, 560mmx 380mm)

2nd July 2008. Juvenile Buzzard, Fairliehope. Overcast, brief sunny periods, cool first thing becoming warmer. Occasional showers. Gusty wind. Chick stood up all the time with occasional wing stretch but no exercising of wings. Surely will not be long, though.

Large Beech in the dean
(watercolour, 1016mm x 660mm)

24th October 2008. Beeches under heavy rain, Amazondean, Carlops. Unsettled start with rain and strong winds throughout the morning and into mid afternoon. Bright by late afternoon. Small skein of Pink-footed Geese south towards West Linton and a surprise: a small group of Waxwing calling low over beeches. Had a quick look around Amazondean but no real berry trees around to attract them. Perhaps I will catch up with them later. Part of a current national large invasion.

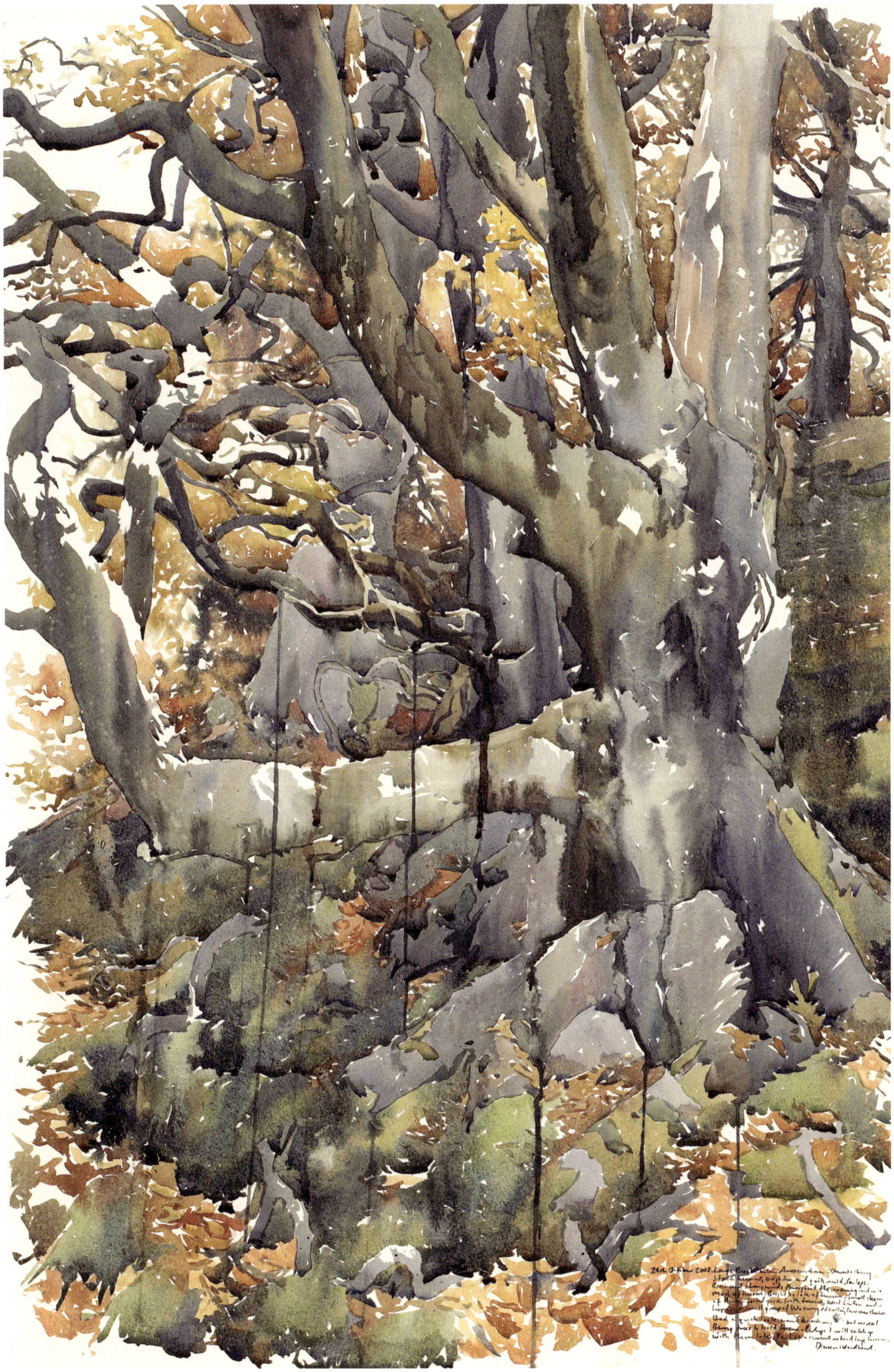

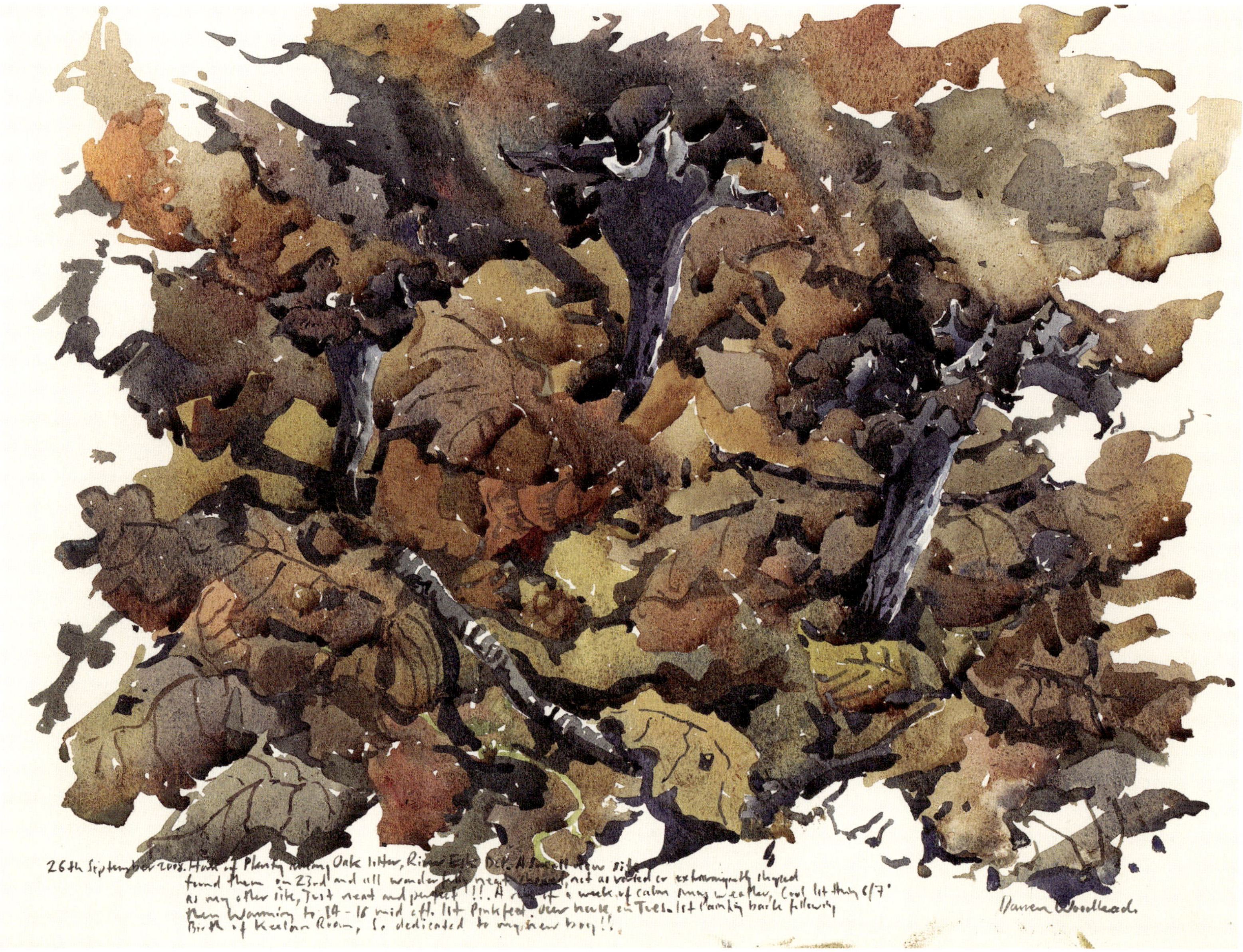

Horn of Plenty
(watercolour, 275mm x 370mm)

26th September 2008. Horn of Plenty among Oak litter, River Esk. A small new site, found them on the 23rd and all wonderfully shaped, not as varied or extravagantly shaped as my other site, just neat and perfect! A run of a week of calm sunny weather, cool first thing 6 or 7 degrees then warming to 14/16 degrees by mid afternoon. First Pink-footed Geese over house on Tuesday 23rd September. First painting back following birth of Keelan Roan, so dedicated it to my new boy!

Autumn 2008 was a surprise. August as well as July was so wet and cold that any dry day was a bonus. I was not sure whether these conditions would mean a good season ahead. Whether this actually encouraged an earlier season for fungi I am not certain, but when I first began looking at the end of August I was amazed by the sheer volume of Horn of Plenty I found already in my usual patch. They must have been out mid month, in total contrast to 2006, when I first saw them in mid October. As I walked through the woods there was little else in the way of fungi, yet the steep bank beneath the Beech with scattered Oak and Holly was literally black with decaying Horn of Plenty. I also found them in another small area slightly later, from mid to late September, but here they were totally different in size, being nowhere near as spectacular and impressive in size and shape as those which occur at my 'regular' place. Chanterelles seemed in good numbers, and I located them in several different locations. They seemed always to be found below Beech in moss, and this year I saw some truly breathtaking examples, some with such huge deep yellow flutes and magnificent wavy gills that I just had to leave them to spore. One of the highlights was the three impressive Giant Puffballs that were suddenly standing like sculptures overlooking the glen. The season flashed by with little in the way of Blewitt feasts that I had had the year before.

Chanterelles and Devil's Coachhorse
(watercolour and pen, 380mm x 280mm)

2nd September 2008. Chanterelle studies, beside North Esk.

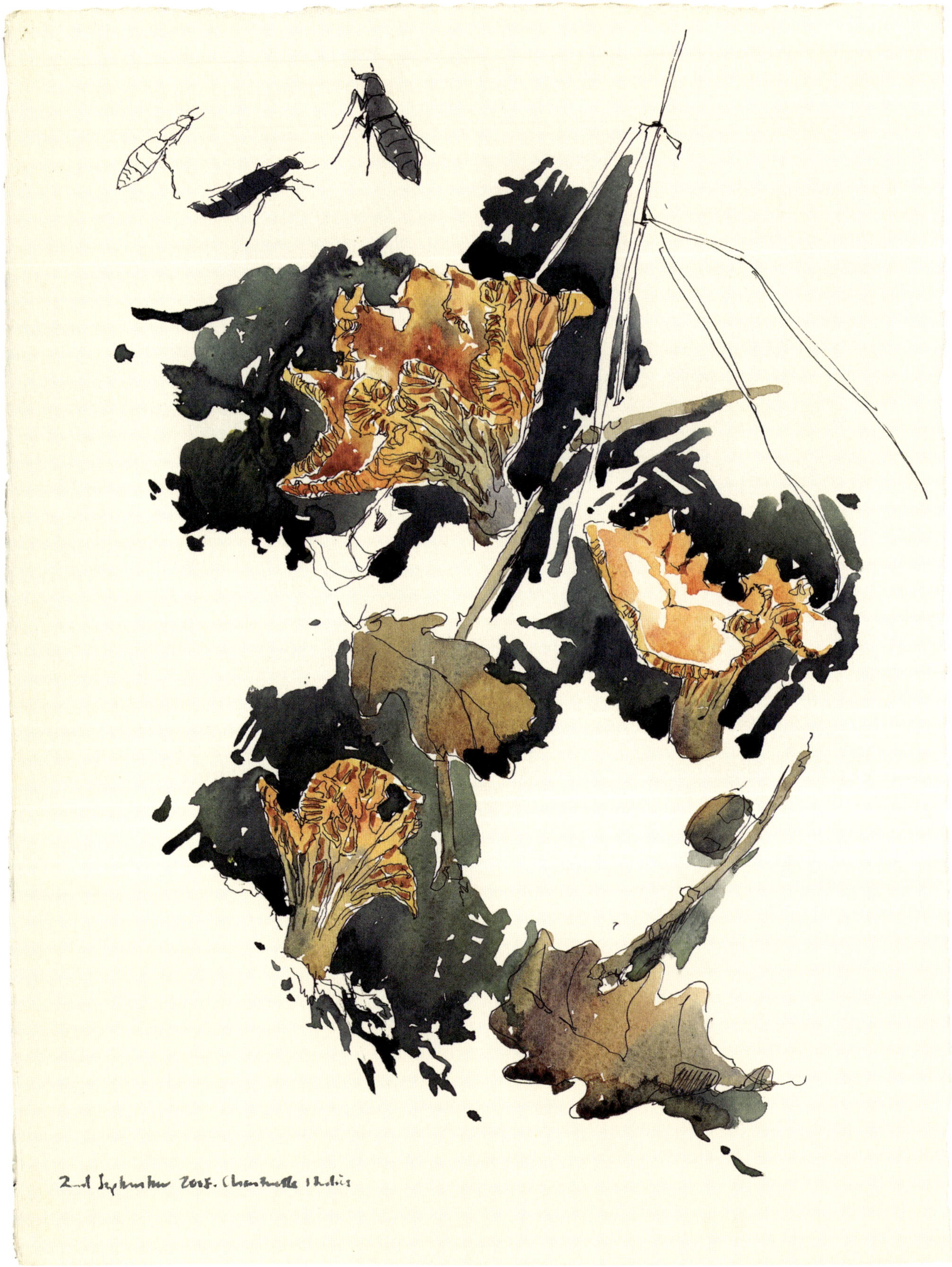

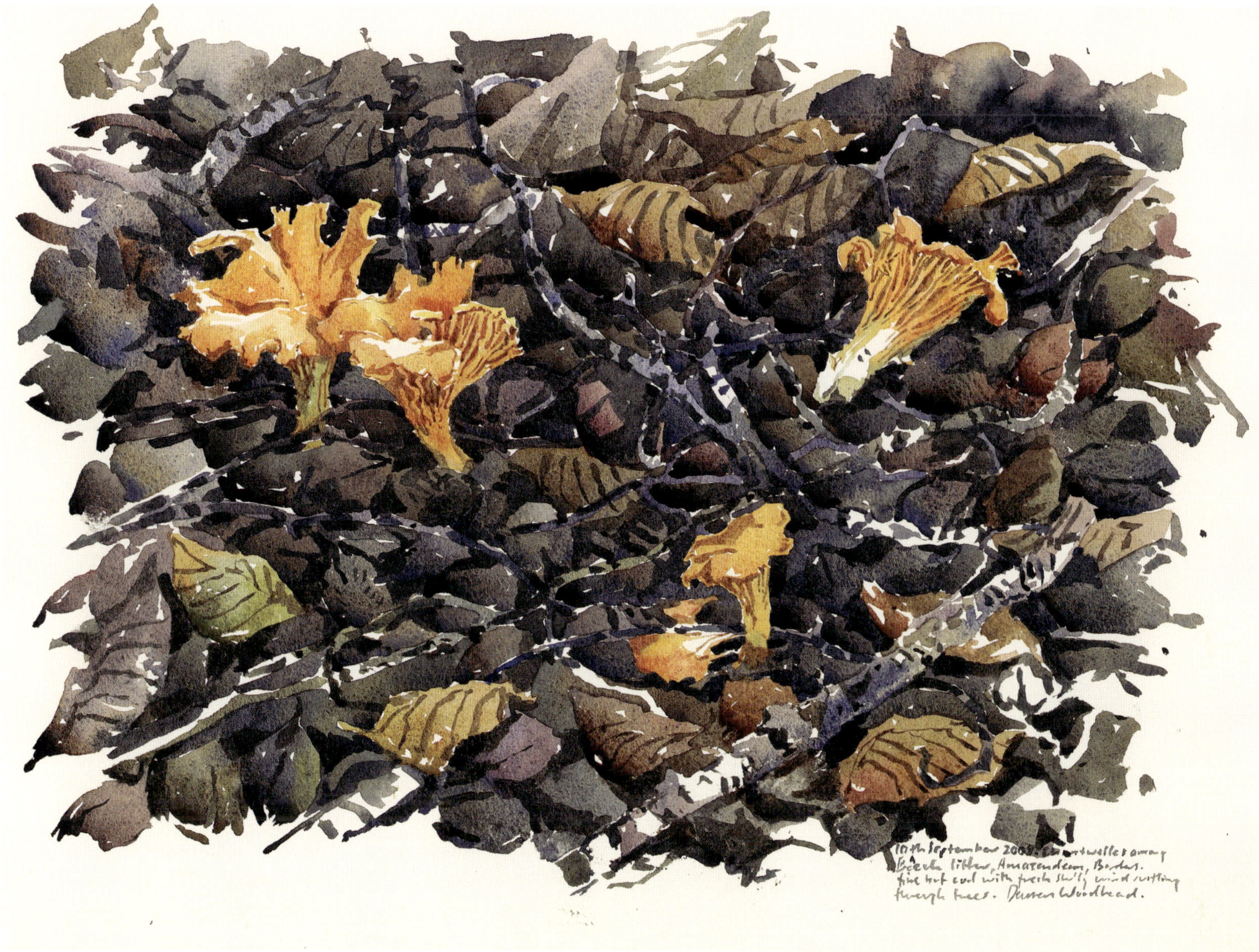

Chanterelles, Habbies Howe *(watercolour, 275mm x 370mm)*

10th September 2008. Chanterelles among Beech litter, Amazondean, Borders. Fine but cool with fresh south-westerly wind rustling through trees.

This group was found nestling in year-old Beechmast on very hard ground. The cooler background colours pitched against the deep yellow fluted caps made a stark contrast to the green of the usual moss. With Keelan due at any time, I began to keep my paintings small in case the phone might ring and I had to head home suddenly. This was the last painting I completed before Keelan was born a few days later on the 16th.

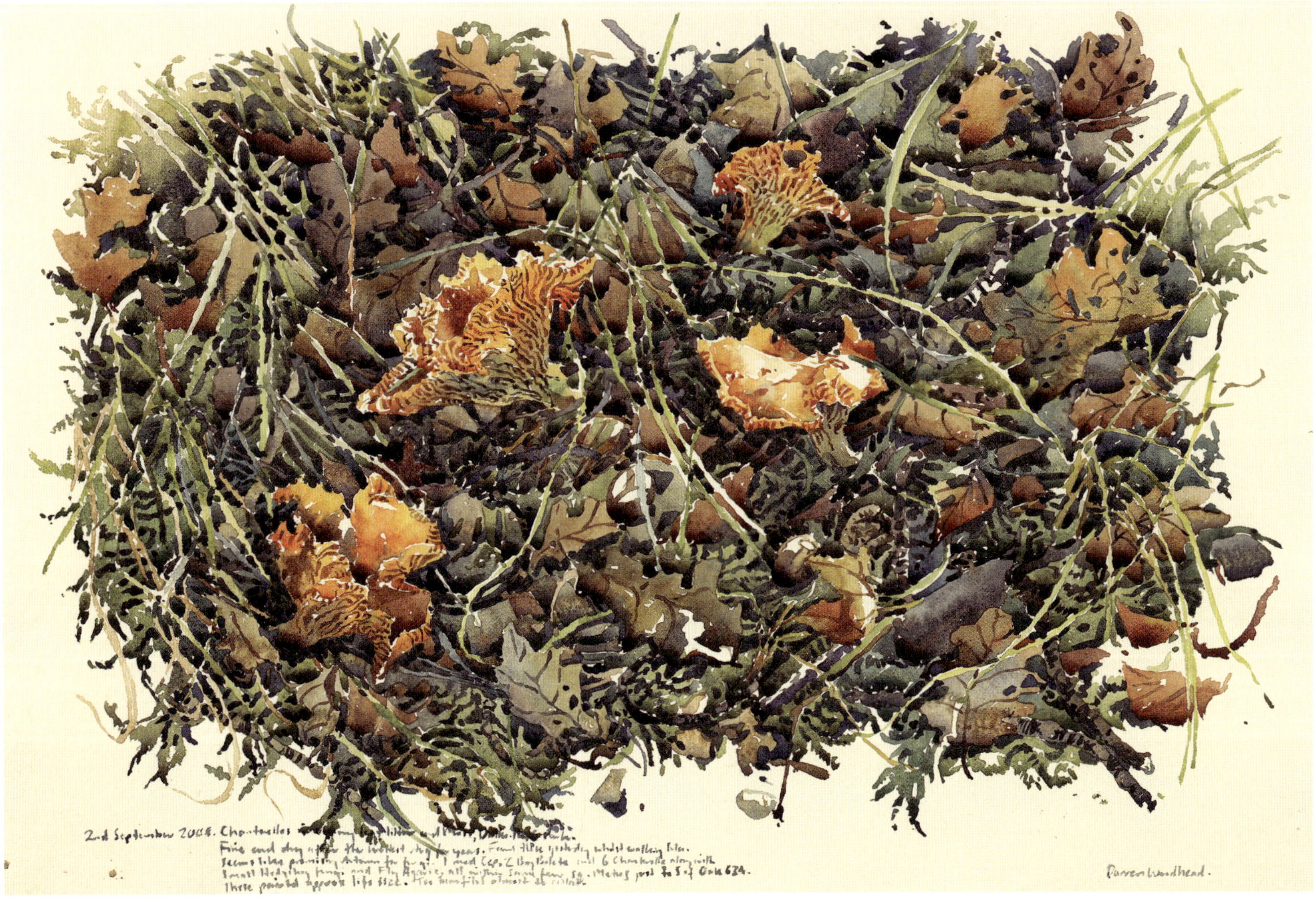

Chanterelles beside North Esk
(watercolour, 380mm x 560mm)

2nd September 2008. Chanterelles among leaf litter and moss. Fine day after the wettest August for years. Found these yesterday whilst walking Sula. Seems like a promising autumn for fungi. One medium Cep, two Bay Bolete and six Chanterelle along with small Hedgehog fungi and Fly Agaric all within same few square metres just to south of Oaks. These painted approximately life size. Too beautiful almost to collect.

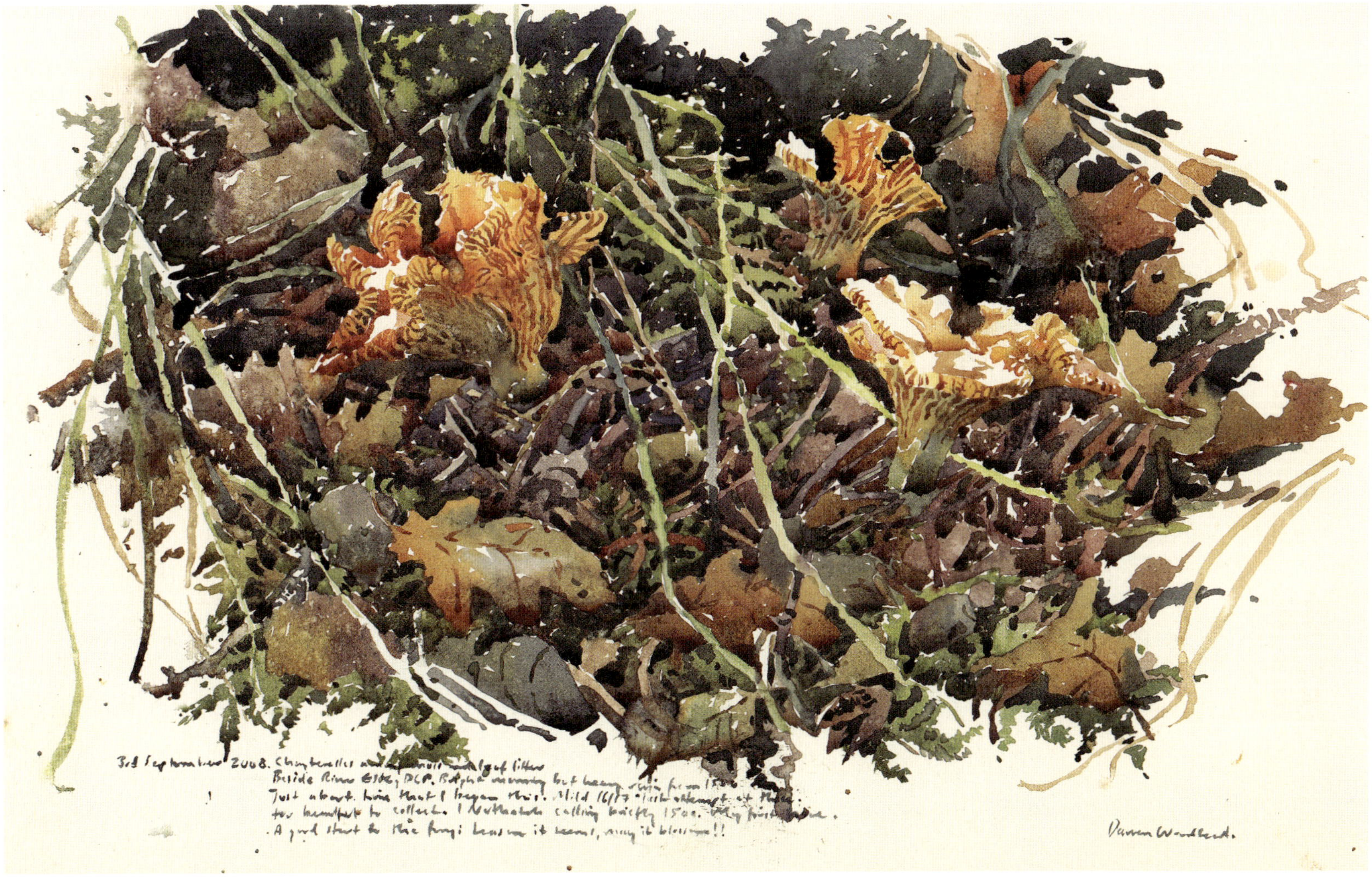

Chanterelles, North Esk
(watercolour, 285mm x 440mm)

3rd September 2008. Chanterelles among moss and leaf litter beside River Esk. Bright morning but heavy rain from 15:00, just about the time I started this. Mild; 16/17 degrees. Last attempt at these, too beautiful to collect. One Nuthatch calling briefly 15:00. My first here. A good start to the fungi season it seems; may it blossom.

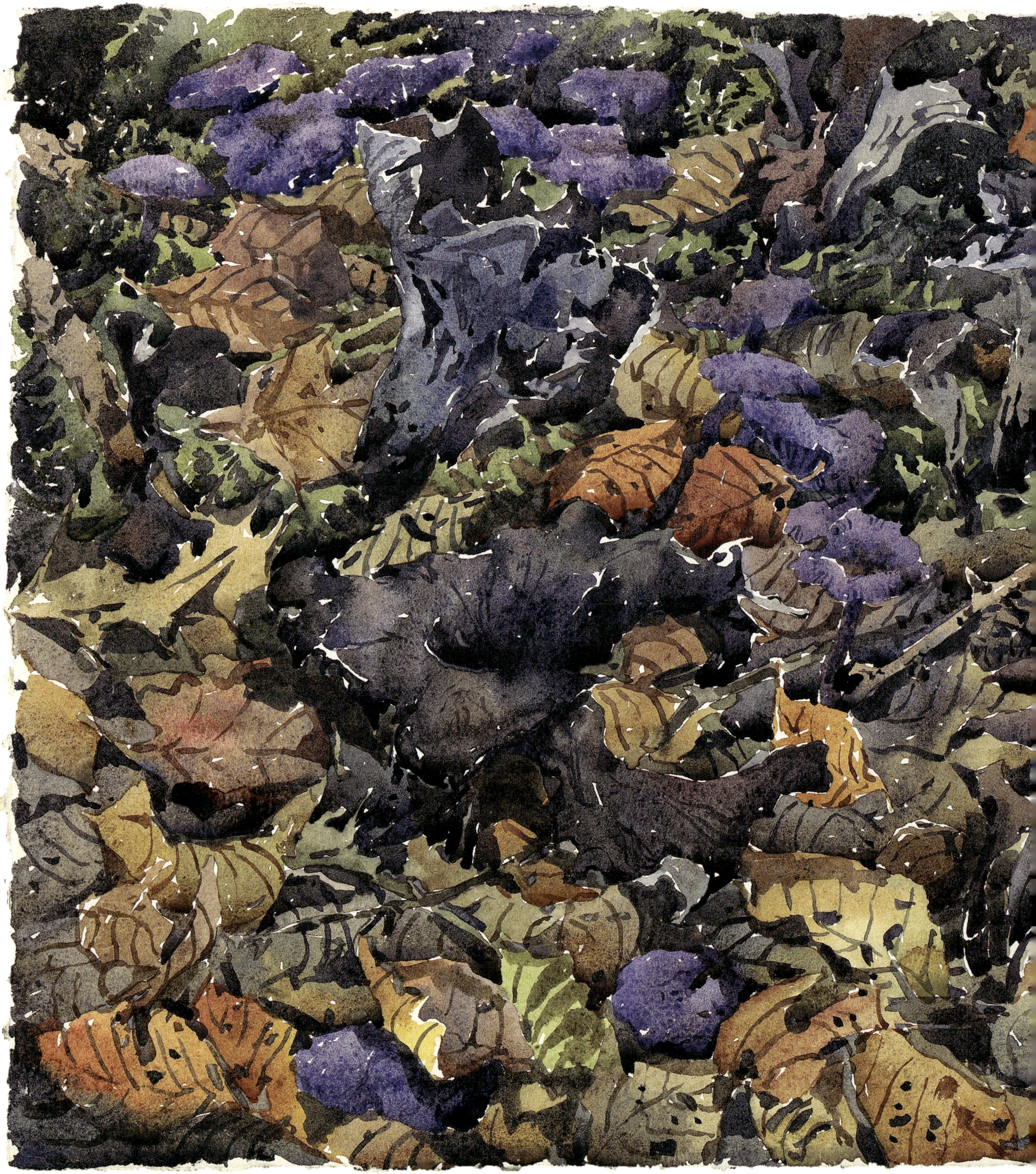

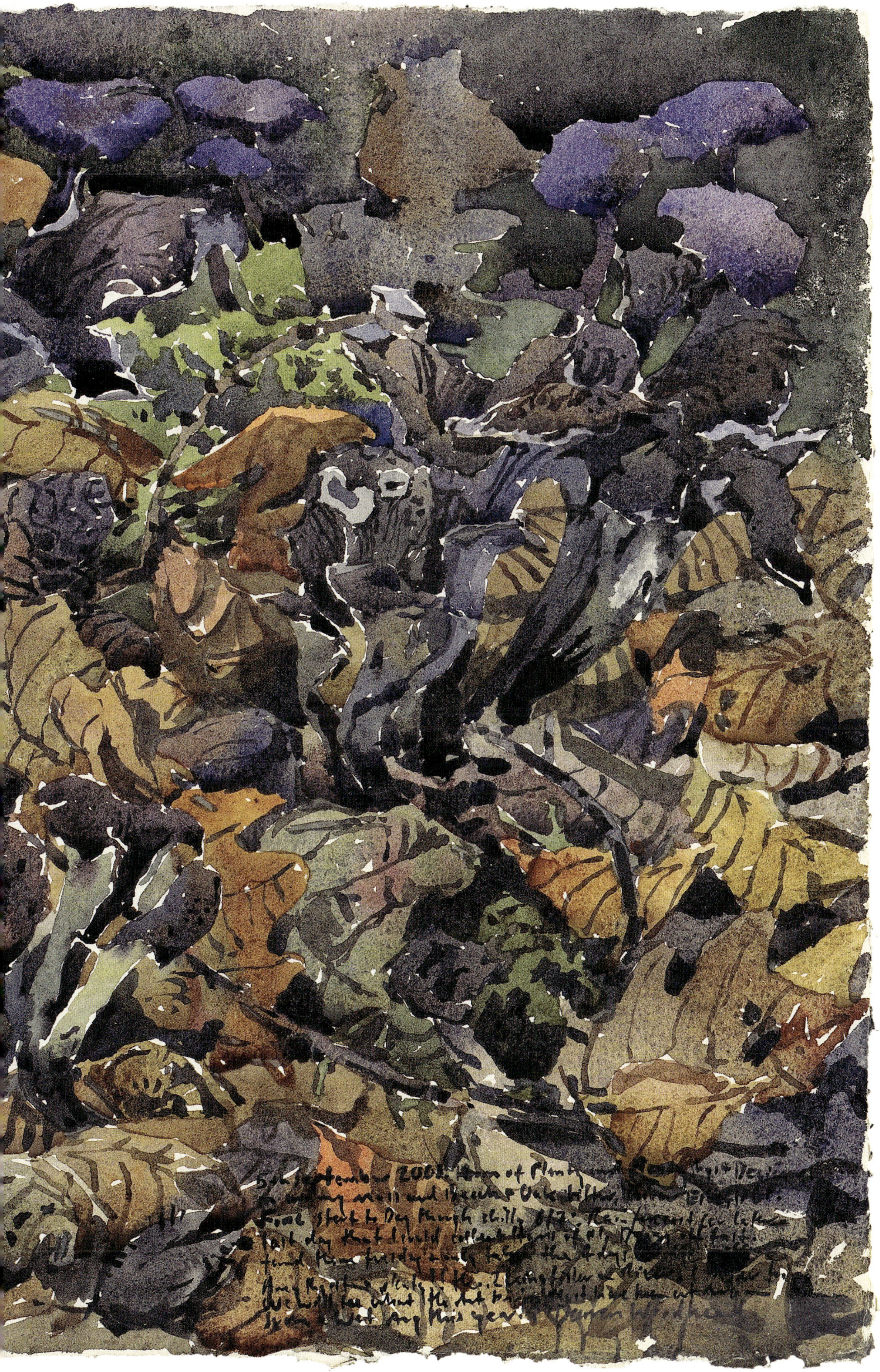

Horn of Plenty and Ameythysts
(watercolour, 285mm x 440mm)

5th September 2008. Horn of Plenty and Ameythyst Deceivers in among moss and beech and Oak litter, besides North Esk. Fine start to the day though chilly, 6/7 degrees. Rain forecast for later. Last day that I could collect them; found them Tuesday. Ameythyst aplenty. Two Kingfishers and onc Dipper on river. Horn of Plenty must have been out in August as a huge carpet of them, more than I have ever seen, but now looking oily and way past their best. Such a wet August this year.

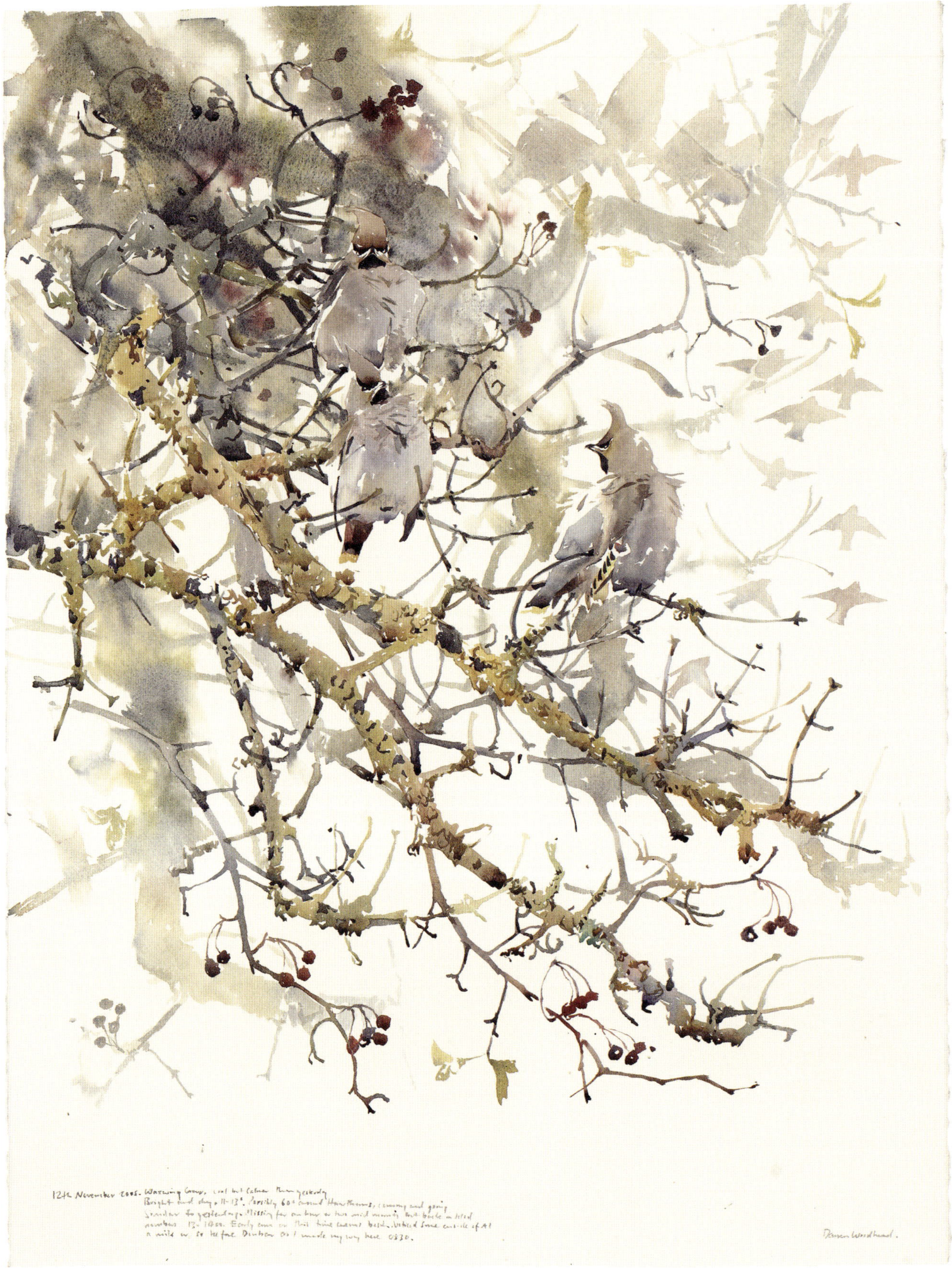

Waxwings in Hawthorn
(watercolour, 760mm x 560mm)

12th November 2008. Waxwing Group. Cool but calmer than yesterday, bright and dry, 11/13 degrees. Possibly sixty plus around Hawthorns, coming and going similar to yesterday. Missing for an hour or two mid morning but back in solid numbers between one and two p.m. First thing or early afternoon seems to be best. Noticed more on side of A1 as I made my way here.

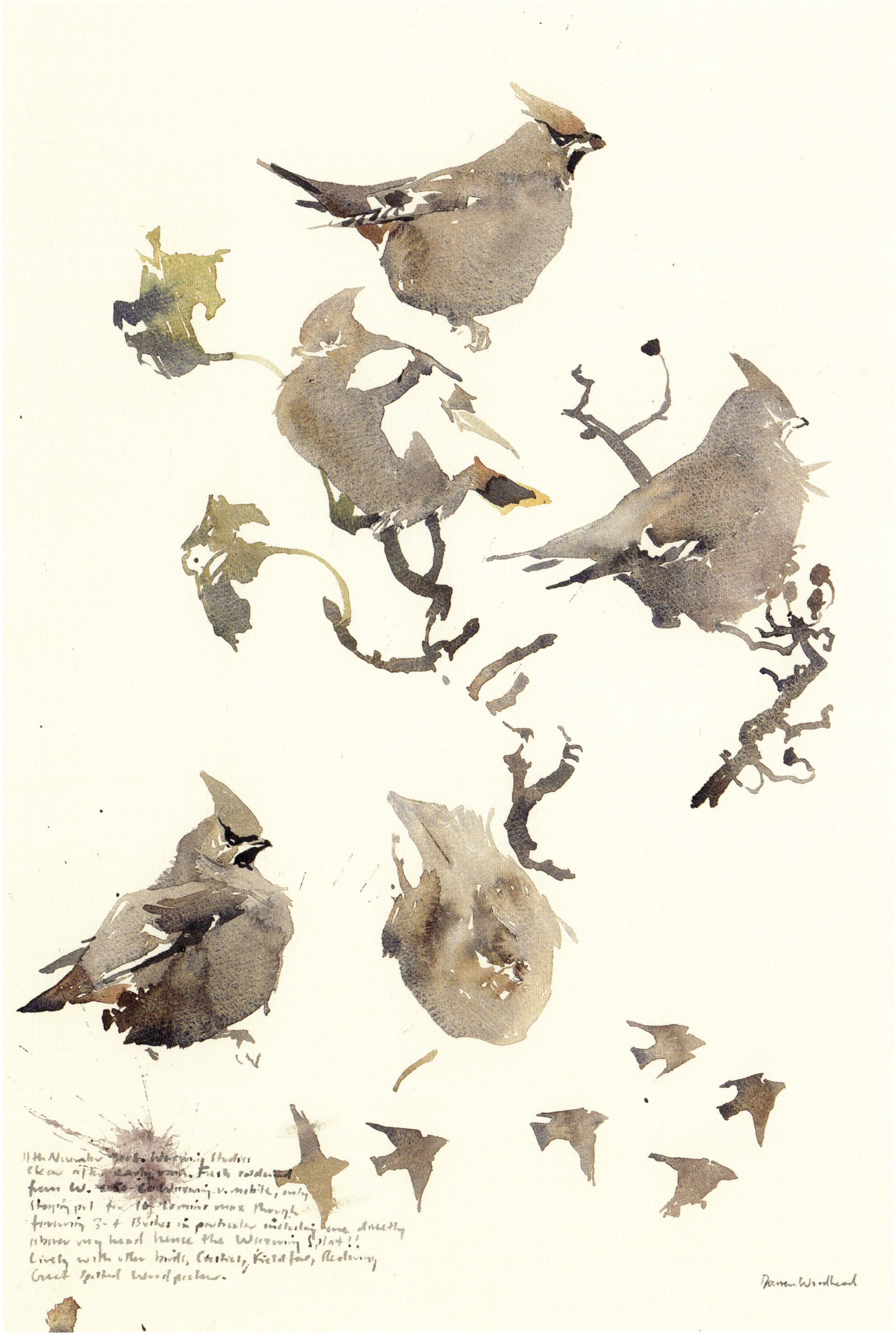

Waxwings

(watercolour, 560mm x 380mm)

11th November 2008. Waxwing studies. Clear after early rain. Fresh cold wind from the west. Approximately fifty to sixty birds but very mobile, only staying for maximum ten to twenty minutes, and favouring the same three or four Hawthorns, including one that I sat below, decorated by a very accurate Waxwing! Alive with other birds: Golcrests, Fieldfares, Redwings and Great-spotted Woodpeckers.

Waxwings and Fieldfare
(watercolour, 560mm x 380mm)

11th November 2008. Waxwings and a lone Fieldfare among Hawthorn. Flock very active today apart from when settling in Hawthorns often above my head! Fifty to sixty at least, favouring three or four particular bushes. At least thirty Fieldfares, twenty Redwings, Goldcrests and two Great-spotted Woodpeckers.

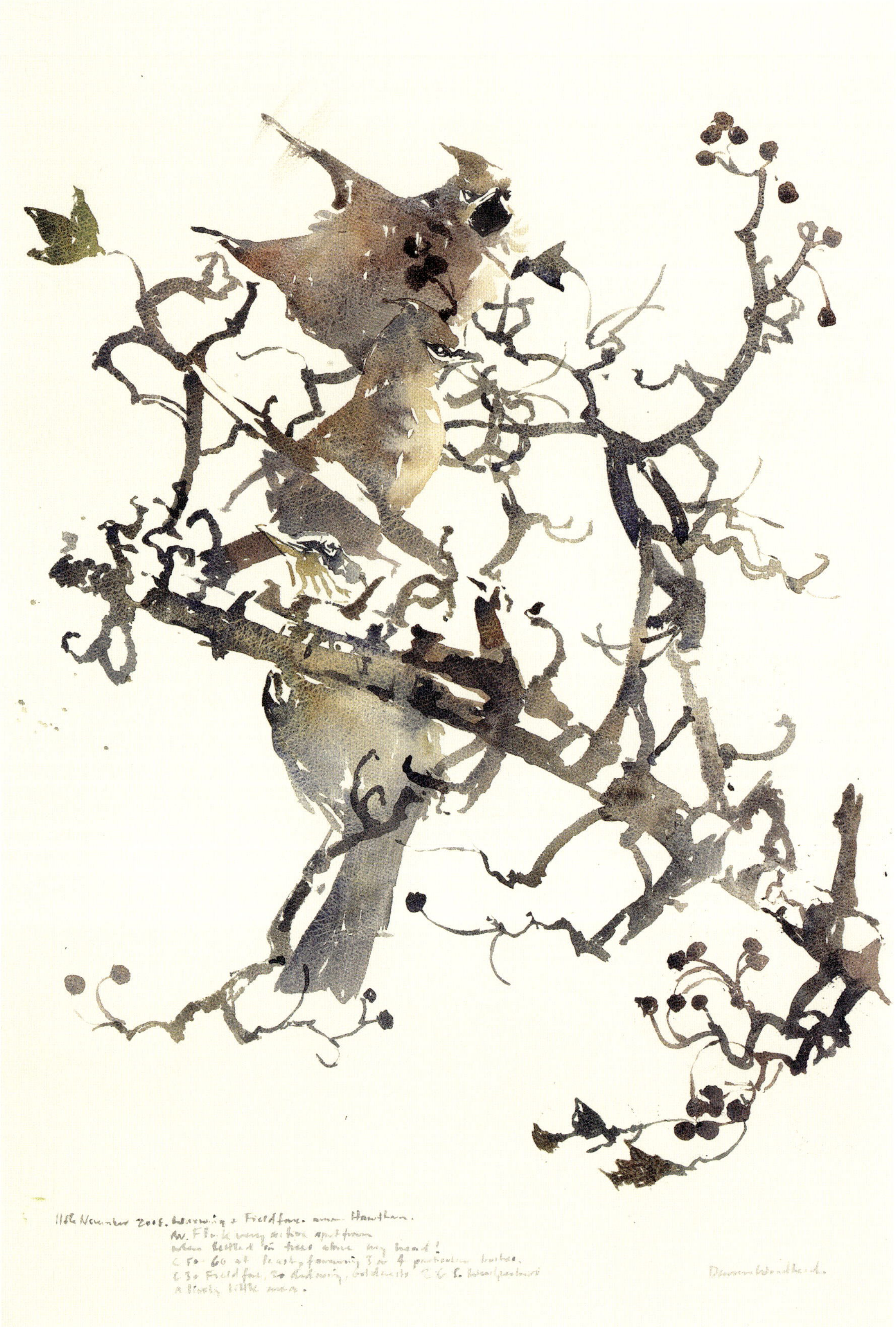

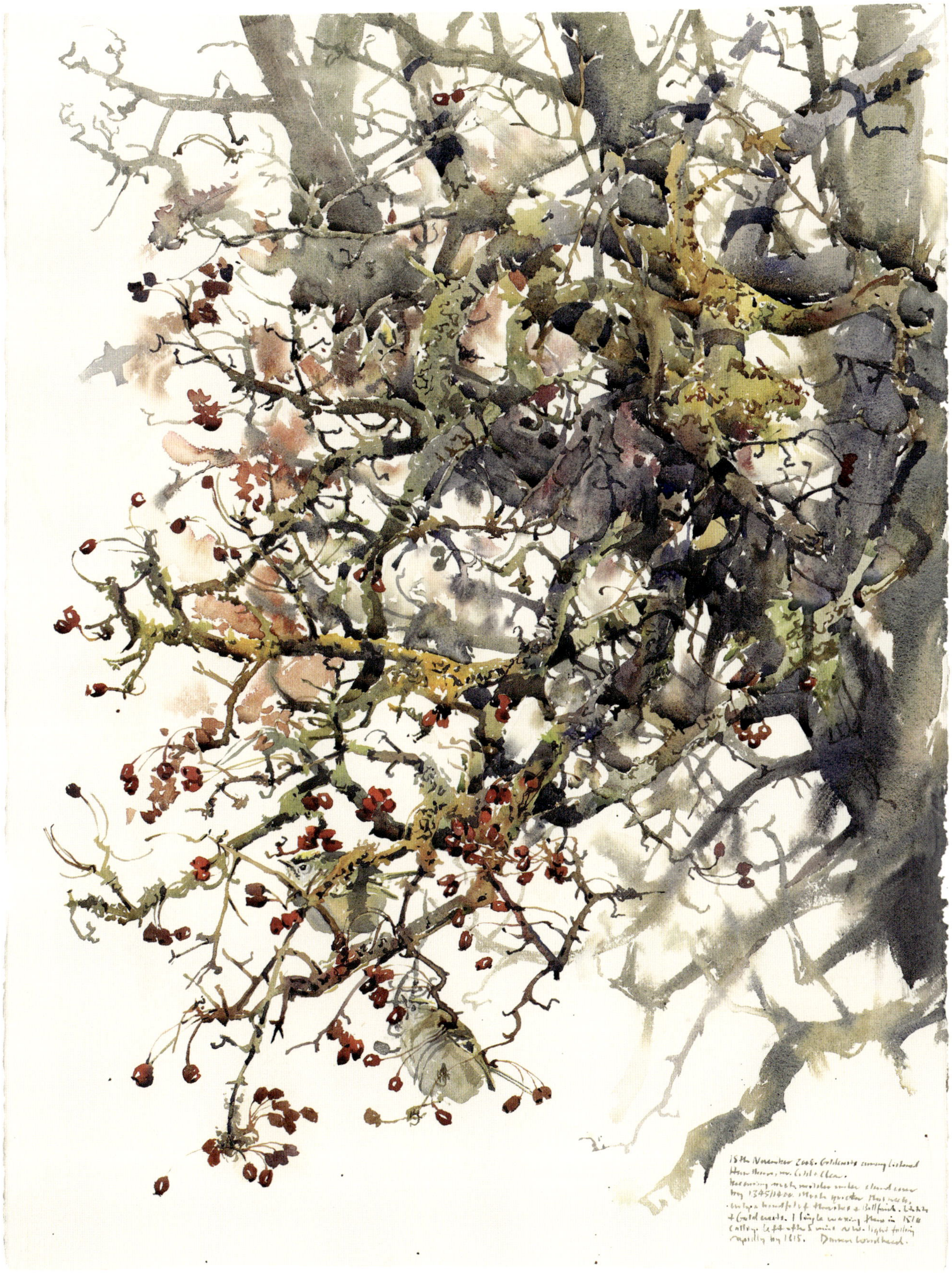

Goldcrests in Hawthorn
(watercolour, 760mm x 560mm)

18th November 2008. Goldcrest among Lichened Hawthorn. Cold and clear becoming much milder with cloud cover by 13:45/14:00. Much quieter this week, only a handful of Thrushes and Bullfinch. Long-tailed Tits and Goldcrests. One single Waxwing flew in 15:10 calling, leaving after five minutes to the north-west. Light falling rapidly by 16:15.

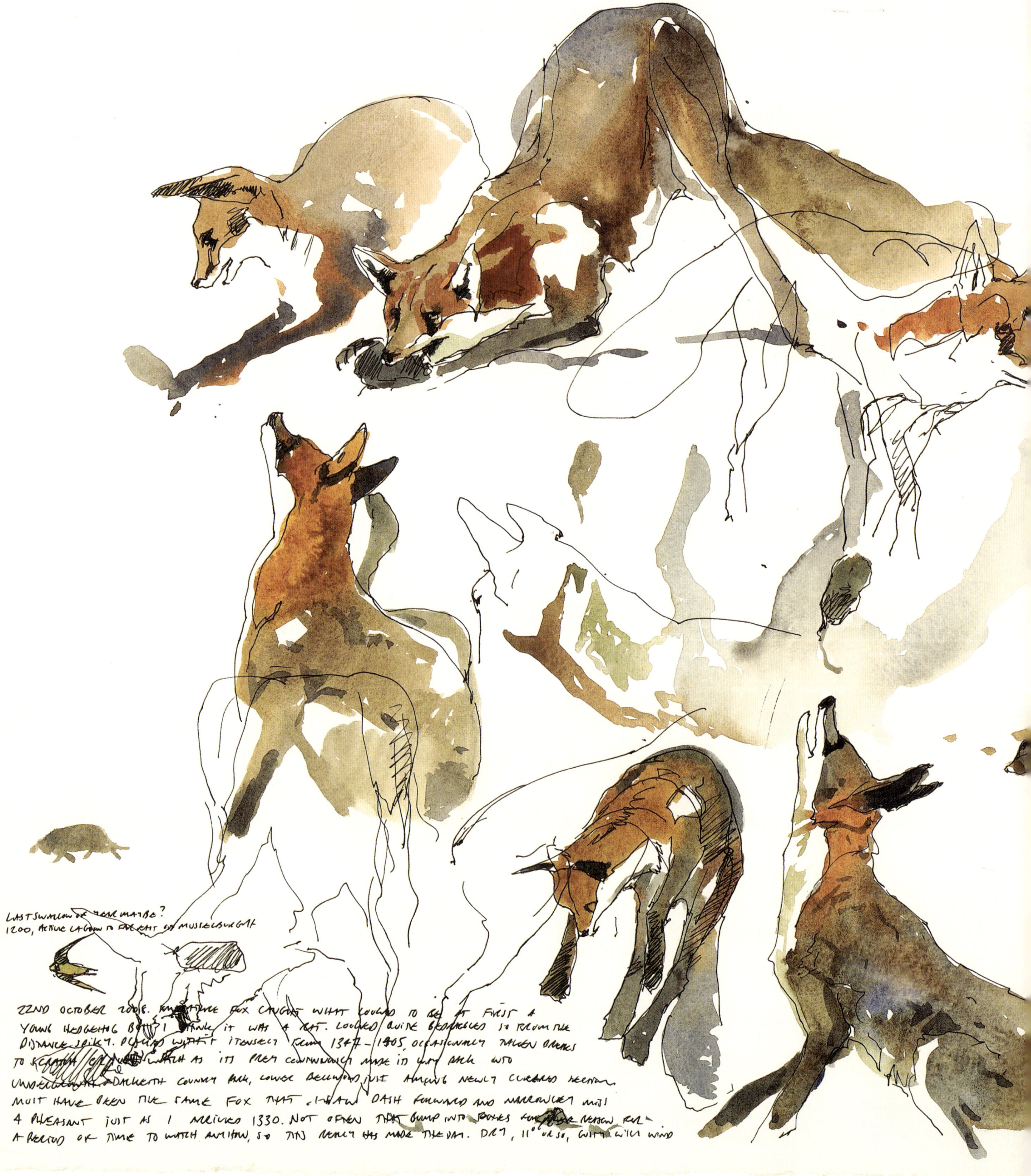
LAST SWALLOW OF YEAR MAYBE?
1200, ACTIVE LAGOON TO FAR EAST OF MUSSELBURGH
22ND OCTOBER 2008. ... FOX CAUGHT WHAT LOOKED TO BE AT FIRST A
YOUNG HEDGEHOG BUT I THINK IT WAS A RAT. LOOKED QUITE BEDRAGGLED SO FROM THE
DISTANCE SPIKY. PLAYED WITH IT ITSELF FROM 1347 – 1405, OCCASIONALLY TAKEN BREAKS
TO SCRATCH ... WATCH AS ITS PREY CONTINUOUSLY MADE ITS WAY BACK INTO
UNDERGROWTH. DALKEITH COUNTRY PARK, LOWER ... JUST AMONG NEWLY CLEARED SECTION
MUST HAVE BEEN THE SAME FOX THAT I SAW DASH FORWARD AND NARROWLY MISS
A PHEASANT JUST AS I ARRIVED 1330. NOT OFTEN THAT I BUMP INTO FOXES FOR ... REASON FOR
A PERIOD OF TIME TO WATCH ANYHOW, SO THIS REALLY HAS MADE THE DAY. DRY, 11° OR SO, WITH ... WIND

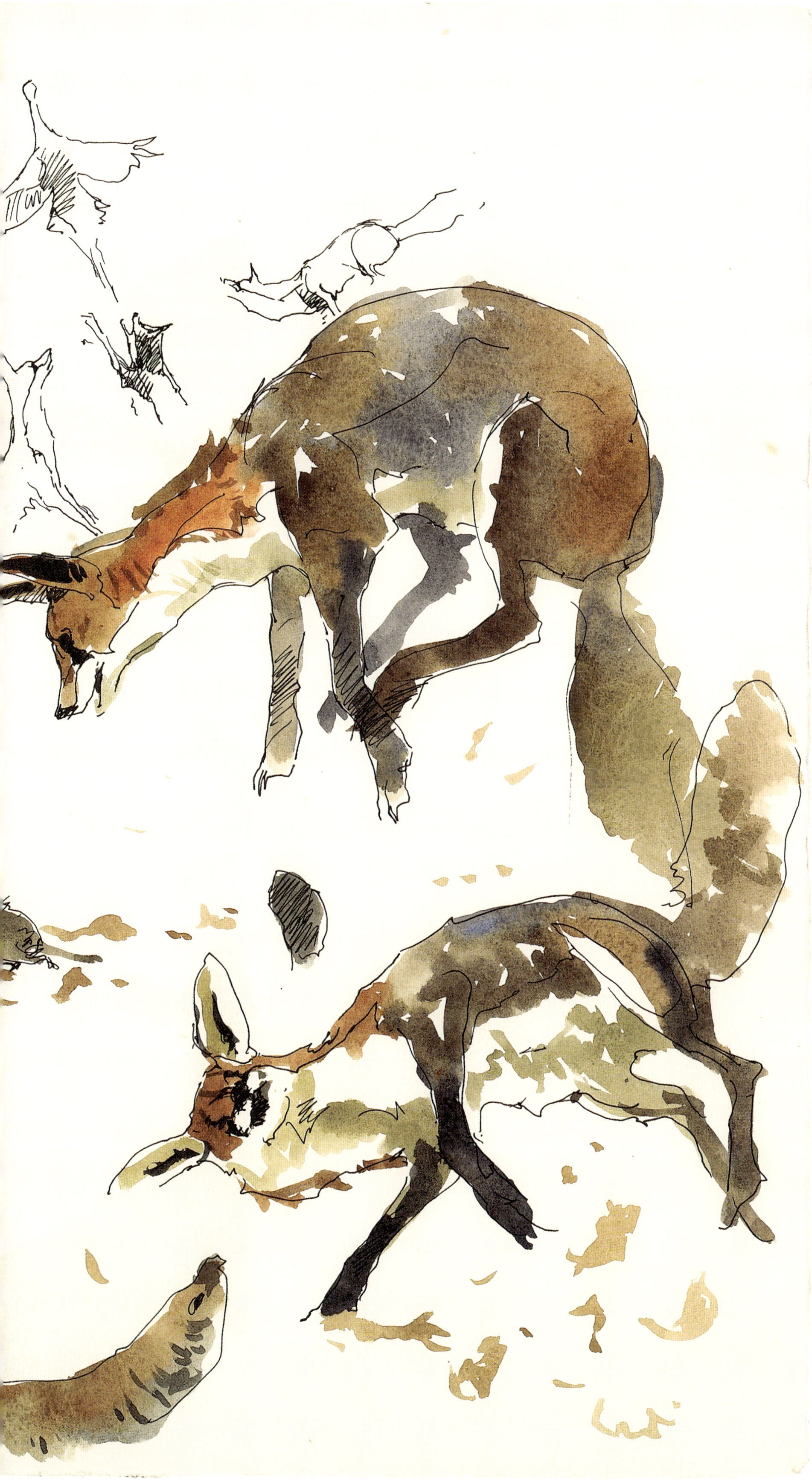

Immature Fox playing with prey beside the Esk
(watercolour and pen, 380mm x 560mm)

22nd October 2008. Immature Fox caught what looked like at first a young Hedgehog, but I think it was a Rat. Looked quite bedraggled, so from the distance spiky. Played with it intensely from 13:47–14:05, occasionally taking breaks to scratch or watch as its prey continually made its way back into undergrowth. Must have been the same Fox that I saw pounce on but narrowly miss a Pheasant – just as I arrived, 13:30. Not often that I bump into Foxes for some reason – for any length of time – so this has really made the day. Feeling cool, temperature 11 degrees or so in a gusting westerly wind.
Last Swallow of year, maybe, at 12 p.m. over active lagoon to the far eastern side of Musselburgh.

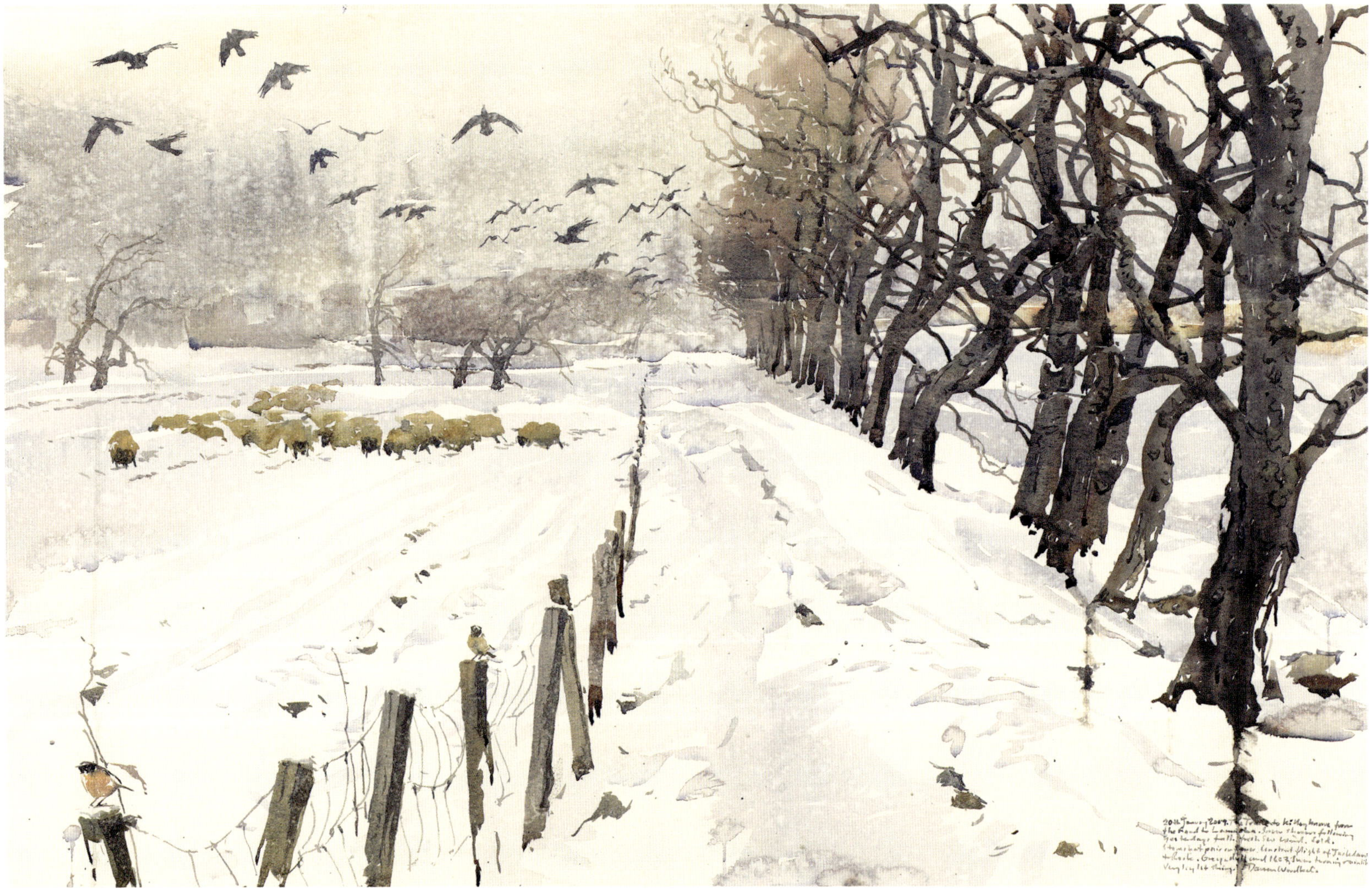

Towards Kitleyknowe
(watercolour, 660mm x 1016mm)

20th January 2009. The Track to Kitleyknowe from the road to Lamancha. Snow showers following yesterday's fall. Fresh south-westerly wind and cold. Stonechat pair actively feeding from fence working their way up the entire length and onto the gate in front before continuing on section to right. Constant flight of Jackdaws and Rook. Exceptionally grey and dull 16:07, with snow turning to rain. Very icy first thing.

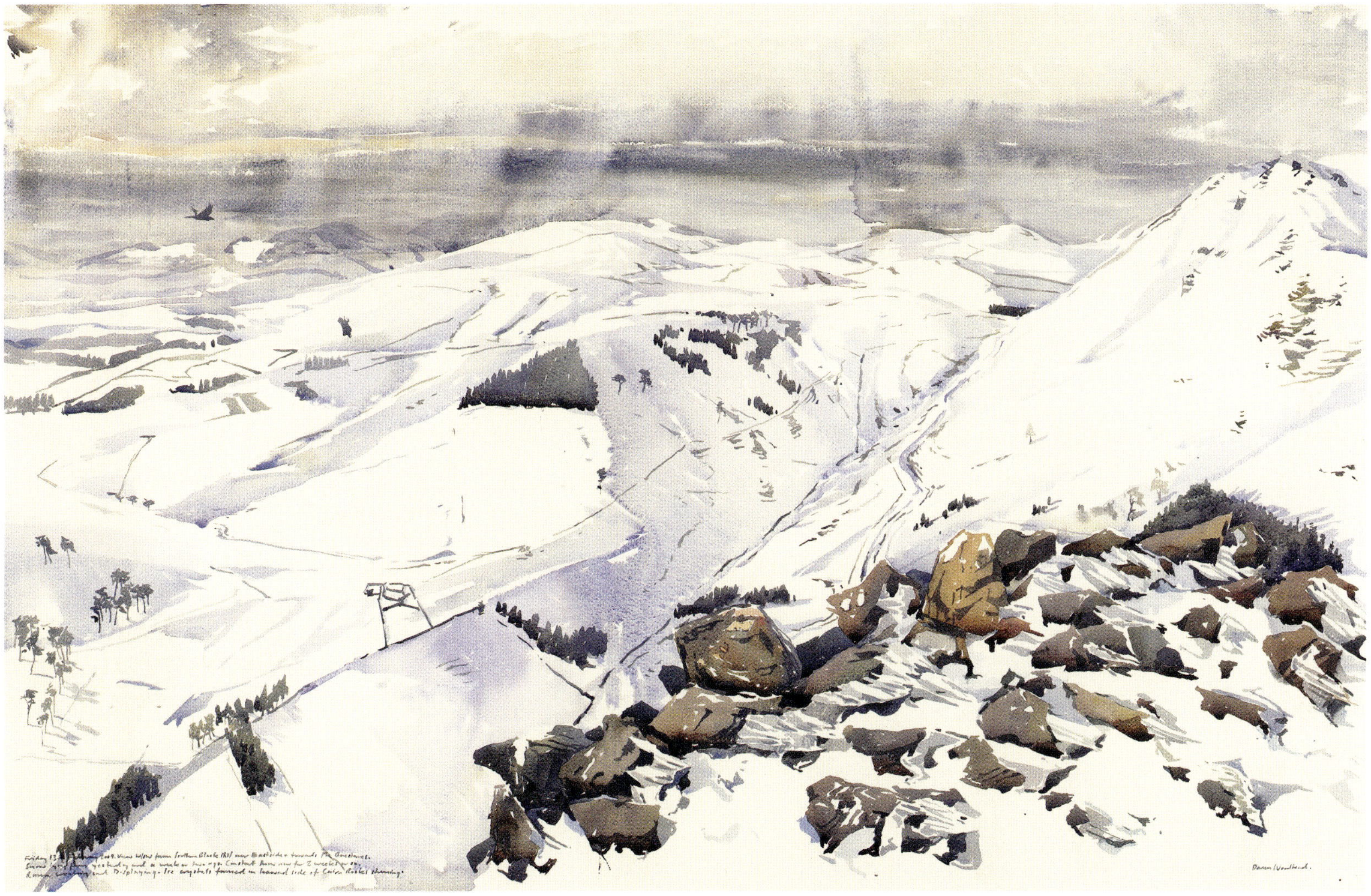

Ice Crystals on the Cairn
(watercolour, 660mm x 1016mm)

Friday, 13th February 2009. View west south-west from Southern Black Hill over Eastside and towards the Borestanes. Snow lying from both fresh fall yesterday and that from over a week or two ago also. Constant falls over the last two weeks or so. Raven croaking and displaying. Ice crystals formed on leeward side of cairn rocks, stunningly beautiful.

Tracks over the bridge, Amazondean *(watercolour, 1016mm x 660mm)*

Wednesday, 4th February 2009. Kitleyknowe Bridge near Amazondean. Fresh fall of snow on weekend, a good four inches or so here. One Roe Deer crept over bridge as I painted. Lots of Jackdaw chatter, odd woodpecker 'chip'. Treecreeper in front of me among Tit flock. Bullfinch calling below. Stunning day, only freezing from 16:00 onwards. Bit of a rush today, only arrived 10.00. On way to quarry where four hundred plus Woodpigeon in field below, but instinct led me here. Not a cloud in sky until light snow from 16:00. The North Esk a patchwork of running water below large ice islands.

With a succession of bitterly cold days the river beneath the bridge was a patchwork of large ice islands standing an inch or two proud of the running water below. These strange forms were the most beautiful of natural sculptures, and amazingly the distance between them and the trickle below appeared to grow as the day progressed.

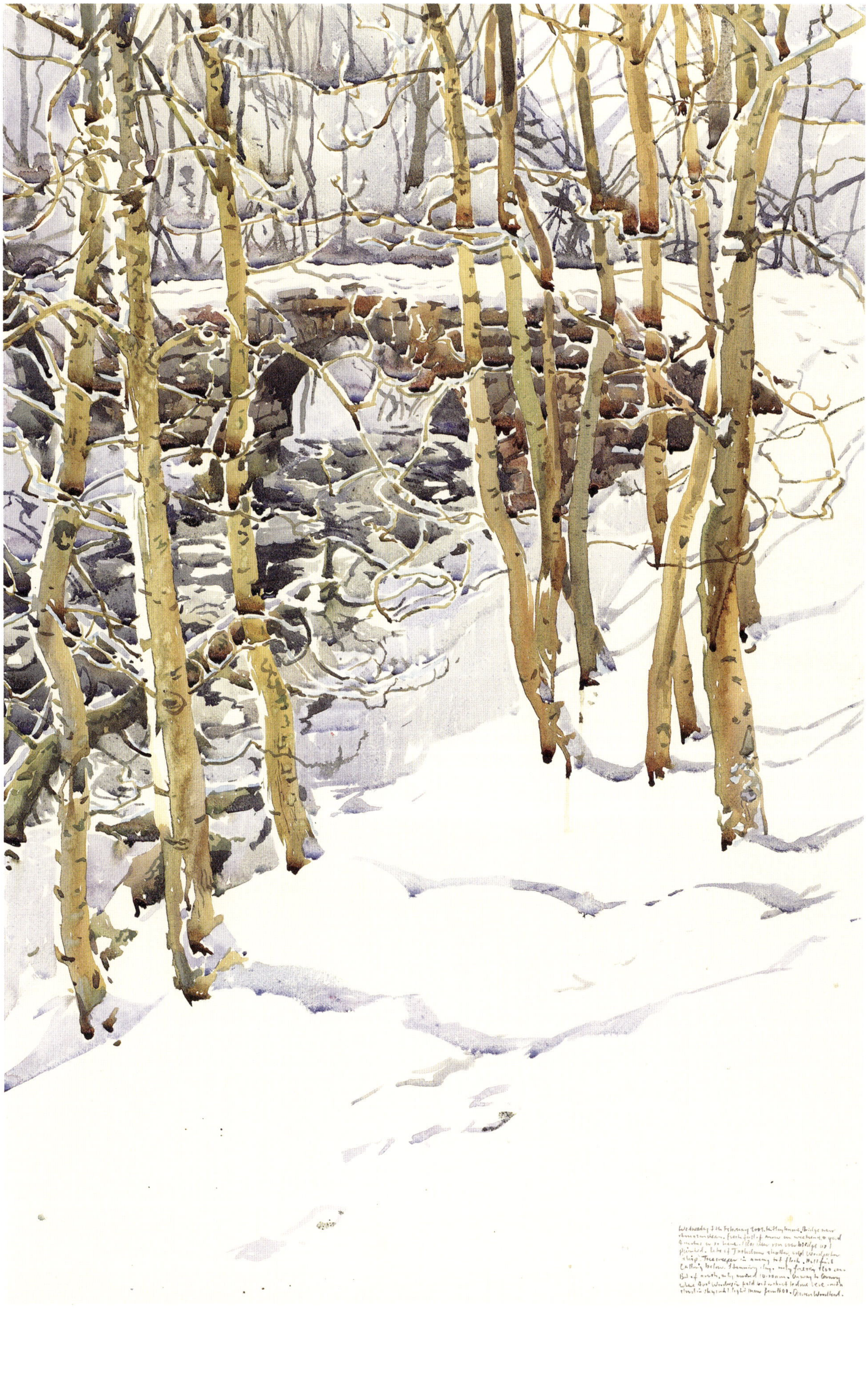

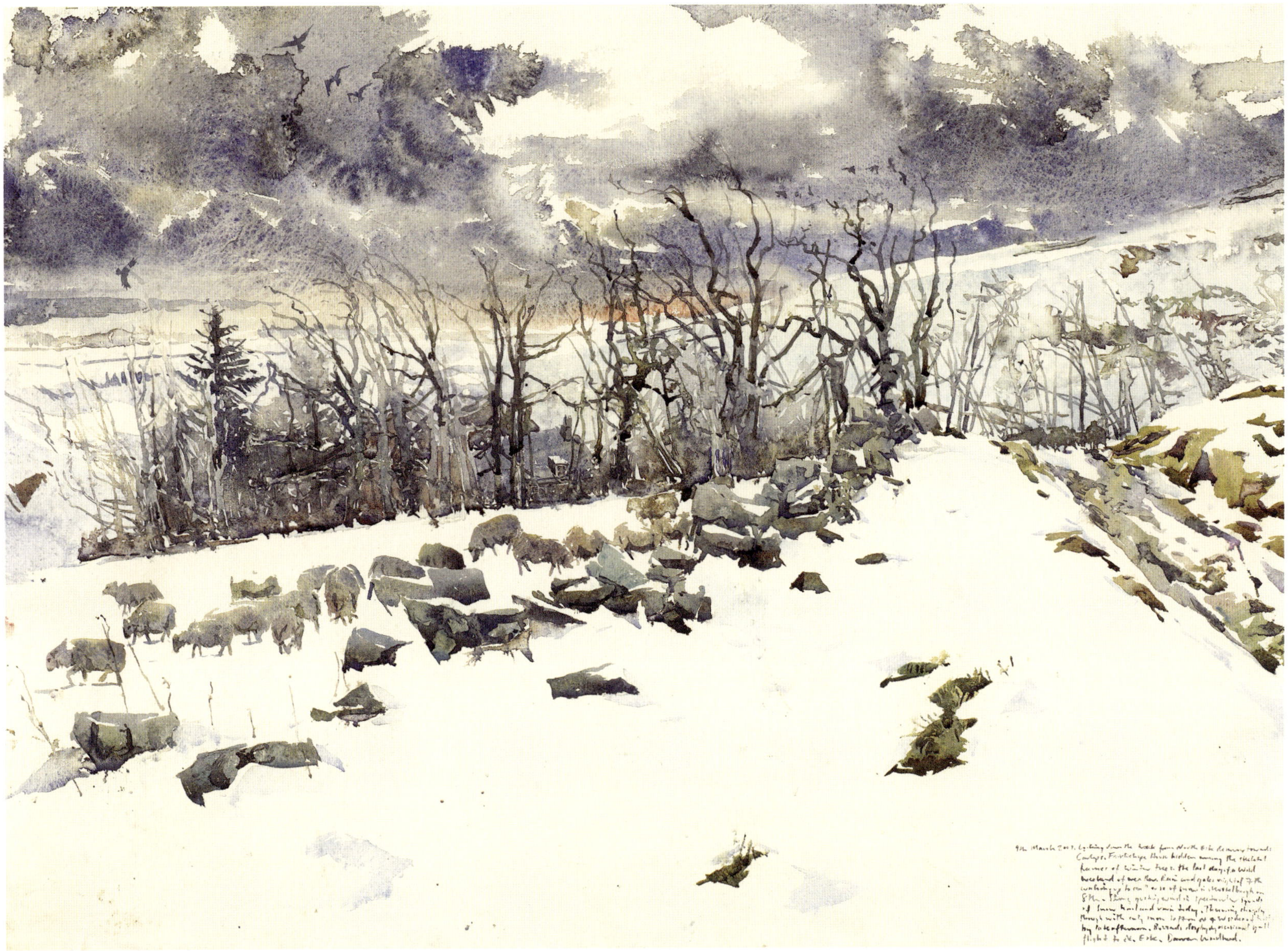

Fairliehope
(watercolour, 560mm x 760mm)

9th March 2007. Looking down track from North Esk reservoir towards Carlops. Fairliehope House hidden among the skeletal frames of winter trees. The last day of a wild weekend of weather. Rain and gales night of 7th waking up to an inch of snow in Musselburgh on the 8th. Strong gusting wind in spectacular squalls of snow, hail and rain today. Thawing sharply though with only snow left on west sides of hills by late afternoon. Buzzards displaying between squalls and occasional gull flight towards reservoir.

Blizzard and Bullfinch
(watercolour, 1016mm x 660mm)

12th February 2009. Bullfinch and Blue Tit feeding on buds among heavy snow. Two to three inches fell during the morning, slowly turning to light rain by the afternoon. Same flock again feeding in trees at edge of wood. Heavy wet snow settling fast, huge flakes landing and staying on the backs of the birds, with earlier wind dropping off totally. Five Roe again in same area first thing, then again late afternoon. Light falling by 17:15.

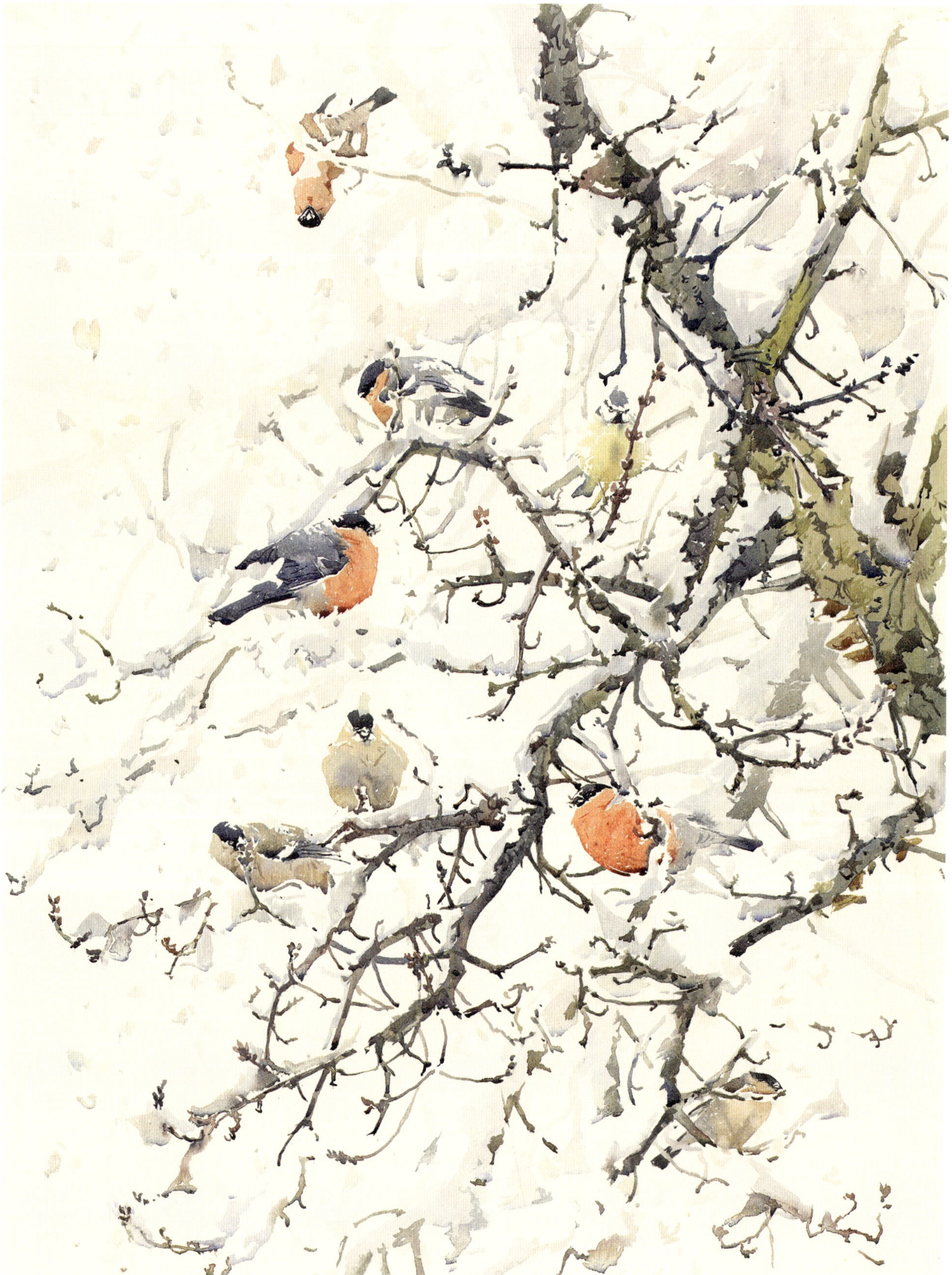

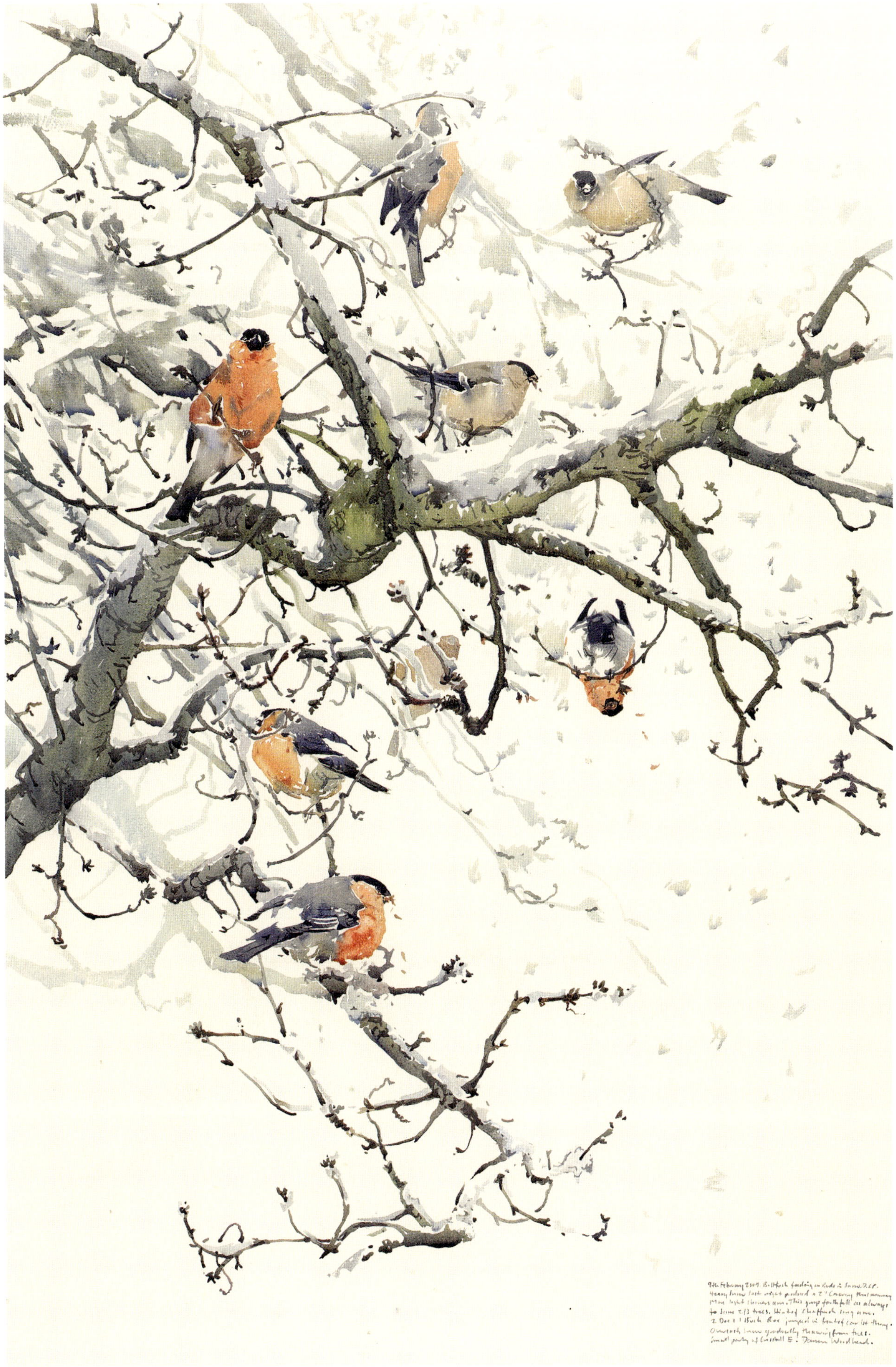

Feeding winter Bullfinch
(watercolour, 1016mm x 660mm)

9th February 2009, Bullfinch feeding on buds in snow beside North Esk. Heavy snow last night produced a two-inch covering this morning. More light showers in the morning. This group were faithful as always to the same two or three trees. Hint of Chaffinch song a.m. Two doe and one buck Roe Deer jumped in front of car first thing. Overcast with snow gradually thawing from trees. Small party of Crossbill flew east.

Acknowledgements

First and foremost, despite the highs and lows of life, it is my family and friends that are my foundation. So I thank Pasci and my two blossoming sons Corin and Keelan, and Mum and Dad, for giving life a meaning and purpose, and for all their belief and support. This is for you, thank you.

Thanks to the many memories that I cherish of times with my Bamp, who as well as bowling the most perplexing 'googlies', has enabled a childhood enthusiasm to develop and prosper. To Martin, Craig, Andrew and Jonathan for so many enjoyable times that we held as youngsters and still do now, and to Dave Gibson for the great friendship over the years.

I am greatly indebted to John and Patricia Kennedy and all the Trustees of The Orcome Trust for having the faith and confidence to fund the unique Artist in Residence position that instigated this whole project. Their kindly support has generated a huge amount of interest as well as an invaluable archive of the beauty and richness of the natural world found in this special part of the Scottish Borders. I am filled with gratitude for the warmth and acceptance that the people of Carlops and nearby communities have given me. Special thanks to Ann Smith for her tireless enthusiasm and dedication; to John and William Aitken for the 'rescues', and Mike Jones of Fairliehope for the emails, chats, Redlegs, etc. To the Vellacott family for putting up with the pestering that my visits to the dean have no doubt caused as well the cheery banter, and to Keir Sword of Carlops and Royal Mile Whiskies, whose additional assistance and belief has helped achieve this book.
To Hugh Andrew, Liz Short, Jim Hutcheson, Andrew Simmons and all at Birlinn, who have had the belief in the project and whose dedication and professionalism has led to such a special publication.

Thanks so much to Julian Spalding, who has written such an eloquent introduction and for his honest enthusiasm and belief in my work.

Much love and admiration to John Busby, who is always a constant inspiration, and Ysbrand Brouwers of the Artists for Nature Foundation for help and support. I must once again thank John Norris-Wood, my tutor at the Royal College of Art, who told me that memorable day to 'just use colour direct in brush', and so established the way my work has developed.

To our Hungarian Viszla, Sula, who has accompanied virtually all my trips and indeed found many subjects that I subsequently painted.

Many of the paintings here are in private collections and so I thank their owners for allowing their reproduction here.

Finally, to Victoria Crowe and Mike Walton, who have been so much more than friends – almost surrogate parents. Their advice, help, encouragement, not forgetting cups of Lady Grey tea, have been a comfort and reassurance on so many occasions. Thank you, Vicky, for being the architect of this whole event and the catalyst for what has followed.

Darren Woodhead
May 2009

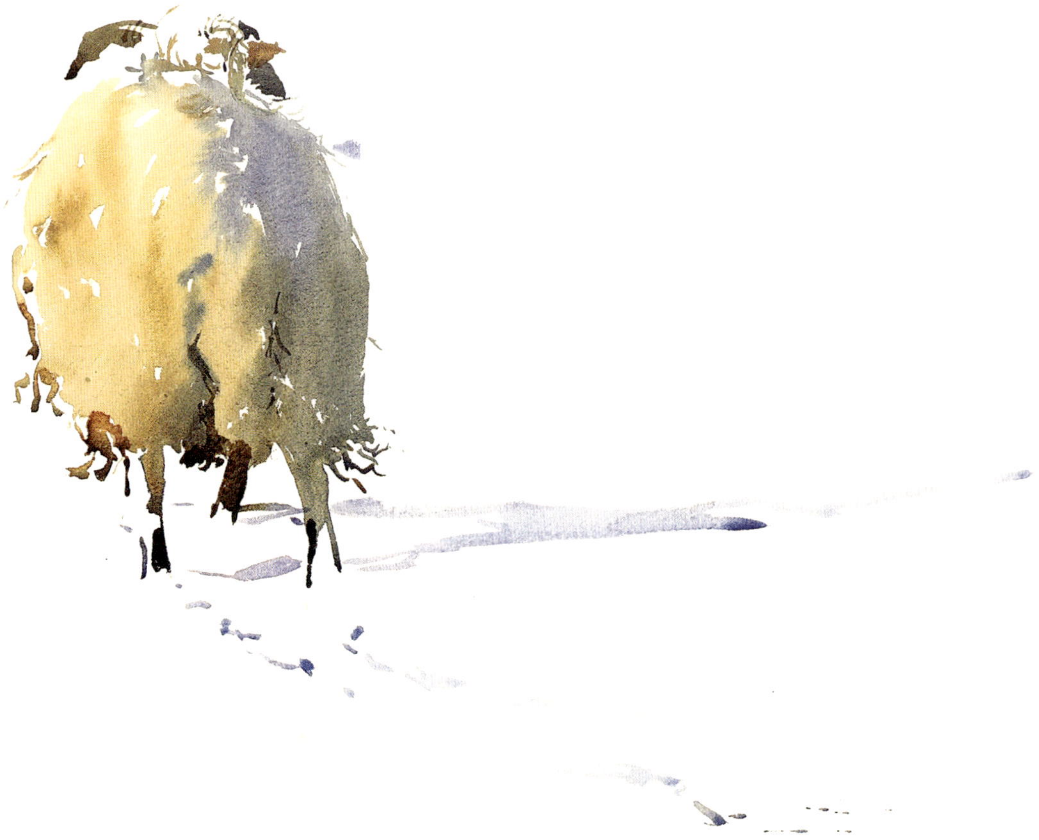

Winter Ewe, 3rd February 2009
(watercolour, 560mm x 760mm)